In a world of unprecedented human movement where faith journeys transcend borders and cultures intermingle, Mehari Tedla Korcho skillfully guides readers on a captivating exploration of Ethiopian American Christianity by tracing the intricate threads connecting the history, church, faith, generations, and mission of an immigrant community in the United States. The insights shared here apply to all diaspora communities everywhere. This book is a testament to the enduring spirit of a dispersed people and their significant contribution to the global tapestry of Christianity.

Sam George, PhD
Catalyst for Diaspora, Lausanne Movement
Director, Global Diaspora Institute, Wheaton College Billy Graham Center

In this book, Mehari Tedla Korcho explores one of the most pressing issues facing not only migrant Christian communities but, indeed, the entire global fellowship of followers of Christ in this age of migration—that of the faith of younger-generation migrants. The lessons he articulates about how Ethiopian churches are doing their intergenerational missional work with younger Ethiopians in the United States should speak to us all. Anyone involved in mission, especially in the context of migration, will find this thesis very helpful. It comes with my highest recommendation.

Harvey Kwiyani, PhD
CEO of Global Connections, UK

This well researched dissertation not only addresses the main problem of Ethiopian diaspora churches but also paints a great picture of what beautiful work the church is positioned to do in the West. The need to attend to the spiritual, emotional, and social wellbeing of the second generation and the benefits of investing in the community as a whole is presented as the best outreach strategy. Mehari has done a great job of capturing the pains, struggles, and resilience of our community as we pursue our call to make disciples of all nations in our new homes. I highly recommend this compelling read for those seeking a deeper understanding of God's work among diaspora communities in the West.

Mekdes Haddis
Advocate for an Equitable and Sustainable Mission Movement

In this timely study, Mehari Tedla Korcho provides insight into mission *by* the diaspora through focusing on the journey of the Ethiopian diaspora church in the United States. A reflective practitioner, Korcho describes the great potential for the Ethiopian diaspora church to play a key role in missions today in the West.

Edward L. Smither, PhD
Dean, College of Intercultural Studies,
Columbia International University, South Carolina, USA

From this body of research, Dr. Mehari Tedla Korcho gives us a rare window into the story of the migration of families, denominations, and the Christian faith itself into the Western world. The story has many trials and triumphs but, as Korcho explains, the narrative has reached a crisis which threatens movement into fuller participation in the Great Commission. While the focus is on the Ethiopian church, the narrative is being repeated in many diaspora groups. Thus the recommendations made herein will be of help to diaspora leaders and those who minister alongside them.

Bob Rasmussen
Executive Team Lead of Near Frontiers, USA

This exceptional book stands out as an invaluable resource, providing essential tools to assist believer immigrant families in the USA, as they navigate the complex journey of raising their families in a foreign land. I am hopeful that the dedication and rigorous research poured into this work will yield fruit, paving the way for our future generations to reach even greater heights by building upon our legacy. I wholeheartedly endorse this book for diaspora families, and anyone committed to effectively serving these communities with a deeper insight into their intergenerational dynamics.

Nigist Fasil
Intergenerational Community Advocate,
The Gathering Networks, USA

Ethiopian Diaspora Churches on Mission

An Intergenerational Perspective on
Ethiopian Churches in the United States

Mehari Tedla Korcho

ACADEMIC

© 2024 Mehari Tedla Korcho

Published 2024 by Langham Academic
An imprint of Langham Publishing
www.langhampublishing.org

Langham Publishing and its imprints are a ministry of Langham Partnership

Langham Partnership
PO Box 296, Carlisle, Cumbria, CA3 9WZ, UK
www.langham.org

ISBNs:
978-1-83973-883-8 Print
978-1-78641-126-6 ePub
978-1-78641-127-3 PDF

Mehari Tedla Korcho has asserted his right under the Copyright, Designs and Patents Act, 1988 to be identified as the Author of this work.

All rights reserved. No part of this publication may be reproduced, stored in a retrieval system or transmitted, in any form or by any means, electronic, mechanical, photocopying, recording or otherwise, without the prior written permission of the publisher or the Copyright Licensing Agency.

Requests to reuse content from Langham Publishing are processed through PLSclear. Please visit www.plsclear.com to complete your request.

Scriptures taken from the Holy Bible, New International Version®, NIV®. Copyright © 1973, 1978, 1984, 2011 by Biblica, Inc.™ Used by permission of Zondervan.

British Library Cataloguing-in-Publication Data
A catalogue record for this book is available from the British Library

ISBN: 978-1-83973-883-8

Cover & Book Design: projectluz.com

Langham Partnership actively supports theological dialogue and an author's right to publish but does not necessarily endorse the views and opinions set forth here or in works referenced within this publication, nor can we guarantee technical and grammatical correctness. Langham Partnership does not accept any responsibility or liability to persons or property as a consequence of the reading, use or interpretation of its published content.

Contents

Abstract xi
Acknowledgements xiii
Chapter 1 1
Introduction
    Rationale and Need for Study 3
    Research Problem, Limitations, and Terms 6
        Research Problem 6
        Limitations 7
        Key Terms 8
    Literature Review 9
        Theories and Practices of Diaspora Mission 9
        Non-Ethiopian Diaspora Churches in Mission 12
        Ethiopian Diaspora Churches in the US 17
        Summary of Literature Review 20
    Statement of Research Methodology 21
        Data Collection 22
        Ethical Issues 23
        Validity and Reliability 24
        Data Analysis 25
    Chapter by Chapter Breakdown 25

Chapter 2 29
History of Ethiopian Evangelical Diaspora Churches in the US
    Country Description 30
    Population and Settlement of Ethiopians in the US 32
        Ethiopian Population in the US 32
        Ethiopians' Settlement in the US 33
    The Three Waves of Ethiopian Migration to the US and the
        Establishment of Ethiopian Evangelical Churches in the US 34
        The First Wave of Ethiopian Migration to the USA
            (1920–1974) 35
        Ethiopian Evangelical Churches in the US During the
            First Wave of Migration 37
        The Second Wave of Ethiopian Migration to the USA
            (1974–1991) 39
        Ethiopian Evangelical Churches in the U.S During the
            Second Wave of Migration 40

    Features of Ethiopian Evangelical Churches in the US During
        the Second Wave of Ethiopian Immigrants to the US 46
    The Third Wave of Ethiopian Migration to the US
        (1991–Present) 53
    Features of Ethiopian Evangelical Churches in the US
        During the Third Wave of Ethiopian Immigrants to the US ... 55
    Chapter Summary 60

Chapter 3 63
Intergenerational Dynamics of the Ethiopian Diaspora Churches in the US

    Description of the First, Second and 1.5 Generation
        Ethiopians in the US 64
        First, Second and 1.5 Generation Age Factor 64
        First, Second and 1.5 Generation Cultural Resonation Factor ... 65
        Some Exceptions in Each Generation 71
    Biblical Examples of First, Second and 1.5 Generations 72
        Nehemiah: First-Generation Example 72
        Joseph: 1.5 Generation Example 73
        Paul: Second-Generation Example 74
    Cultural Adjustment of the First, Second, and 1.5 Generation
        Ethiopians in the US 75
        First-Generation Cultural Adjustment 76
        Challenges of the First-Generation in Cultural Adjustment 79
        1.5 Generation Cultural Adjustment 80
        Second-Generation Cultural Adjustment 82
        Challenges of the Second-Generation in Cultural Adjustment 88
    Current Intergenerational Trends of the Ethiopian Diaspora
        Churches in the US 92
        First Generation Trends 93
        1.5 Generation Trends 95
        Second Generation Trends 95
    Chapter Summary 100

Chapter 4 101
Research Findings on Participants' Demography, Church Features and Interaction Across Generational Lines

    Understanding the Research 102
    Demography of Participants 103
        Age Demography 104
        Gender Demography 104
        Ministry Role 104

    Full-time and Voluntary Correlations 105
    Ministry Motivation 105
Features of Ethiopian Evangelical Churches in the US 106
    Year of Amharic and English-Speaking Churches'
        Establishment 106
    Size of Amharic and English-Speaking Congregations 107
    Church Growth Since Establishment 108
    Features of First, Second and 1.5 Generation Ministries 111
Interactions Across Generational Lines 113
    Openness of the First, Second, and 1.5 Generations
        Across Each Other's Context 114
    How First Generation Migrants are Open to Their
        Children's Cultural Context 114
    How The Second Generation is Open to Their Parents'
        Cultural Context 115
    How Open 1.5 Generation is to Both First and Second
        Generation Context 115
    Challenges of Interaction Across Generational Boundaries 115
    Challenges of the First Generation in Their Relationship
        with the Second Generation 116
    Challenges of Second Generation in Their Relationship
        with the First Generation 117
    Other Challenges Across Generational Lines 118
Church Structure 120
    Perceptions of Second Generation Toward Their Parents'
        Ethnic Church 120
    Exodus and Destiny of the Second Generation 121
    What Model of Church Structure Brings the Three
        Generations Together? 123
Chapter Summary 130

Chapter 5 133
*Research Findings on Definition and Practices of Missions Among
Ethiopian Diaspora Churches in the US*
    Factors That Shape Participants' Definition of Missions 133
        Factor One: Participants' Views on Missionary Sending
            and Receiving Countries 134
        Factor Two: Participants' View on Missions Activities in
            the Recipient Countries 138
        Factor Three: Participants' Own Missions Experience in
            the US 143
        Factor Four: Participants' Biblical Views on Missions 146

    Participants' Definitions of Missions 148
        Missions is Partnering with God in His Mission 149
        Missions Involves Both Gospel Proclamation and
            Humanitarian Work 150
        Missions Involve Going to All Nations 152
        Missions Involves Disciple-Making 153
    The Practice of Missions Among Ethiopian Diaspora
        Churches in the US 155
        Mobilization and Recruitment for Missions 155
        Church Organizational Structure for Missions 156
        Transnationalism in Missions 156
    Strengths, Weaknesses, and Challenges of Ethiopian-Diaspora
        Churches in Missions 159
        Strengths of Ethiopian Diaspora Churches and Lessons
            that Churches in the US Can Take 160
        Weakness of Ethiopian Diaspora Churches in Missions 165
        Challenges of Ethiopian Diaspora Churches in the US 168
    Chapter Summary 175

Chapter 6 177
    Conclusion and Recommendations
    Conclusion 177
    Recommendations 180
        Continue Spiritual Fervency and Community Life 181
        Grow From Inward to Outward Focus 181
        Consider Family Approach 190
        Partner with Local US Churches and Mission Organizations .. 193
        Evaluate Church Structure 196
    Further Recommendations 202
    Final Words 204

Appendix 1 205
    Online Survey for Church Ministers and Members

Appendix 2 217
    Interview Questionnaire for Independent Ministry Leaders

Appendix 3 219
    Interview Questionnaire for Second Generation Church Planters

Bibliography 221

List of Tables

Table 3.1 Age and Community Factors Affecting Bilingual Competency of 1.5 Generation Migrants 70

Table 3.2 Summary of the Four Acculturation Strategies 91

Table 6.1 Different Church Models to Engage the Three Generations Together 202

List of Figures

Figure 3.1 Process of Growing Toward or Away from Bilingual and Bicultural Fluency 71

Figure 3.2 Adjustment Process of First Generation Migrants 77

Abstract

Diaspora missiology is a relatively new dimension in missions. People are on the move more than ever before. This phenomenon presents a tremendous opportunity for the global church to reach out to non-believer migrants and collaborate with believing migrants in the country of destination. Many works on diaspora missions tend to discuss missions *to* the diaspora, while little attention is given to missions *by* the diaspora and lacks an intergenerational perspective. Therefore, this research aims to develop an understanding of missions from the Ethiopian diaspora churches in the United States in order to create a working strategy that will effectively mobilize their intergenerational context for missions.

Ethiopians are the second-largest African diaspora community in the US, and there are over 140 Ethiopian diaspora churches established in the USA. To effectively mobilize their members for missions, these churches need to consider their intergenerational aspects and factors such as their definitions and mission practices, including their mobilization, recruitment, church structure, and transnationalism. This researcher also explores the history, strengths, weaknesses, and challenges of Ethiopian diaspora churches in the US for a deeper analysis.

Research findings of this study indicate that Ethiopian diaspora churches have a great potential for missions. However, they are self-focused in their establishment and ministry approach. In other words, the missional mindset of reaching out to communities beyond their own is weak or missing among Ethiopian diaspora churches' first, second, and 1.5 generations. The first and 1.5 generation take an isolationist approach where they design their ministry exclusively for themselves while neglecting the task of reaching out to the second generation and the hosting communities. The second generation is embedded in the majority culture; however, being embedded in the missional mindset is an issue of discipleship. Disciple-making is crucial among the second generation so that they may take Christianity as their primary identity to impact their surrounding community here in the US and beyond with the gospel. This researcher offers comprehensive strategic recommendations to help the first, second, and 1.5 generations engage in missions together. These strategic recommendations are developed around elements such as spiritual fervency and community life, inward versus outward missions approach, partnering with local US churches and missions organizations, focusing on family, and evaluating church structures.

Acknowledgements

I first and foremost praise the Lord for his grace that strengthened me throughout the whole process of writing this dissertation. This work would not have been possible without the support I have received from God. I give thanks to God, for his mercy endures forever!

I am grateful for the financial support of the Billy Graham Lausanne Scholarship. I especially would like to thank Dr. Ed. Smither, CIU Dean of Intercultural Studies, for connecting me with the scholarship opportunity and for his encouragement during the initial steps into this Ph.D. journey. Your leadership and heart for the nations is always inspiring!

Many people came alongside to provide their important input during this work. However, due to limited space I can only list a few. My sincere appreciation goes to all participants in this study for taking the time to fill out the online survey and answer my interview questions. I thank Dr. Anthony Casey for his insightful comments and encouraging guidance throughout the writing process of this dissertation. I am also grateful for the personal and professional support I have received from my friend, Dr. Abeneazer Urga.

I am so thankful to my friends and family members for their encouraging support and prayers. My heartfelt appreciation goes to my teammates at Near Frontiers for their prayers and encouragement. I thank Bob Rasmussen, Don Kerby, Bob Mossman and Jason Livingston for their encouragement and support in proofreading. I also thank Andinet Bekele and Betel Getachew for their encouraging friendship.

I give a special thanks to my mother, Getenesh Kebede, my father, Tedla Korcho and my aunty Genet Kebede. I got to this point because you raised me up in the Lord's way. I always thank God for you! Finally, I wish to thank my loving and supportive wife, Nazrawit Kasa, for her sacrificial commitment to me and our two children, Elroi and Efrata. Thank you for patiently walking this journey with me.

CHAPTER 1

Introduction

Today, people are on the move more than any time ever. Ethiopians' migration to the USA is one such phenomena amid today's massive people's movement globally. Approximately 251,000 Ethiopian immigrants and their children live in the US.[1] This makes Ethiopian immigrants the second-largest African immigrant community in the US next to the Nigerian diaspora.[2] According to Getahun Solomon, "the migration history of Ethiopians to the US, among other things reflects the nature and development of the Ethiopian-American diplomatic relationship since 1903."[3] Ethiopian migrants came to the US in three migration waves.[4] The first wave began in the 1920s and ended in 1973.[5] During this wave, Ethiopians came to America as students, businessmen, and government officials. The second wave happened in 1974.[6] During that time, many Ethiopians were forced to leave their country because of killings and persecution by the Communist government. The third wave began in the 1990s and continues to the present day.[7] During this wave, many Ethiopians

---

1. *The Ethiopian Diaspora in the United States*, 1. It is difficult to tell the exact number of Ethiopians living in America. The Migration Policy Institute (MPI) estimated that approximately 251,000 Ethiopians are living in America. However, most Ethiopians do not agree with this figure. They argue that this figure may reflect only Ethiopian population in the Washington DC area.

2. *The Ethiopian Diaspora in the United States*, 1.

3. Getahun A. Solomon, *History of Ethiopian Immigrants*, 249. Robert P. Skinner, *Abyssinia of Today: An Account of the First mission Sent by the American Government to the Court of King of Kings, 1903–1904* (Montana: Kessinger Publishing, LLC, 2010), 304.

4. Solomon, *History of Ethiopian Immigrants*, 249.

5. *Mapping of Ethiopian Diasporas*, 4.

6. *Mapping of Ethiopian Diasporas*, 4.

7. *Mapping of Ethiopian Diasporas*, 4.

have come to America mainly through the Diversity Visa Lottery Programs (DV) and family reunification.

At present, it is difficult to determine the exact number of Ethiopian diaspora believers in the US However, according to Gizaw D. Dersoh, the North American Ethiopian Evangelical Churches Association director, there are over 140 Ethiopian diaspora churches in America.[8] Most of these churches are planted in metropolitan areas following the pattern of Ethiopian immigrant distribution in the US Because most Ethiopian immigrants arrived during or after the year 2000, Ethiopian diaspora churches in the US have a very young second generation who were born and raised in the US Looking into the number of Ethiopian diaspora churches in US and their young generation, their potential for global missions becomes apparent.

This research explores an intergenerational perspective on diaspora missiology from Ethiopian churches in the US Diaspora missiology has two wings. The first wing is missions to diaspora or immigrants as mission fields.[9] Reaching out to non-believing immigrants with the gospel of Christ is the focus of this wing. The second wing is missions by and with diaspora or immigrants as mission participants.[10] This refers to believing immigrants carrying out missions by themselves or in collaboration with other believers in the country of destination. In this regard, Ethiopian diaspora churches are one of the mission forces in the US.

The purpose of this research is to establish an understanding of missions from the Ethiopian diaspora churches in the US by analyzing their history, intergenerational dynamics, definitions, and practices of mission. Included in mission practices are mobilization, recruitment, missions to future generations and transnationalism. Another purpose of this research is to develop comprehensive mission strategies to effectively mobilize them for global missions. This means that to analyze their practices in missions, Ethiopian diaspora churches in the US would need to consider their intergenerational dynamics and other factors such as mobilization, recruitment, missions to future generations, and transnationalism, because these factors would help

---

8. Derash, in person meeting, July 26, 2018, MD.

9. Enoch Wan, *Diaspora Missiology: Theory, Methodology, and Practice*, Second Edition. (Portland: Institute of Diaspora Studies, 2014), 3.

10. Wan, *Diaspora Missiology: Theory, Methodology and Practice*, 3.

them to develop comprehensive missions strategies to effectively mobilize their members for global missions.

Rationale and Need for Study

The need for scholarly research on missions in regard to Ethiopian diaspora churches in the US is threefold. First, little scholarly research has been done regarding missions from Ethiopian diaspora churches. To this researcher's knowledge, there is no book on missions from Ethiopian diaspora churches in the US, particularly with consideration to their intergenerational aspect. Again, to this researcher's knowledge, only two papers have been written to directly address missions from the Ethiopian diaspora churches in the US. One is by this researcher[11] and the other is by Jessica Udall.[12] However, both articles are descriptive studies focused on explaining the opportunities and challenges of Ethiopian diaspora churches in missions, rather than on helping them develop a comprehensive missions strategy to mobilize their intergenerational dynamics more effectively. Therefore, this researcher sought to contribute a thorough research to fill the gap.

Secondly, this study is needed because there has been little emphasis given to missions from believers in the diaspora. We now live in an era where people are more on the move than ever before, which creates tremendous mission opportunities for churches globally. Several books, articles, and papers have been written about the mission opportunities presented from these massive movements. In other words, diaspora missiology is gaining increased consideration. Yet, little attention is given to engaging believing migrants in missions.

Diaspora missiology has two wings: missions to the diaspora or immigrants as mission fields,[13] and missions by and with the diaspora or immigrants as mission participants.[14] The former focuses on reaching out to non-believing migrants with the gospel of Christ, while the latter refers to

---

11. Mehari Korcho, "The Case for Missions in Ethiopian Diaspora Churches of America." in *Churches on Mission: God's Grace Abounding to the Nations*, eds. Geoffrey Hartt, Christopher Little, and John Wang (Pasadena: William Carey Library, 2017), 233–254.

12. Jessica Udall, "The Ethiopian Diaspora," 183–195.

13. Enoch Wan, *Diaspora Missiology: Theory, Methodology, and Practice*, 3.

14. Wan, 3.

believing migrants carrying out missions by themselves or in collaboration with other believers in the country of destination. Many works on diaspora missions have focused on describing the phenomenon and encouraging churches and mission organizations to consider the global migration trend in their missions endeavors. For instance, diaspora mission scholars such as Enoch Wan,[15] Sadiri Joy Tira and Tetsunao Yamamori,[16] Jehu J. Hanciles,[17] and Jared Looney[18] did not expound the diaspora phenomenon beyond describing it methodologically. They mostly focused on mobilizing churches in the West to respond to the diaspora missions call. However, little has been done to increase missions by believing immigrants in the diaspora.

These scholarly works *Diaspora Missiology* by Enoch Wan, *Scattered and Gathered* by Sadiri Joy Tira and Tetsunao Yamamori and *Crossroads of the Nations* by Jared Looney addressed missions by the diaspora through case studies. However, these case studies only indicate the potential that diaspora churches could have in missions, but not success stories with working missions strategies.

The Lausanne Movement is another initiative playing an instrumental role in bringing the diaspora missions agenda to the forefront. In 2004, the Lausanne Movement added a new missions track called "the diaspora peoples" because it was becoming a key issue in global missions.[19] A call to reach the unreached in the diaspora and partnering with believing immigrants in the diaspora have been the two major focuses of this movement over the past decade. In other words, the Lausanne Movement's works are more focused on mobilizing churches and mission organizations in the host countries than helping the diaspora churches themselves. While helpful, a gap still exists in addressing the issue of missions by believing immigrants themselves.

Thirdly, the need for this research is due to the lack of a comprehensive look into the intergenerational context of the diaspora churches for effective missions. Most works on diaspora missions are either exclusively focused on the parents' generation (first generation) or their children (second generation).

---

15. Wan, 3.
16. Tira and Yamamori eds, *Scattered and Gathered*.
17. Hanciles, *Beyond Christendom*.
18. Looney, *Crossroads of the Nations*.
19. Wan and Tira, "Diaspora Missiology and Missions in the Context of the Twenty-First Century," 53.

The 1.5 generation, those who arrived in the country of destination at a young age, are not taken into consideration. A handful of scholars have written articles and dissertations about Ethiopian evangelical Christians in the US; however, their works do not reflect a comprehensive approach as they emphasize only one or two generations and disregard the others. For instance, Yared Halcheonly discussed the first-generation,[20] Tesfai Tessemafocused on the second and 1.5 generations,[21] and Mohammed Mussa explored the interaction between the first and second generations while neglecting the 1.5 generation.[22] While studying each individual generation is helpful, the diaspora missions field is missing a comprehensive look at how the three generations relate to each other. Therefore, this study seeks to fill the gap in the field.

In short, the need for scholarly research in the case of Ethiopian diaspora churches in the US is threefold. First, little scholarly research has been done regarding missions from Ethiopian diaspora churches. Therefore, this research provides additional resource to the field. Second, much emphasis has been given to missions to the diaspora. However, this study aims to go a step further and deal with missions by and with the diaspora. In this case, this study takes the discussion a step further and aims to develop a working mission strategy for diaspora churches by investigating a deeper analysis of their practices. Third, the intergenerational aspect of the diaspora churches is not given enough attention. Hence, this research explores the opportunities and responsibilities of mobilizing the intergenerational dynamics of Ethiopian diaspora churches in the US

In the context of this study, a working mission strategy for diaspora churches can be understood as a strategy that involves the three generational dynamics together, namely the parents (first generation), their children who were born and raised in the diaspora (second generation) and those who came to the country of destination at a young age (1.5 generation).

In addition to helping to fill the void in research, this study will help Ethiopian diaspora churches in the US actively engage in missions as diaspora witnesses in their host nation and beyond. Non-Ethiopian immigrant

---

20. Halche, "A Socio-Cultural Analysis," xvi.
21. Tesema, "Global Nomads," xviii.
22. Mussa, "Sociocultural Problems," ii.

churches and local US churches will also gain insight into further missional partnerships from this study.

Research Problem, Limitations, and Terms

In this section, this researcher presents five sub-questions to discuss research problems and four limitations and delimitations to indicate the scope and boundary of the study. Furthermore, key terms used in the entire study are defined for clarity.

Research Problem

The overarching research question that this study sought to answer is: what are the best practices that will help improve mission engagement from the Ethiopian diaspora churches in the US? To effectively explore this research issue, this researcher will lay out five important sub-questions.

The first sub-question is historical: what is the history of Ethiopian diaspora churches in the US? Here this researcher will discuss important historical periods contributing to Ethiopians' migration to the United States, focusing primarily on the second and third migration waves that helped birth and expand Ethiopian diaspora churches in the US Included in this section are issues that have influenced the US to open its doors to Ethiopians during those periods.

The second sub-question is sociological: what are the trends among Ethiopian diaspora churches in handling the challenges and opportunities of cultural adjustment and missions engagement of the first, second and 1.5 generation in the diaspora? This question delves into developing an understanding of the intergenerational aspect of Ethiopian diaspora churches in the US.

The third sub-question deals with the analysis and research findings of the study. That is, what do the participants' demography, church features, and interaction across generational lines look like? Answering this sub-question will offer a deeper understanding into who the participants are, what their churches look like, and how they interact across generational lines.

The fourth sub-question explores participants' historical and theological views of missions. Namely, what are some of the elements that shape the definition and practices of missions among Ethiopian diaspora churches in the US? To identify participants' historical views on missions, this researcher asked participants to reflect on the history of the global movement of missionary sending and receiving nations. Concerning theological views, this researcher discusses the prevailing theology and biblical concepts of missions observed among Ethiopian diaspora churches in the US.

Next, this researcher examines the practices of missions among Ethiopian diaspora churches, including their mobilization, organizational structure, and transnationalism. Mobilization includes investigating methods, training, and resource allocation to missions. Regarding organizational structure, this researcher considers programs that Ethiopian diaspora churches have designed toward missions. When it comes to transnationalism, this researcher probes the missionary sending or cross-cultural ministry activities of Ethiopian diaspora churches in the US Finally, this researcher explores the strengths, weaknesses, and challenges of Ethiopian diaspora churches in missions. In particular, this researcher considers aspects such as attitudes, culture, and resources.

The fifth and the final sub-question refers to future strategy. Specifically what new strategies can be developed to effectively mobilize and equip Ethiopian diaspora churches in the US for global missions? To answer this question, this researcher focuses on evaluating responses and identifying those that would help Ethiopian diaspora churches develop comprehensive missions strategies that enable them to be more effective in missions work in the US and beyond.

Limitations

This study includes five limitations and delimitations. First, this research analyzes both best practices and challenges that limit Ethiopian diaspora churches in missions from the mid–1990s to the present. This researcher chooses to delimit his investigation to that timeframe in order to follow the arrival of majority Ethiopian immigrants to the US through Diversity Lottery programs and family reunification. Second, this study is focused on Ethiopian diaspora churches located in the metropolitan areas where most Ethiopian immigrants live. These cities include Silver Spring, MD; Denver, CO; Atlanta GA; Seattle, WA; Dallas, TX; Los Angeles, CA; and Chicago, IL. Third, this study is not focused on every aspect of Ethiopian diaspora churches in mission. Rather, attention will be centered on examining whether factors such as their mobilization, intergenerational aspect, and transnationalism could contribute to the development of comprehensive missions strategy to effectively equip Ethiopian diaspora churches for global missions. Fourth, it is also important to note that this study is focused on believing Ethiopian immigrants rather than non-believing Ethiopian immigrants. Fifth, to encompass the different generational contexts and its implications on missions, this study will focus on a wide age range of Ethiopian diaspora church leaders between twenty-one and seventy years of age.

Key Terms

The following list includes definitions of key terms used throughout this dissertation.

Amharic: There are 83 different languages spoken in Ethiopia. Amharic is one of them. "Only 29% of the Ethiopian population are native Amharic speakers, compared to the approximately 34% who speak Afan Oromo."[23] Amharic is the official language in Ethiopia because it is widely used across the nation outside of the Amhara ethnic group, which is not the case for Afan Oromo.

Comprehensive strategy: A plan of action developed by comprehending nearly all elements or aspects to achieve a major goal of a certain entity.

Diaspora: Refers to the dispersion of any people from their original homeland.

Diaspora churches: Any ethnic churches established by believing immigrants outside of their home country.

Diaspora missiology: A missiological study that studies the missional aspect of people dispersed outside of their homeland.

First generation immigrants: Refers to the first immigrants of a particular family to move to the new host country at the age of 22 and over. They are characterized by their attachment to their country of origin.

Second generation immigrants: Refers to children of immigrants who came to the country of destination in their early age (0–10), or who were born and raised in the country of destination. They are mostly characterized

---

23. Alpha Omega Translations, "Top 4 Languages of Ethiopia," Alpha Omega translations, accessed March 27, 2020. https://alphaomegatranslations.com/foreign-language/top-4-languages-of-ethiopia/.

by their attachment to the country of destination more than their parents' home country.

1.5 generation immigrants: Refers to immigrants who came to the country of destination at an older age than the second generation, between eleven and twenty-one. They are usually characterized by their role as a bridge between the first and the second generation since they have the experience of both cultures; that of their homeland and of the country of destination.

Transnationalism: A social phenomenon that creates a greater interconnectedness between individuals, communities, and societies across borders, which influences the cultural, economic, and political landscape of both the country of origin and destination.

Literature Review

In this section we review existing research on diaspora missiology and diaspora missions. Reviews are presented in three categories, global diaspora missions, missions work among diaspora churches both in the West and non-Western contexts and Ethiopian diaspora churches in the US.

Theories and Practices of Diaspora Mission

This section focuses broadly on the issue of global diaspora missiology. This helps the study to develop an understanding of diaspora missions based on the wider context of the field of study.

Enoch Wan, in his prominent book, *Diaspora Missiology*, described the diaspora phenomenon methodologically.[24] He identified three types of diaspora missions: missions to the diaspora (reaching out to non-believer immigrants), missions with the diaspora (mobilizing non-diasporic Christians to partner with Christians in diaspora), and missions through, by, and beyond the diaspora (motivating and mobilizing diaspora Christians for cross-cultural missions).[25] Wan's methodological description of diaspora missions is helpful to develop a clearer understanding of the current diaspora phenomenon. However, his work focuses on the first two categories (missions to the diaspora and missions with the diaspora) rather than the third category (missions

---

24. Wan, *Diaspora Missiology*, 5.
25. Wan, 6.

by and beyond the diaspora). In other words, his work is more about mobilizing churches and missions organizations in the receiving countries than helping the diaspora churches themselves.

In a study on missiology and missions in the context of the 21st century, Enoch Wan and Sadiri Joy Tira give an overview of diaspora missiology and suggest the practice of diaspora missions as a new missions strategy that can supplement the traditional missiology to effectively respond to the demographic changes in the 21st century.[26] Wan and Tira further elaborate that unlike traditional missions approaches, diaspora missions can operate locally and globally, because its perspective is multi-directional, borderless, and transnational, with no geographical dichotomy of "here" and "there".[27] Wan and Tira suggest that diaspora missions has to be introduced to the global community of missiologists and mission leaders since diaspora missiology is a relatively new paradigm.[28] This means that churches in the hosting countries must recognize the immense potential for ministering to and through the diaspora.

Wan and Tira's study is helpful to better understand diaspora missiology compared with the traditional missions approaches; however, it is more focused on missions to the diaspora rather than missions by the diaspora. In other words, much attention is given to mobilizing Western churches rather than raising mission forces from the diaspora churches themselves. The discussion on providing working mission strategies to mobilize diaspora churches for global missions is overlooked in the study.

Matthew Krabill and Allison Norton, in their article, "New Wine in Old Wineskins," critiqued Wan and Tira's problematic assumptions and methodological issues within diaspora missiology.[29] Krabill and Norton agree with Wan and Tira that diaspora missiology "represents a non-spatial, borderless, transnational, and global perspective."[30] However, Krabill and Norton disagree with Wan and Tira claiming that their work reflects a narrow understanding of diaspora missions as their primary emphasis is outreach to diaspora,

---

26. Enoch Wan and Sadiri J. Tira, *Diaspora Missiology*, 45–56.
27. Wan and Tira, 48.
28. Wan and Tira, 55.
29. Matthew Krabill and Allison Norton, "New Wine in Old Wineskins," 442–455.
30. Krall and Norton, "New Wine," 451.

which falls short in fully grasping the significance of non-Western Christian initiatives and movements for the future of global Christianity.[31] It is true that non-believing immigrants are coming to the West where they can access the gospel more easily; however, one should not forget that believing immigrants are also coming to the West. For instance, "the United States continues to be the world's primary destination for Christian migrants, with three-quarters of migrants to the USA self-identifying with the Christian faith."[32] Here it can be asserted that unlike Wan and Tira, Krabill and Norton suggest that "the more central question regarding the relationship between mission and migration is not how Christians from the West can reach out to unreached diasporas, but rather how the initiatives and movements of Christian migrants are shaping the American religious landscape."[33] Therefore, their study shows that missions by believing immigrants is underutilized and indicates a need for this study.

Works of other diaspora mission scholars like Jehu J. Hanciles[34] and Jared Looney[35] are also focused on raising awareness about doing missions with diaspora, while little has been discussed about missions by diaspora. In their books, both authors call Western mission organizations and churches to change their traditional missions approaches to respond to the new missions opportunity presented by the global diaspora movement. They only attempt to address the issue of "missions by and beyond the diaspora"[36] through case studies, but most of these attempts discuss only the potential that diaspora churches could have in missions and not actual success stories with tangible working mission strategies for diaspora churches. For instance, Jehu J. Hanciles, in his book *Beyond Christendom*, included three case studies on missions by African diaspora churches in America.[37] As inspiring as the stories are for both local and diaspora churches in the US, they do not provide practical strategies for missions by these African diaspora churches.

---

31. Krall and Norton, 451.
32. Krall and Norton, 451.
33. Krall and Norton, 451.
34. Hancciles, *Beyond Christendom*.
35. Jared Looney, *Crossroads of the Nations*.
36. Wan, Diaspora Missiology, 131.
37. Hancciles, *Beyond Christendom*, 324–349.

Sadiri Joy Tira and Tetsunao Yamamori have also shed light on diaspora missiology by editing the book *Scattered and Gathered*.[38] This expansive volume addresses many aspects of diaspora ministry including trends, theological background, strategic ministry, challenges, church ministry and case studies. While helpful, the book did not expound the issue of diaspora missions beyond providing information about the diaspora phenomenon and the need to reach out to the people on the move globally. For instance, though the third section of the book was dedicated to the strategic direction of diaspora missions, much emphasis in this section was given to missions to the diaspora and it did not present a working strategy for missions by the diaspora. However, the second category of the book reveals different diaspora churches and their missions work both in the West and non-Western contexts. These reviews of preliminary works on the case of different diaspora churches will help this study to gain insights, draw lessons, and identify research gaps.

Non-Ethiopian Diaspora Churches in Mission

This section reviews mission practices of non-Ethiopian diaspora believers across the globe. John Stanley, in his article, "Are Migrant Churches Missional: A Case for Expanding Our Geography of Mission?," explores the case of Kerala Pentecostal Church, an Indian church in Kuwait, to show that neither the "going principle," cross-cultural engagement in missions, nor the "staying principle," embracing the local neighborhood in missions, fit diaspora missions.[39] Stanley argued that "the two principles have a limited view of the geographic scope of missions that prevent them from adequately understanding the missional involvement of diaspora churches."[40] In this case one can understand that the limited interaction of diaspora churches with local people and their luck of global cross-cultural missions does not imply that they failed in missions. Instead, their engagement in missions has shown by how social networks and transnationalism ministries back in their home land. For the Kerala church, ministering to the church members in Kuwait, supporting churches back home financially, supporting Christians in the

---

38. Tira and Yamamori, *Scattered and Gathered*.
39. John, "Are Migrant Churches," 2–4.
40. John, 9.

south to cross-culturally reach out to Northern India, and returning home for ministry are all missions work.[41]

Though Stanley's work addressed the issue of transnationalism in diaspora missions, he did not discuss how this concept fit the second generation, who are more open to global networking and tend to think beyond their parents' country of origin.

In his qualitative research, Stanley Nwoji studied the missional status of African diaspora Christians in the United States. Findings of his study showed that "though there are missionary programs in the African Christian community in the United States, they have an overall floundering missional identity and ineffective utilization of diaspora networks for missions."[42] Nwoji added that their ministry mainly reflects a replication of the churches in Africa and they have poor networking among themselves.[43] Also, lack of strategies to reach out to their children who are born and raised in the diaspora are their major challenges.[44] Nwoji's study concludes that "African Christians in the diaspora must sit with God, the Word itself, and the host and sending countries to formulate a strategy that would reach Americans, Africans, and the rest of the world."[45] Nwoji's research relates to my research in the sense that it identifies some of the challenges of diaspora churches in missions and calls for strategy development to respond to those challenges.

In his research, Sinyil Kim investigates the Christian identity and missional implication of South Korean diaspora churches in North America. Kim shares his own personal experience of "identity transformation" that helped him become more missional as a South Korean immigrant pastor. He explained this transformation as a change from "negative/passive" to "positive," from "victimized" to "blessed," and from "American Dream" to "Kingdom Dream".[46] In the light of his own experience, Kim explored the case of six South Korean diaspora churches in North America that needed to have the same identity transformation encounter for missions. Kim noted, South Korean immigrant churches generally have not clearly understood their

---

41. John, 5–7.
42. Nwoji, "The missional status", 175.
43. Nwoji. "The missional status" 211.
44. Nwoji, 213.
45. Nwoji, 214.
46. Kim, "South Korean," 6.

creative Christian identity and therefore cannot articulate the relevant missional implications.[47] In his study Kim's suggestion was that these churches need a kind of "Missional Identity Transformation" that has been exhibited in his own personal life and in the experiences of the six churches presented in his study.[48]

While helpful, this study is primarily focused on first-generation South Korean immigrants and did not incorporate the 1.5 and second generations, for whom the issue is much more relevant.

In her book, *Mission Through Diaspora: The Case of Chinese Churches in the USA*, Jeanne Wu noted that the mission practices of Chinese churches in the US are self-centered. Using the model proposed by Zephaniah Yu, Wu noted that Chinese diaspora churches in the US tend to reflect the three stages of missions.

> The first stage is "Local Local" which refers to Chinese diaspora churches in the US reaching out to non-believing Chinese in the US. The second stage is "Global Local" where the Chinese diaspora churches in the USA organize short-term outreach to Chinese in Taiwan, Hong Kong, mainland China, and other non-Chinese countries. The third stage is "Global Global" which refers to Chinese diaspora in the USA reaching out to non-Chinese in other countries.[49]

From the above three stages, Wu suggested that the missions activity of Chinese churches in the US reflects more of the second stage, missions through diaspora, and that their missions activity is progressively growing towards the third stage, missions by the diaspora.

Wu's study is helpful as it develops a progressive understanding of diaspora missions and the importance of transnational networking in missions. However, it does not discuss the role of the second generation which could help Chinese diaspora churches in their growth toward "missions by diaspora," reaching out to communities beyond their own globally.

---

47. Kim, 183.
48. Kim, 188.
49. Wu, *Mission Through Diaspora*, 56.

Miriam Adeney contributes a chapter, "Latino Diaspora Ministries in the USA," in Tira and Yamamori's volume where she discusses the Latino diaspora ministries in the USA.[50] According to Adeney, even though "some Latinos have lived in America for more than ten generations, many struggle with substandard living conditions which left Latinos to have few prospects to escape lower class status, and they are among the Americans most likely to live in poverty."[51] Adeney also noted that legal residency is another challenging issue where "about eleven million people reside illegally in the US."[52] Because of the economic and migration status situations "Latino churches like New Life Covenant Ministries in Chicago and Victory Outreach Ministry in California are focused on ministering to the hurt among the Latino community in the US."[53] Adeney remarked that "while combating these local burdens, Latino diaspora churches in America are also reaching out in foreign missions, not only through church-based outreaches, but also through networks like Pueblos Muslims (Muslim Peoples) and Cooperación Misionera de los Hispanos Norteamerica (COMHINA)."[54] Adeney's article discussed the local and global attempts of mission work by Latino diaspora churches in the US However, it did not show us the role of the next generation in missions, identifying them as mission fields rather than mission forces.

Manuel J. Gutierrez argues that the Western mission models do not fit non-Western missionaries. Gutierrez is a Mexican who was born and raised in the US In the process of preparing the future generations of Latino believers for mission, he was faced with challenges from the Western mission sending and funding models. In his article, "Missions from a Personal Latin American Perspective," Gutierrez noted that the Latino mission movement is growing, yet "the approach to getting believing Latinos started and involved in missions is not easy because they do not fit in with the mission sending process of the Western missions agencies, or the concept of regularly contributing funds for the agencies' support."[55] When Gutierrez explained the alternative approach that they are utilizing, he said, "instead of taking the expensive

---

50. Adeney, "Latino Diaspora Ministries," 423–429.
51. Adeney, 427.
52. Adeney, 427.
53. Adeney, 427.
54. Adeney, 425.
55. Gutierrez, "Missions from a Personal Latin American Perspective."

mission-sending approach, Latino missionaries give a boost to the existing local church and when they arrive in a place with no established church, they learn how to plant churches in order to have others with whom they can worship."[56] Gutierrez added that they also use the tentmaking ministry method to carry out missions work in a foreign land. This study is helpful to my research as it ventures new strategies to effectively mobilize diaspora churches for global missions.

Philip Jenkins, in his article, "From Lagos to All Nations," discussed the global impact of the Redeemed Christian Church of God (RCCG). This church aims to plant churches "within five minutes' walking distance in every city and town of developing countries; and within five minutes' driving distance in every city and town of developed countries."[57] The contemporary Nigerian diaspora is the driving force for the global mission while the headquarters is based in Nigeria. They want people to be able to find the Redeemed Church wherever believing Nigerians live. Jenkins highlighted that the church operates in almost 200 countries and claims five million members, despite the challenges of power struggles and charges of exploitation and financial malpractice by some pastors.[58] Though this study provides a practical example of a missions initiative from an African diaspora church, it did not discuss whether the expansion of this church encompasses reaching out cross-culturally, beyond Nigerians. Also, the study did not say anything about the engagement of their children (the second generation) in missions.

J. Kwabena Asamoah-Gyadu, in his article, "Migration, Diaspora Mission, and Religious Others World's Christianity: An African Perspective," observes that "African believing immigrants are perceived by their Western compatriots as religious others, a minority group that might need some support, while the presence of these churches with their practices of faith and spirituality is important in missions."[59] Asamoah-Gyadu added that believing African Christians and their churches in the diaspora are perceived as "creation of boundaries charged with 'ghettoizing' religion."[60] In other words, because

---

56. Gutierrez, "Missions From a Personal."

57. Philip Jenkins, "From Lagos to all Nations, Notes from the Global church." *Christian Century* (2018): 44–45.

58. Jenkins, "From Lagos," 44.

59. Asamoah-Gyadu, "Migration, Diaspora Mission," 189–192.

60. Asamoah-Gyadu, 190.

of the isolation approach "witness of presence is the only contribution that believing African immigrants could make to the world Christianity."[61] This study sheds light on my research in developing an understanding of missions by believing immigrants. However, it lacks strategies on how these churches could overcome their self-focus challenge so that they would communicate their spiritual zeal with communities beyond their own (cross-culturally) and to their own children, who were born and raised in diaspora (intergenerationally).

Harvey Kwiyani highlighted missions from the Christian African diaspora in Europe. He noted that these churches need a missiological framework in Europe because, unlike the rest of the world, the continent is becoming increasingly secular. Therefore, African believing immigrants "need to learn the secular context to effectively reach Europe."[62] Kwiyani also highlighted the importance of prayer in the plans, strategies, and visions of these churches. "Prayer is essential because God has sent these churches in the form of many prayerful and zealous Christians who would open the gates and shine God's light in Europe."[63] Kwiyani challenged European Christians to think of their continent as a mission field and to receive help from non-Westerners living among them.[64]

Kwiyani's study is relevant for my research because it suggested some ways to help diaspora churches be more effective in missions. However, the study is more focused on helping European churches realize the mission force from the diaspora living in their midst rather than discussing how these churches are doing missions apart from their presence in Europe. Moreover, the study did not discuss the role of second-generation immigrant children in missions, except to identify them as victims of the European secular system.

Ethiopian Diaspora Churches in the US

Preceding studies on the history of Ethiopian diaspora churches in the US and their practices in relation to missions will be reviewed in this category, highlighting research possibilities that have been overlooked. Jessica Udall

---

61. Asamoah-Gyadu, 190.
62. Kwiyani, "Rethinking Mission," 10.
63. Kwiyani, 11.
64. Kwiyani, 11.

contributes a chapter, "The Ethiopian Diaspora: Ethiopian Immigrants as Cross-cultural Missionaries; Activating the Diaspora for Great Commission Impact." in Michael Pocock and Enoch Wan's volume.[65] In the chapter she discusses Ethiopian believing immigrants as cross-cultural missionaries in the West. In her study, Udall emphasizes the need to help Ethiopian diaspora churches realize their responsibility and opportunity to reach other immigrants as well as those in the host culture.[66] Cultural proximity is the major missions opportunity. As immigrants themselves, Ethiopian diaspora Christians have cultural proximity to other immigrants that can open doors for the gospel. There are several challenges that Ethiopian evangelicals face in their mission work. Udall noted that believing Ethiopians in the US "are zealous and passionate about their faith; however, enclave mentality, lack of cross-cultural missions, the notion of professionalization of ministry, and lack of unity pose real challenges to missions."[67] Udall offers several suggestions including the need to strive for unity as well as training church leaders, members, and the younger generations to help them be more mission-minded.[68] Udall's study shed light on my research in relation to identifying challenges that Ethiopian diaspora churches face in missions. However, her work lacks strategy development on how the suggestions can be implemented.

Migration Policy Institution presented detailed demographic and socioeconomic characteristics of the Ethiopian diaspora community in the US. The report noted that "sixty percent of Ethiopian immigrants to the United States arrived during or after 2000 through family reunification and diversity visa programs."[69] Thus Ethiopian diaspora communities are the most recently settled and have the youngest populations in both the first and second generations. The vast majority of the Ethiopian diaspora population in the US is working age, with a median age of 37 and the median age of their children (the second generation) is 7.[70] Even though most Ethiopians are heavily concentrated in Washington D.C., they can also be found in other metropolitan areas such as Chicago, Minneapolis, Seattle, and Atlanta, as well as in states

---

65. Udall, "The Ethiopian Diaspora, 183.
66. Udall, 184.
67. Udall, 187.
68. Udall, 187.
69. *Ethiopian Diaspora in the United States*, 1.
70. *Ethiopian Diaspora in the United States*, 1.

such as California, Texas, and Colorado.⁷¹ This article relates to my research as it explains the historical and demographic context of the Ethiopian diaspora in the US However, this work did not specifically discuss Ethiopian evangelicals in the US and their missional components.

Yared Halche conducted a qualitative case study by interviewing twenty-two Ethiopian immigrant church pastors and elders. His study investigates the implications of leadership styles on missions within Ethiopian diaspora churches in the US. Halche noted that "leadership style cannot be viewed or studied apart from the socioeconomic and spiritual realities that immigrant leaders face in the new land."⁷² Halche added,

> Adjustment challenges stir power tension which is one of the major variables that brings about poor leader-member relations, entangled task structure, and impoverished missionary roles. These churches are suffering from power-fueled conflicts. Transnationally, these churches are contributing to missions work back home; however, due to overwhelming social demands, these churches lose sight of the bigger picture of evangelistic roles among various ethnic communities and the second generation in the US and beyond.⁷³

Halche recommended that "for the Ethiopian immigrant church to engage in a dynamic transforming mission, critical leadership formation needs to be articulated, recontextualized, and implemented."⁷⁴ Halche's study is helpful for my research as it discusses some major challenges of Ethiopian diaspora churches in missions. However, the study did not discuss missions strategy development that reflects the intergenerational and transnational context of Ethiopian diaspora churches in the US.

In his qualitative study, Mohammed Mussa examined sociocultural problems experienced by Ethiopian immigrants in the US and the communication of the gospel. For his study, Mussa interviewed sixteen second-generation and twenty-five first-generation Ethiopian believing immigrants in the US Mussa's study revealed that immigrants face racism, assimilation, prejudice,

---

71. *Ethiopian Diaspora in the United States*, .
72. Halche, "A Socio-Cultural Analysis," 243.
73. Halche, 237.
74. Halche, 245.

and discrimination.[75] The study gives recommendations on how Ethiopian believing immigrants should respond to these problems as Christians and that gospel communicators should use these problems as opportunities to share the gospel with both the first and second generation in the midst of this sociocultural crisis. Mussa's study clarifies the context behind Ethiopian diaspora communities in the US and their sociocultural challenges. However, his study focuses more on missions to the Ethiopian immigrants rather than missions by Ethiopian diaspora churches in the US.

Summary of Literature Review

In summary, this literature review investigates secondary resources containing broader issues of diaspora missiology - those that discuss the cases of different diaspora churches and those specifically focusing on the Ethiopian diaspora churches. Helpful insights have been drawn from these sources in relation to understanding diaspora missiology as relatively new missions paradigms. These sources also add value to this study by expounding how diaspora ministry brought a tremendous missions opportunities for churches in the twenty-first century. However, gaps still exist in providing a working comprehensive strategy to effectively mobilize diaspora churches for global missions.

Most of the literature reviewed by this researcher gives an informative methodological description of the diaspora phenomenon. Much emphasis has been placed on "missions to" or "missions with" the diaspora, while little attention is given to "missions by" the diaspora. Those that discussed "missions by" the diaspora widely discussed potential and challenges of diaspora churches in missions. Most of these writings indicated that diaspora churches are characterized as zealous and spiritual with great potential for missions. However, these churches face challenges, including not understanding their new context, being soley concentrated on their own community, splitting as a result of leadership power struggles, and being unable to properly reach the second generation. Though most of the writings attempt to give suggestions as responses to the presented challenges, none of them discuss the need to develop a comprehensive missions strategy to overcome challenges and maximize their potential for global missions. Thus, this study is designed to fill a critical gap in the research and provide a comprehensive strategy for

---

75. Mussa, "Sociocultural Problems," Publishing. 1.

missions by the diaspora; a strategy that considers the whole context of diaspora churches, including their intergenerational dynamics and other elements such as organization, transnationalism, and intergenerational dynamics.

Statement of Research Methodology

This researcher employed a qualitative and quantitative case study. According to Creswell and Poth, case study research is the qualitative approach that involves "identification of a specific case or multiple cases so that they can be compared."[76] Creswell and Poth added that case studies "may also be distinguished in terms of the intent of the case analysis as single instrumental case study, collective or multiple case studies, and intrinsic case studies."[77] For this study, this researcher utilized a single instrumental case study. Hence, the aim of this study is to explore the issue of missions from the Ethiopian diaspora churches in the US from an intergenerational perspective.

Creswell and Poth highlighted that "in case studies the investigator explores a real-life case that is in progress so that accurate information can be gathered that is not lost by time."[78] In other words Creswell is stressing that "the key here is defining a case that can be bounded or described within certain parameters, such as a specific place and time."[79] Though there are many Ethiopian diaspora churches worldwide, investigation of this study is only focused on Ethiopian diaspora churches in the US The study also limited the investigation period and focused on exploring the mission work among Ethiopian diaspora churches in the US from the mid-1980s to the present. Ethiopian diaspora churches in the US began to rapidly grow in number in the 1980s, followed by the arrival of majority Ethiopian migrants through asylum seeking and then through Diversity Visa lottery programs and family reunification from 1991 to date.

Creswell and Poth noted that "a hallmark of a good qualitative case study is that it presents an in-depth understanding of the case."[80] This research is

---

76. Creswell and Poth, *Qualitative Inquiry*, 15.
77. Creswell and Poth, 99.
78. Creswell and Poth, 98.
79. Creswell and Poth, 98.
80. Creswell and Poth, 98.

intended to develop an in-depth description and analysis of missions in the Ethiopian diaspora churches in the US This includes studying their intergenerational dynamics and factors such as mobilization, recruitment, missions to future generations, and transnationalism. By analyzing implications of the intergenerational aspect and the above factors on missions, this research aims to develop a working comprehensive missions strategy to effectively mobilize and equip Ethiopian diaspora churches in the US for global missions.

Creswell and Poth underline that "relying on one source of data is typically not enough to develop this in-depth understanding."[81] Hence, this researcher gathers quantitative data and many forms of qualitative data ranging from "interviews to observation, to documents, to audiovisual materials."[82] In other words, this research draws data using multiple resources such as online survey, interviews, observations, different report documents, journals, and websites.

Data Collection

This researcher gathered data in two ways: through an online survey and a follow-up interview. The online survey was developed through Google Forms and includes thirty-seven participants from fourteen Ethiopian diaspora churches across the US. The survey was distributed to church ministers and members from the first, second, and 1.5 generations. Interviews were conducted with twelve participants, two independent ministry leaders, three second-generation church planters, two 1.5 generation members, and five first-generation church leaders.

To encompass this generational dynamic, this study focuses on a wide range of Ethiopian diaspora church leaders between twenty-one and seventy years of age. This researcher found participants based on the connections he developed over the last two years of traveling to visit and minister to the Ethiopian churches across the US. This researcher considers these participants good fits for this study because they represent and reflect the intergenerational and intercultural dynamics of Ethiopian diaspora churches in the US.

This researcher used purposeful sampling to select participants to glean the most helpful and relevant feedback from eight Ethiopian diaspora churches

---

81. Creswell and Poth, 98.
82. Creswell and Poth, 98.

across the United States using the following criteria: (1) A broad sampling based on the size of the church with the number of members ranging from 300 – 600. (2) A broad sampling based on their locations, including Silver Spring, MD; Denver, CO; Atlanta, GA; Seattle, WA; Dallas, TX; Los Angeles, CA; Chicago, IL; and St. Paul, MN. These cities are metropolitan areas with a high density of Ethiopian immigrants. (3) Churches that this researcher knows have relatively strong second-generation ministries. (4) Churches that this researcher knows are open to grow in the area of cross-cultural missions.

Both the survey and interview were conducted in the spring and summer of 2021. Interviews were conducted through phone and Zoom calls. This researcher sent interview questions to participants prior to the interviews so participants would be familiar with the questions. Each interview took approximately one hour and fifteen minutes. Participants were asked to respond to seventeen questions about missions in the Ethiopian diaspora churches. Regarding the survey questions, a survey link was distributed to participants through regular text, WhatsApp, Viber, Facebook Messenger, and email. Participants were asked to respond to sixty-five questions and the survey took approximately 25 – 30 minutes to complete.

Language barrier was one the challenges that this researcher faced in the study. It was not easy for first-generation responders to adequately communicate their responses in English as conveniently as it was for second-generation responders. To solve this problem, this researcher conducted some interviews in Amharic with first-generation respondents, depending on their preferences. Results were carefully translated into English. Here one can raise the issue of reliability when it comes to interpreting and relaying accurate responses. This is a valid concern, and this researcher invited some participants and others with a good grasp of Amharic to participate in the validation process. This researcher will do a further discussion on this concern under the section "Validity and Reliability." When it comes to the survey, participants were given options to respond orally to the open-ended questions or to write their responses in Amharic.

Ethical Issues

Ethical research applies to both quantitative and qualitative studies when a researcher uses primary sources, such as those who directly participate in the research by completing a survey or conducting an interview. Conducting ethical research primarily requires having the participants; consent before the study begins. This includes clarifying the research subject, explaining the purpose of the research, and describing how the data will be used. In this case, this researcher will first connect with participants through phone calls and emails to explain the purpose and process of the study and ask if they are willing to participate in the study. Once they agree, this researcher will ask them to sign an informed consent form. This form indicates that participants have clearly understood the purpose and process of the study and that they are willing to take part in the study.

Another important issue when conducting ethical research is to explain both the benefits and risks involved in the study. How will the results benefit participants? What are the risks involved in the research? And how does this researcher minimize the risks? This researcher will mention to participants that he will share findings of the study at the completion of the research. To minimize risks, this researcher will give assurance that participants' information will not be used outside of the study. Confidentiality of participants in the process of the study will be kept by allowing each person to remain anonymous and their specific work and location undisclosed. This researcher will also mention that participants have a right to withdraw from the study at any time, even after the interview is completed.

Validity and Reliability

Edgar J. Elliston noted that "in a qualitative study, validity and reliability require consistent serious attention."[83] Elliston further explained that "validity refers to asking the right questions, securing the right information, and making the appropriate applications, while reliability relates to consistency or stability of the result."[84] In this case, a researcher must ask, "Does the study indeed address the issues it claims to address?" For this study, this researcher will seek to incorporate at least three methods of validation of the analyzed conclusions for accuracy. First, this researcher will engage in persistent observation on the subject and those involved in the research process. Doing so will help this researcher make a reliable conclusion that will not stem from superficial first impressions, but from his real experience through deep

---

83. Edgar J Elliston, *Introduction to Missiological Research Design*, 54.
84. Edgar J Elliston, 235.

observation. Second, in addition to observation, using multiple sources of information, such as different report documents, journals, and websites, will also lead to result validation. Third and finally, this researcher will invite people, including participants in the study and others who understand diaspora ministry well, to participate in the validation process by reflecting on the findings of the study.

Data Analysis

The case study approach has three paths of data analysis: descriptive, thematic, and cross-case themes. This study employs a descriptive data analysis that follows a thematic approach. Creswell and Poth noted that a good case study research involves a description of the case.[85] This researcher will identify key patterns, trends, and repeated themes that shape thinking and practices as a result of the case study. In the data analysis section, this researcher thematically interprets the collected data to describe how Ethiopian diaspora churches in the US have practiced missions and why. Based on the interpretation, this researcher will determine what procedures or practices might be necessary in the future to replicate a desired outcome or avoid undesired outcomes.

No standard format exists for reporting case study research. Some case studies generate theory, some are simply descriptions of the case, and others are more analytical in nature and display cross-case or interstice comparisons.[86] The anticipated final outcome of this study is to develop a comprehensive missions strategy by taking practical lessons from the analysis.

Chapter by Chapter Breakdown

This study is divided into six chapters. The first chapter provides an introduction to the study, along with the needs of the study, research problem, literature reviews, and methods of the study.

Chapter two discusses the historical background of Ethiopian Diaspora churches in the US In this chapter, this researcher presents important historical periods contributing to Ethiopian migration to the US, including issues that have influenced the US to open its doors to Ethiopians during those

---

85. Creswell and Poth, *Qualitative Inquiry and Research Design*, 55.
86. Creswell and Poth, 236.

periods. In particular, attention will be given to discussing the history of Ethiopian diaspora churches in the US.

Chapter three deals with the intergenerational dynamics of Ethiopian diaspora churches in the US In this chapter, this researcher first lays out the definition and description of each generation, along with their sociological views of cultural adjustment in the diaspora. Then the current trend of Ethiopian diaspora churches in handling their intergenerational dynamics is discussed.

Chapter four offers data analysis and research findings across three subtopics, including participants' demography, church features, and interaction among generations. Demography of participants discusses the age, gender, ministry role, full-time and voluntary correlations, as well as participants' motivation to join their current ministry in the church. Church features consist of both the Amharic and English-speaking congregations of the Ethiopian diaspora churches in the US The year of establishment, size, operation, and structure of these churches is discussed in detail. Regarding interaction across generational lines, this researcher explores how open the first, second, and 1.5 generations are to each other's context, the challenges they face when they want to communicate across the boundaries of their generational circles, and church structures that can bring the whole generations together for effective missions.

Chapter five also presents data analysis and research findings, this time focused on definition and practices of missions among Ethiopian diaspora churches. First, this researcher probes participants' observations on the historical missionary sending and recipient countries, as well as missionaries' activities in host countries. Next, this researcher explores the theological views of participants in relation to missions to see how these factors have shaped participants' definition of missions. When it comes to mission practices, this chapter analyzes participants' responses on mobilization, recruitment, missions to future generations, transnationalism, strengths, weaknesses, and challenges of Ethiopian diaspora churches in missions.

The sixth and final chapter offers conclusions and recommendations of the study. In this chapter, the researcher puts forth the conclusion of the study. Then, by taking practical lessons from the analysis, this researcher develops a comprehensive mission strategy that allows the first, second, and 1.5 generations to engage together in missions. Here, this researcher determines what procedures or practices might be necessary for the future to replicate the desired outcome or avoid undesired outcomes. This researcher uses a thematic approach to identify key patterns, trends, and repeated themes that shape the thinking and practices as a result of this case study. This will be done by taking into consideration the mobilization practices, theological convictions, intergenerational dynamics, and transnational opportunities of Ethiopian diaspora churches in the US. These strategic recommendations, along with the recommendations for further study, will be shared in this chapter. It is the researcher's hope that the recommendations will help Ethiopian diaspora churches effectively mobilize and equip their communities in the US for global missions. Also, other diaspora believers in the United States and US mainstream churches and mission organizations can take their lessons accordingly.

CHAPTER 2

History of Ethiopian Evangelical Diaspora Churches in the US

This chapter provides the history of Ethiopian evangelical diaspora churches in the US in light of their country description, population, and settlement in the US and the three waves of their migration to the US.

Obtaining the relevant resources to study the history of Ethiopian evangelical churches in the US presents a challenge, as there is a scarcity of literature and data that addresses this topic. Consequently, this researcher used unpublished internal documents and primary data by interviewing six pastors from the first generation, one pastor from the second generation, and one person who formerly served as an elder in one of the oldest Ethiopian evangelical churches in the US.

The term "Ethiopian evangelical church" is used throughout this study to describe all Ethiopian migrant communities that affiliate with a Protestant faith. Halche noted, "the word 'evangelical,' besides denoting affiliation to a Protestant faith, also signifies a non-Ethiopian Orthodox *Tewahido* (EOTC)."[1] Moreover, the term "evangelical" is used here as a unifying name across different Protestant church denominations in Ethiopia. The campus ministry in Ethiopia, Ethiopian Evangelical Students and Graduates Association (EvaSUE), with whom this researcher served prior to traveling abroad, is a good example of this classification. EvaSUE uses the title "evangelical" to signify the unity of non-Ethiopian Orthodox *Tewahido* Christian students from different denominations of Protestant churches across the country.

---

1. Halche, "A Socio-Cultural Analysis," 23.

The same is true for believing Ethiopian migrants in the US In their home country, Ethiopian immigrants may be part of varying denominations such as Lutheran (Mekane Yesus), Mennonite (Meserte Kirstos), Pentecostal (Muluwengel), and so on. However, once here in the US, they come under the umbrella "evangelical" to distinguish themselves from the diaspora Ethiopian Orthodox *Tewahido* Christians, and to signify unity across their Ethiopian-origin denominational backgrounds.

In this chapter, the author first presents the country description to develop an understanding of Ethiopian identity. Second, the author discusses the population and settlement patterns of Ethiopians in the US Third, the author offers an in-depth study of the three waves of Ethiopian migration to the US and the growth of Ethiopian evangelical diaspora churches corresponding to the three waves of migration. Here the author seeks to understand the timing and methods of church planting and growth among the Ethiopian evangelical diaspora churches in the US by asking the question, "How do the three waves of Ethiopian migration to the US impact the establishment and growth of Ethiopian evangelical diaspora churches within the US?"

Country Description

Since Ethiopian diaspora communities in the US are a reflection of their country of origin, it is important to begin by laying out a general description of the Ethiopian identity. Ethiopia is an African country located in the horn of Africa. It borders Eritrea to the north and northeast, Djibouti and Somalia to the east, Kenya to the south, South Sudan to the southwest, and Sudan to the west. Ethiopia is the tenth-largest country geographically and the second most populated nation in Africa, after Nigeria.

Ethiopia is home to over eighty ethnic groups and people that have diverse religious affiliations. There are eighty-three different languages spoken in Ethiopia. Under the constitution, all Ethiopian languages enjoy official state recognition. However, Amharic is the "working language" of the federal government. Together with Oromo, it is one of the two most widely spoken languages in the country.[2] Only 29 percent of the Ethiopian population are

---

2. "Ethiopia-Ethnic Groups and Language", accessed October 15, 2020, https://www.britannica.com/place/Ethiopia/Ethnic-groups-and-languages

native Amharic speakers, compared to the approximately 34 percent who speak Afan Oromo.³ However, Amharic is widely used across the nation outside of the Amhara ethnic group, which is not the case for Afan-Oromo.⁴

Economically, Ethiopia is one of the poorest countries in the world. According to the World Bank Report, Ethiopia's economy experienced strong, broad-based growth of average 9.4 percent a year between 2010 and 2020.⁵ However, in spite of this, the country remains poor due to the challenges of sustaining positive economic growth and accelerating poverty reduction, both of which require significant progress in job creation, as well as improved governance.⁶ Moreover, the COVID-19 pandemic and the civil war between the central government and the Tigray rebel forces (both recent phenomena at the time of compiling research and writing this dissertation) have posed a huge challenge to Ethiopia's economy.

Regarding religious affiliation in Ethiopia, the 2016 World Factbook estimates that the Ethiopian Orthodox *Tewahido* accounts for 43.8 percent of the population, Islam accounts for 31.3 percent, Protestants 22.8 percent, Catholics 0.7 percent, traditional religion 0.6 percent, and others 1 percent.⁷ Geographically, Orthodox *Tewahido* believers are predominant in the north, while Islam is prevalent in the southeast, and Protestantism in the south and southwestern parts of Ethiopia.

Historically, Ethiopia is unique among African countries because it has never been colonized by Western powers. The ancient Ethiopian monarchy maintained its freedom from colonial rule, with the exception of the 1936–1941 Italian occupation.⁸ This freedom has enabled Ethiopians to have a strong and solid cultural identity unbiased by European colonial influence. However, this remarkable national identity is currently challenged by Ethiopia's ethnic-based politics. Consequently, this ethnic-based politics

---

3. "Top Four Languages of Ethiopia," Alpha Omega Translations, accessed October 27, 2020, https://alphaomegatranslations.com/foreign-language/top-4-languages-of-ethiopia/

4. Alpha Omega Translations, "Top Four Languages."

5. "World Bank Country Overview," World Bank, accessed December 16, 2021, https://www.worldbank.org/en/country/ethiopia/overview#1.

6. "World Bank Country Overview."

7. "The World Factbook," accessed October 15, 2020, https://www.cia.gov/the-world-factbook/countries/ethiopia/

8. "Global Atlanta Snapshots: A Look at Ethnic Communities in the Atlanta Region," accessed October 17, 2020, http://documents.atlantaregional.com/gawsnapshots/ethiopian.pdf

created internal division. The current reformist government that came to power in 2018 is undertaking a national unification project across the myriad ethnic groups through its philosophy of *medemer* which means to be summed up.

Population and Settlement of Ethiopians in the US
Ethiopian Population in the US

It is difficult to tell the exact number of Ethiopians living in the US. The MPI study reveals that Ethiopian-born immigrants constitute the United States' second-largest African immigrant group, after Nigeria.[9] However, according to the 2014 MPI study, approximately 251,000 Ethiopian immigrants and their children (the first and second generations) live in the United States, and Ethiopian-born immigrants account for 0.5 percent of the US foreign-born population.[10] Another study by International Organization for Migration (IOM) in 2018 indicates approximately 305,800 Ethiopian immigrants live in the United States.[11]

Many Ethiopian communities in the US do not agree with the figures reflected in either the MPI or IOM studies. They say that those figures reflect only the Ethiopian population in the Washington, D.C. area. A prominent Ethiopian historian, Solomon, also suggests that these figures may represent only Ethiopian immigrants who came to the United Sates between the 1950s and 1990s.[12] James Jeffery summarizes what the Ethiopian community believes about the population of Ethiopians in the US saying, "Though there is no census data, a million Ethiopians are estimated to live in the US, of whom about 250,000 are concentrated across Washington, D.C., Virginia and Maryland."[13] Regardless of the view one takes, it is safe to say that the number of Ethiopians living in America is likely somewhere between three hundred thousand to one million.

---

9. *Ethiopian Diaspora*, 1.
10. *Ethiopian Diaspora*, 1.
11. "Mapping of Ethiopian Diasporas," 2.
12. Solomon, *The History of Ethiopian Immigrants*, 1.
13. Jeffrey, "How did US?" BBC, accessed October 19, 2020, https://www.bbc.com/news/world-us-canada-47203691

Similarly, it is difficult to tell the exact number of Ethiopian evangelical Christians in America,[14] but most Ethiopian diaspora believers agree that the number is growing significantly. The growth of Ethiopian evangelical Christianity in the US has a direct relationship to the growth of Christianity in Ethiopia. According to Eshete, the evangelical Christianity that accounted for only less than one percent of the Ethiopian population in the early 1960s has been growing rapidly to number in the millions over the last three decades alone.[15] Further, Eshete notes that the 1994 government census records the number of evangelical Christians as being close to six million. The World Factbook estimate in 2016 also witnessed the growth of evangelical Christians in Ethiopia accounting for 22.8 percent of the total population.[16] This clearly shows that prior to the 1970s, most Ethiopians who migrated to the US were not evangelical Christians, but their presence has increased over time as evangelical Christianity has rapidly expanded in Ethiopia. The North American Ethiopian Evangelical Churches Association director, Gizaw D. Derseh, says that currently there are over 140 Ethiopian diaspora churches in America.[17]

Ethiopians' Settlement in the US

The number of Ethiopians who settled in the US prior to the 1980s was small, and dispersed throughout the United States, largely pursuing higher education. Getahun Solomon states that the main reason for the absence of Ethiopian community organizations, restaurants, and shops in the US during this time was due to the nature of this dispersed settlement.[18]

The settlement of Ethiopians who came to the USA in the 1980s was shaped by refugee resettlement programs. According to MPI study, over one thousand Ethiopian refugees were resettled in the US each year from 1981 to 1993 and 1999 to 2007 (with the exception of 2002).[19] The settlement of these refugees in America was ultimately determined by their religious, ethnic, and regional affiliations. In other words, these factors played major roles in

---

14. Jeffrey, "How did US?" 2.
15. Eshete, *The evangelical Movement in Ethiopia*, 27.
16. "The World Factbook," accessed October 15, 2020, https://www.cia.gov/the-world-factbook/countries/ethiopia/
17. Derseh, in person interview by author, April 19, 2020.
18. Solomon, *The History of Ethiopian Immigrants*, 43.
19. *Ethiopian Diaspora*, 3.

the attraction and concentration of immigrant groups to a certain US cities or states.[20] For instance, Ethiopians who are ethnically Gonderes (Amhara people) are predominantly in Seattle and Los Angeles, while Oromo are largely in Minnesota, and Tigrigna speakers are more concentrated in Ohio.[21]

The majority of the Ethiopian diaspora population in the US arrived from 1991, and the current settlement of Ethiopians in the US is widely distributed across a number of metropolitan areas. These recent Ethiopian migrants who have come to the US, mostly through the Diversity Visa (DV) Program, have the subsequent freedom to settle wherever they choose to live in the US These immigrants may still take their religious or ethnic affiliation into consideration when deciding where to settle, but given the larger degree of freedom they have under the DV Program, considerations such as cost of living and finding environments conducive to raising their children are more strongly determinative. The 2014 Migration Policy Institute study reports that Ethiopians are concentrated in California, Washington, Virginia, Maryland, Minnesota, Colorado, and Texas, each having about 15,000 Ethiopians, with the Washington, D.C. area having a population of 35,000, making it the largest population center for Ethiopians in the US.[22]

Unsurprisingly, following the recent settlement patterns of Ethiopians in the US, the largest concentrations of Ethiopian evangelical diaspora churches can be found in the Washington, D.C. area, California, Colorado, Texas, Washington, Georgia, Florida, Minnesota, North Carolina, New York, Kansas, and Illinois.

The Three Waves of Ethiopian Migration to the US and the Establishment of Ethiopian Evangelical Churches in the US

Ethiopian migration to the US reflects the nature and development of diplomatic relationships and the political atmosphere of both countries over the course of history. Factors such as the 1965 Immigration Act, the 1980

---

20. Solomon, *The History of Ethiopian Immigrants*, 120–121.

21. Solomon, *The History of Ethiopian Immigrants*, 124–131.

22. *Ethiopian Diaspora*, 5. The numbers indicated here do not reflect what the Ethiopian communities in each state believe to be accurate. They believe that the number is two or three times higher than what is indicated in the study.

Refugee Act, the 1990 Immigration Act, and the Diversity Visa program have shaped the pattern of Ethiopian migration to the US This migration history is often characterized as the three waves of Ethiopian migration to the US For the purpose of our discussion, we will emphasize those issues that have prompted the US to open its doors to Ethiopians, and the subsequent establishment and growth of Ethiopian evangelical churches in America during each of the three periods.

The First Wave of Ethiopian Migration to the USA (1920–1974)

The first wave of Ethiopian migration to the US took place between 1920–1974, catalyzed by a new diplomatic relationship between Ethiopia and the US Ethiopia-US relations officially began in 1903 with the arrival of an American trade missionary, Robert P. Skinner, in Addis Ababa, making Ethiopia one of the first African countries with a diplomatic relationship with the US[23] During this time, Ethiopia was also sending government officials and students to the US Accordingly, Ethiopians' arrival in the US began with Ethiopia sending a handful of its citizens for further education in the 1920s.[24] Empress Zewditu sent a group of students in 1922 to the Muskingum College in Ohio. The second group came to the East Coast in the 1930s to study in prestigious universities such as Harvard and Cornell.[25]

Among these students, Melaku Beyan was one of the most significant for two reasons: he played a prominent role in connecting African Americans with Ethiopia, particularly during the Italo-Ethiopian war in 1936; and he became the first Ethiopian to settle in America.[26] His case is of particular interest because permanent migration to the US by Ethiopians was virtually unknown before the revolution in 1974.[27] For instance, in the 1930s, the United States Immigration and Naturalization Bureau allotted a quota for 100 Ethiopian immigrants. However, this quota was never reached because prior to 1960 Ethiopians were largely averse to migration due to their limited

---

23. Solomon, *The History of Ethiopian Immigrants*, 11.
24. Solomon, 3.
25. Skinner, *Abyssinia of Today*, 103.
26. Solomon, *The History of Ethiopian Immigrants*, 18.
27. Solomon, 3.

exposure to the outside world in general and America in particular.[28] The number of Ethiopians who came to the US increased in the late 1960s and early 1970s as their awareness about life abroad increased. Solomon noted that Ethiopian migration to America, commenced by a select few who sought higher education in the 1920s as noted above, grew into the thousands by the 1970s.[29] In addition to those Ethiopians on a student visa program, who constituted the majority of new arrivals, others migrated as tourists, businesspeople, and government officials.[30] The arrival of Ethiopians to the US during this time as tourists and businesspeople is a strong indicator of an increased awareness among Ethiopians of the world at large, and the US in particular. Arguably, this new growth of a broader global awareness among Ethiopians was fostered primarily by the arrival of a comparable number of Americans to Ethiopia in the early 1970s. In the intervening years, about ten thousand Americans have worked in Ethiopia with other expatriates.[31]

Out of the six participants in this study who came to the US in the early 1970s, four of them indicated that they came to the US because of the awareness and support they received from missionaries who resided in Ethiopia. It is not clear how many believing Ethiopian immigrants were present in the US during that time. However, according to Getachew Metaferia and Maigenet Shifferaw, the estimated number of Ethiopians in the US (both believers and non-believers) before the 1974 Revolution was about thirty thousand.[32]

Despite the increased number of Ethiopians in the US resulting from an enlarged awareness of the outside world, it is interesting to note that the "sojourner" mindset among Ethiopian migrants in this period remained intact; in other words, these migrants still felt their primary identity to be rooted in their home country, and therefore felt no desire nor made any effort to establish a permanent Ethiopian community in the United States until the late 1970s and early 1980s.[33]

---

28. Solomon, 19.
29. Solomon, 3.
30. Solomon, 6.
31. Solomon, 3
32. Getachew and Maigenet, *The Ethiopian 2nd Revolution of 1974*, 63.
33. Getachew and Maigenet, *The Ethiopian Revolution*, 63.

Ethiopian Evangelical Churches in the US During the First Wave of Migration

No Ethiopian church was planted in the United States before 1981. However, the establishment of the Ethiopian Evangelical Christians Association (EECA) in the US was one of the major accomplishments of the Ethiopian diaspora Christians who arrived in the first wave. One of the participants who arrived during that time and is currently pastoring an Ethiopian diaspora church said, "The beginning of the 1970s is an important time for Ethiopian evangelical churches because that was the time when few believers started to arrive in the United States as students."[34]

In 1974 something remarkable happened among the Ethiopian diaspora evangelical Christians in the US At the invitation of Bete Mengistu and his wife Sophia Assefa, a small number of believing Ethiopian immigrants, including Mikal Bayisa, Amakelech Sahele, Yalew Kebede, Guenetu Yigzaw, Rahel Mesfin, and a few others met at their home in Wheaton, IL. One of the participants in this study who was present at the meeting says, "Bete Mengistu shared his vision of bringing Ethiopian evangelical Christians across the United States together for a time of fellowship and worship at least once a year." The participant adds: "The following year, in 1975, we had our first conference at Goshen College, in Goshen, Indiana." Another participant points out that this gathering, which they later called the "Chicago Conference," was the only place to go for all Ethiopian evangelical Christians across the United States. He adds, "Every year around August, we would all migrate to Chicago from all the corners of the United States for five days conference, which was a source of encouragement for us to enjoy fellowship and keep our faith in the diaspora and not be swallowed by the secular world in America."[35]

Under this overarching purpose, the gathering benefitted participants in two significant ways. First, the conference helped participants to maintain the ardor of their spiritual life while living in the diaspora. One of our participants explains it this way: "The purpose of our gathering back then was to encourage one another to keep the spiritual fervency."[36] He adds:

---

34. Zoom Interview, first generation participant 1, December 7, 2020.
35. Zoom Interview, first generation participant 1, December 7, 2020.
36. Zoom Interview, first generation participant 2, December 12, 2020.

> While still we were in Ethiopia in the city of Nazareth, we had heard many prophetic voices from the Lord. One of the messages was that God would send us overseas for the advancement of His kingdom. We did not understand it at that time. Today, it is that generation that dispersed around the world, expanding God's kingdom particularly in the West, including Canada, Europe, and America.[37]

Second, the gathering helped participants form a community in which they could enjoy their native culture together. By then, most of them were students scattered across the US, and many were experiencing homesickness. They missed their country, their food, their music, their coffee ceremony, and the opportunity to converse with their fellow countrymen about the things going on back home. A participant describes the situation:

> We were always longing for the Chicago Conference to spend five days with brothers and sisters from across the United States. Life was not easy for most of us, particularly with the atmosphere of the American culture fueled by ethnic division back then. So, coming to the Chicago Conference helped us get the encouragement and the love we needed. I remember how it was so hard for us to leave Chicago five days after the conference was over.[38]

Another participant says, "The conference was a blessing for us, even some of us were able to get our spouses from there."[39]

As more believing Ethiopian immigrants began to join the conference, they realized the need to change the gathering into a formal institution that could function beyond simply organizing annual conferences. In 1979 they appointed their first leader, Alemu Biftu. Since most of those who participated in the discussion were students, they named it Ethiopian Evangelical Christian Students Fellowship in America.

---

37. Zoom Interview, first generation participant 2, December 12, 2020.
38. Zoom Interview, first generation participant 1, December 7, 2020.
39. Zoom Interview, first generation participant 3, December 17, 2020.

The Second Wave of Ethiopian Migration to the USA (1974–1991)

The second wave of Ethiopian migration to the US occurred between 1974 and 1991. The relationship between Ethiopia and America during this period was highly influenced by the political atmosphere of the time. The Ethiopian-American diplomatic relationship was almost entirely dissolved when Ethiopia came under the rule of the Communist government in 1974. Consequently, the number of Americans in Ethiopia dropped significantly while the number of Ethiopians living abroad, mainly in America, increased by tens of thousands.[40] Therefore, US immigration policy during this period primarily accounted for the significant flow of Ethiopian refugees to the US At that time, the US immigration policy was highly influenced by Cold War politics, under which America invited all who were fleeing Communism. In other words, this political climate favored Ethiopians who wished to begin a new life in America.[41]

The 1951 UNHCR refugee convention defined a refugee as "someone unable or unwilling to return to their country of origin owing to a well-founded fear of being persecuted for reasons of race, religion, nationality, membership of a particular social group, or political opinion."[42] Factors that forced Ethiopian refugees in the 1980s to flee their country include harsh political realities such as the mass killing ("Red Terror"), mass detention and torture, war, and economic conditions like famine. "Chief among the causes of misery in Ethiopia during this time was the aforementioned "Red Terror," which lasted into the early 1990s."[43]

Ethiopian refugees, who made their initial migration to neighboring countries like Sudan and Kenya, were desperate to make America their final destination. Solomon stated that "most Ethiopians who arrived in the USA in the 1980s were from refugee camps, mainly from Sudan."[44] Solomon further explains that "fifteen hundred Ethiopian refugees were granted admission into the United States annually between the years 1980 and 1999, making

---

40. Getachew and Maigenet, *The Ethiopian Revolution*, 3.
41. Kobel, "Countries and their Cultures: Ethiopian Americans."
42. "What is a Refugee," UNHCR, accessed October 17, 2020, https://www.unhcr.org/what-is-a-refugee.html
43. Getachew and Maigenet, *The Ethiopian Revolution*, 49.
44. Solomon, *The History of Ethiopian Immigrants*, 18–19.

Ethiopians the second-largest recent African immigrant group in the United States."[45]

Another important phenomenon which merits discussion here is diaspora Ethiopians who were already residing in the US before the revolution happened in their home country in 1974. This group had the sojourner mentality discussed above, and so had thus far been unwilling to establish a permanency to their lives in the US However, Ethiopia's political change left them with no option but to reevaluate this stance and to choose long-term settlement in the US as refugees.

Ethiopian Evangelical Churches in the U.S During the Second Wave of Migration

It was during this period that the Ethiopian evangelical churches began to appear in the US In 1981, the first two Ethiopian evangelical churches were planted in the US at the same time. One on the East Coast (Washington, D.C.) and the other on the West Coast (California). In the following years, a number of other Ethiopian churches were established in several states including Texas, Colorado, and Georgia, to name a few.

Ethiopian Evangelical Church in California

A significant number of Ethiopian diaspora believers who were present for the church planting in California were also regular attendants of the Chicago Conference. One of the participants in this study, reflecting upon the formation of the church in California, has this to say: "Those of us who were regularly going to the annual Chicago Conference asked an important question to ourselves. 'Why do not we become a church?'"[46] Among those present in this discussion were Shewangizaw Zeleke, Enrico Giorgio, Addis Erku, Tamiru Agune, Tsehay Hailu, and Meaza Matt. In 1981, they began to have a weekly house church in Orange County in southern California. Bible study, fellowship, and prayer were the focus of this house church. The benefit of this gathering was twofold. First, they received spiritual blessings through their prayers and Bible study; and second, they were able to enjoy community and

---

45. Solomon, *The History of Ethiopian Immigrants*, 3.
46. Zoom Interview, first generation participant 1, December 7, 2020.

fellowship unique to the Ethiopian diaspora. For example, the women played a significant role in preparing Ethiopian food for their fellowship.

After the initial formation and fostering of the community at the house church, the members were able to find a place at one of the Baptist churches where they were permitted to meet on Saturdays. It was at that time this group asked themselves another important question: "Why do not we have a conference?"[47] Organizing a conference is one of the most effective evangelism strategies utilized by Ethiopian evangelical Christians, and the first one was held in 1982. Haile Woldemichael was the guest speaker, and he subsequently became the church pastor the following year. After finding a place at one of the Lutheran churches in Los Angeles, Haile immediately decided to move the church from Orange County to Los Angeles. One of the participants says, "The reason Haile wanted to move the church to Los Angeles is because there were more Ethiopians in that city." Two years after the church moved to Los Angeles, Badeg Bekele was appointed as associate pastor. Another participant says, "We had invited Badeg to move from Boston to Los Angeles to be our associate pastor not because we have many members, but it was because we were planning to reach out to Ethiopians in the city more effectively."[48] Today, that church bears the name Ethiopian Christian Fellowship Church, and it is the biggest Ethiopian evangelical church in Los Angeles with about six hundred to eight hundred members.

Ethiopian Evangelical Church in Washington D.C.

In different locations and contexts in Ethiopia, two more consequential figures simultaneously heard God's voice. One of them was Hanfere Aligaz. When he was traveling from Addis Ababa to Asmara, Eritrea, God's voice came to him, saying, "Do you remember your prayer? You prayed that you would serve the true God if you knew Him. Now you came to know me for the last two years. Now, I will send you to the USA to plant a church in Washington, D.C."[49]

When he shared his experience, Hanfere said,

> I had a mixed emotion after I heard the Lord's voice. On the one hand, I was so excited to hear the Lord's voice, but on the other

---

47. Zoom Interview, first generation participant 1, December 7, 2020.
48. Zoom Interview, first generation participant 1, December 7, 2020.
49. Zoom Interview, first generation participant 2, December 12, 2020.

hand, it was challenging for me to decide because at that time, I was a pilot at Ethiopian Airlines, and my wife had a well-known bakery. We had a good life and leaving these all behind and moving to America for ministry was a challenging decision.[50]

At this same time, in another part of Ethiopia, Daniel Mekonnen received this same message. God spoke to him, saying that he would send him to Washington, D.C. to plant a church for the Ethiopian diaspora currently living there.

After some time, these two people connected fortuitously in Addis Ababa and shared what they had both heard from God. They were both compelled to find a way to go to the US First, Daniel Mekonnen arrived in America in 1981 through a tourist visa. A few months after Daniel came to America, Hanfere also got a visa for technical training and joined him in Washington, D.C. Upon his arrival to the US, Hanfere found out that the ministry his friend had attempted to form was not as effective as he expected. By then, Daniel was preparing to leave the ministry in Washington D.C. to join a Mennonite Bible school at Virginia Beach.

Compared to Daniel, Hanfere had little experience in ministry. At the time, Daniel was a well-known preacher in Ethiopia while Hanfere was a new believer. It had been only two years since Hanfere had come to Christ. Therefore, Hanfere did not know how to preach, and he did not have any idea what was required to plant a church. Hanfere's only advantage was his knowledge about the city and Ethiopians living there. His previous job as a pilot had given him a chance to travel to Washington, D.C. Since Hanfere knew the city and its Ethiopian residents, they decided that he would be responsible for bringing people to the church, and his friend who was more experienced in ministry would handle the teaching and preaching.

In 1981 they started their house church at Olana Terkena's home. Hanfere said, "I knew that I came here for a purpose. I have left my country and all that I have for the gospel. Therefore, I was preaching the gospel day and night and inviting Ethiopians to come to our house church."[51]

After some time, people began to come, and church attendance grew to the point where Olana's house was not large enough for them. The next step was

---

50. Zoom Interview, first generation participant 2, December 12, 2020.

51. Zoom Interview, first generation participant 2, December 12, 2020.

to find a space at one of the churches in the area. Sharing his first experience with American churches, Hanfere remarks,

> I saw white people helping the poor in Ethiopia and generously share their resources. With that in mind, my presumption was that American churches would help us provide the space we need. However, none of them were willing to give us the space we need. Instead, they asked us to pay rent, and we did not have anything to pay. Let alone pay rent; some of us did not have a residence permit yet.[52]

Remarking upon another early experience with US Christians, Hanfere adds,

> Steve connected me with Christian lawyers who come from different denominations to study the Bible. The first day I joined them, I felt rejected because they did not ask my name or allow me to say a word. I said to myself, 'I will never come back here.' However, the following week the Lord's voice came to me and said, 'Go back to that Bible study.' I called Steve and asked him to take me to the Bible study. I became a regular attender, and two months passed by, but they never gave me a chance to speak. After two months they showed interest to know me and asked me to say some words. As I started to share my story, I felt the presence of God filling the place, and all of them were in awe. I shared how I came to Christ and how God called me to go to the USA to plant a church. After I finish sharing, they began to promise to support the ministry that God has given me. One of them promised to help me with my immigration process. The other one said that he would help me in the legalization process of the church with the IRS. The other one promised to connect me with his pastor at the Episcopal Church for financial support. The other one said that he will bring 100 Amharic Bibles. The other one decided to ask for a space at his local church. As promised, we find a place at Presbyterian church for our Sunday

---

52. Zoom Interview, first generation participant 2, December 12, 2020.

service, and the Episcopal church supported us financially to cover our rent and ministry expenses.[53]

Daniel Mekonnen traveled back and forth from school to serve with his two friends during this period. After he finished school in 1985, he became a full-time pastor at the church while Yohannis left for school in Seattle. After serving with Hanfere for about a decade, Daniel took another direction and started the Gospel Light Ministries in Ethiopia. He began the ministry in 1992 while traveling back and forth from the US, and he moved permanently to Ethiopia in 2000. Currently, the US church is led by Hanfere. The name of the church is International Ethiopian Evangelical Church, and it is the biggest Ethiopian evangelical church in Washington, D.C. It has two Sunday services for about three thousand members.

Ethiopian Evangelical Church in Atlanta

The Ethiopian Evangelical Church of Atlanta was started in in 1982. What began as a fellowship of two people grew to be a Bible study of more than eight believing Ethiopian immigrants at the First Baptist Church in Atlanta. These believers also attended the international student ministry at the First Baptist Church in Atlanta. An American serving in that ministry brought some more Ethiopians from the Farmers Market (a place where many Ethiopians work in Atlanta) and told them to start an Ethiopian church at the First Baptist church facility. At that time, Alemu Biftu, Director of the Ethiopian Evangelical Churches Association in America, traveled to Atlanta to encourage Sister Azeb Gebrekiros and others to continue their Bible study and prayer. After they established their Bible study, the First Baptist Church promised to sponsor them, if they could find a pastor. At their request, the Ethiopian Evangelical Churches Association sent Tolosa Gudina to be their pastor in 1986. For the thirty-three years since then, Tolosa has pastored the church, and currently they have about eight hundred members.

Ethiopian Evangelical Baptist Church in Dallas

The Ethiopian Evangelical Baptist Church in Dallas, Texas, was planted in 1984. Marta Zekiros was one of the women who played an instrumental role

---

53. Zoom Interview, first generation participant 2, December 12, 2020.

in establishing the church. Before 1984, about 20 people came together at a park to discuss how to start an Ethiopian church. Among those present with Sister Marta were Mengistu Lema, Captain Yohannis, and Seyifu Kebede. At the invitation of Marta, Zeleke Alemu came from Sweden to help with the church planting. At that time, the Highland Park Baptist Church supported Zeleke and the church planting initiative. The Highland Park Baptist Church offered on numerous occasions to process a visa for Pastor Zeleke and his family; if he wanted to resettle in Dallas.[54] However, after a two month stay in Dallas, Pastor Zeleke preferred to go back to Sweden, agreeing with the Highland Park Baptist Church that they would help his church planting upon his return to Dallas. In 1984, Zeleke returned to Dallas with his family. His church planting strategy was to reach out to the Ethiopian community in the Dallas area through spiritual conferences. The first such conference lasted for four days, with guest speakers such as Tesfa Workineh, Daniel Mekonnen, and Alemu Biftu. Baptism in the Holy Spirit was another area of focus in his church planting strategy. During this time, Aster Birihane, Kiros, Bekelech, Wubshet, Siyoum, and Mesfin were among those who received the Holy Ghost's power to advance the kingdom of God.[55] "What began in 1983 with eight Ethiopians meeting in parks and homes and later in spaces lent by various North Texas churches to worship in their Amharic tongue had now ballooned into a congregation of over one thousand members."[56]

Ethiopian Evangelical Church in Denver

The Ethiopian Evangelical Church in Denver was planted in 1989 and began as a fellowship led by Sister Sofia, with the help of Alemu Biftu. This fellowship and Bible study had about seven Ethiopian believers. As members grew in number, they were granted a place by the Cleverly Church for their Sunday service. It was during that time Zeleke moved from Dallas to Denver to help with the church planting. Zeleke notes that it was relatively easy for him to

---

54. Zeleke Alemu, ሕይወቴ እና ጰንጠቆስጣዊአዊ እንቅስቃሴ አጀማመር በኢትዮጵያ, (Gaithersburg: Signature Book Printing, 2009), 185–194.

55. Alemu, ሕይወቴ እና ጰንጠቆስጣዊአዊ እንቅስቃሴ አጀማመር በኢትዮጵያ, 185–194.

56. Ethiopian Evangelical Baptist Church Gets New Texas Site," *Longview News Journal*, accessed October 17, 2020. https://www.news-journal.com/features/religion/ethiopian-evangelical-baptist-church-gets-new-texas-site/article_1e806b9e-69c2-11e8-945c-878ef1147c82.html

start a church in Denver compared to his experience in Dallas because their fellowship was well organized.[57] The church grew under his leadership, but after two years, Zeleke changed direction and moved back to Dallas to work with Baptist General Convention as a church planting director for African immigrants. He appointed Endashaw Kelkele to take his place in Denver, and Kelkele has led the church since 1992. Today the church has two services with about six hundred members.

Features of Ethiopian Evangelical Churches in the US During the Second Wave of Ethiopian Immigrants to the US

During this period, Ethiopian evangelical churches in the US reflected the following features:

Home Church Bible Study, Prayer, and Fellowship

Bible study, prayer, and fellowship were the hallmark beginnings of each church plant. As such, a church plant offered both spiritual and cultural values to its members. As one participant says, "There was no Ethiopian restaurant back then, and we used to say, '*Enate diresh be-ayer honeshi be hamberger hode teweterelish*.' Meaning, please Mom, fly and come to me, my stomach is so inflated with hamburger."[58] He added, "Today there are many Ethiopians living in Los Angeles and we have a street called 'Little Ethiopia' where we can see Ethiopian culture and enjoy Ethiopian food."[59] He elaborates, "Back then, the home gathering was so important for us to enjoy our culture and grow in our Christian life together."[60]

Spiritual Conference as Evangelism Strategy

During this time, believing Ethiopian immigrants were very active in evangelizing their own community. Organizing spiritual conferences remained a primary evangelistic strategy for these immigrants to reach out to the Ethiopian community in their respective cities. Church members would invite

---

57. Alemu, ሕይወቴ እና ጸንጠቆስጥጤአዊ እንቅስቃሴ አጀማመር በኢትዮጵያ, 201.
58. Zoom Interview, first generation participant 1, December 7, 2020.
59. Zoom Interview, first generation participant 1, December 7, 2020.
60. Zoom Interview, first generation participant 1, December 7, 2020.

nonbelievers to attend conferences, take part in the fellowship, and hear the gospel. One of our respondents explains this strategy in this way:

> You know how Ethiopian food smells powerful . . . so we would go to an apartment complex and walk around for a while and if we smell Ethiopian food in one of the apartments, we simply knock on their door to invite them to come to our conference. We also would go to the mailboxes and if we saw an Ethiopian name on the box we would go knock on their door and invite them to our conference. That is how we were witnessing the gospel.[61]

Role of Women in Church Planting

The role of women in the establishment of Ethiopian evangelical churches in the US is astonishing. Women were actively involved on multiple fronts, which included everything from leading and organizing Bible study groups to providing community services such as preparing food for fellowship. Mikal Bayisa was one such woman who played a major role in the establishment and growth of Ethiopian Evangelical Churches Association in America. She served in the association as a board member while it was assisting many church planting initiatives in the 1980s. Azeb Gebrekiros, another noteworthy woman, led the first fellowship and Bible study in Atlanta, which later grew to be the biggest Ethiopian evangelical church in the city. Sister Marta Zekiros was another woman of faith who gathered believing Ethiopian immigrants to discuss how they could begin a church in Dallas. Through her invitation, Zeleke was able to come to Dallas in order to plant the church. When Marta left Dallas, it was another woman, Bekelech Kiros, who continued church planting with Zeleke. Sister Sofia, yet another influential woman, built a strong fellowship in Denver prior to the arrival of Pastor Zeleke.

Relationship with Local US Churches

The relationship between Ethiopian evangelical churches in the US and local US mainstream churches can be described in two ways. First, their

---

61. Zoom Interview, first generation participant 1, December 7, 2020.

relationship between the Ethiopian church in Los Angeles and other local churches was like the relationship between landlords and tenants. A respondent says:

> Ethiopian churches in Los Angeles had no relationship that was based on doctrine or resource exchange. We were paying rent for using their facilities. We never became part of either Baptist church when we start our church in the Orange County or the Lutheran church after we moved to Los Angeles. We were open for the gospel and to love them as brothers and sisters in Christ. However, since most of us who planted the church were from *"Mulu Wongel"* (Ethiopian Pentecostal Church) and some were from other denominations like Lutheran and Mennonites background. We were not ready to leave our doctrines and be part of Baptist or Lutheran church here in America.[62]

Second, the relationship with other churches planted during this period was characterized mostly by resource exchange, where local US mainstream churches supported Ethiopian diaspora churches materially and financially. Particularly, the relationship between the Ethiopian Evangelical Baptist church in Dallas and the American Baptist church was characterized not only by resource exchange but also by mutual engagement in ministry. The researcher will discuss how this relationship continued to grow during the period of third wave of Ethiopian migration to the US.

Hiring Versus Developing Leaders from Within

The growth of Ethiopian evangelical churches in the US took the route of appointing pastors from outside instead of developing leaders from within. For instance, before Haile Woldemichael became a pastor, the first Ethiopian evangelical church in California was led by leaders from within such as Shewangizaw Zeleke and Enrico Giorgio. Since most of them, including the two leaders, were students at that time, it was determined to be useful to appoint Haile Woldemichael as their pastor initially in order to start the church in an organized way. However, it shows that they were not intentional in developing leaders from within as they wanted to expand the church. One

---

62. Zoom Interview, first generation participant 1, December 7, 2020.

participant stated, "As our church in Los Angeles grew in number, the elders asked me to become an assistant pastor, but I did not feel that that was a right time for me to say yes . . . then they bring Badeg Bekele from Boston and appointed him as an associate pastor in 1985."[63] While the willingness to invest their resources early on in order to bring in an experienced associate pastor is laudable, it began a pattern of seeking external expertise in leadership which has continued to the present day. This pattern has likely been a detriment to the church's development as since the church's planting in 1981, it has been led by six different pastors.

Missions and Cross-Cultural Ministry

One of the participants notes that the survival-refugee mentality had an influence upon the Ethiopian evangelical diaspora churches' missional endeavor during this period. Another participant said,

> One of the weaknesses we have in the Ethiopian evangelical churches in America is that we never had the vision to reach out to Americans. All our effort at that time was to minister to the Ethiopians in providing them a community where they can feel at home, conserve their culture, and keep their Ethiopian version of Christian practice.[64]

In short, the church's preoccupation with a survival-refugee mindset resulted in neglect of its missional calling in the diaspora. The church was serving Ethiopians' cultural values and Christian heritage, but its focus did not extend beyond the Ethiopian diaspora community.

Ministry in Their Home Country

All participants agree that almost all Ethiopian evangelical churches in the US have maintained a connection to their home country through participation in various ministries in Ethiopia. This passion is undoubtedly healthy. However, if they are not careful, it can hurt the ministry that God has given them here in the US First, if Ethiopian churches in the US are highly focused on ministering to their home country, it could negatively affect their internal

---

63. Zoom Interview, first generation participant 1, December 7, 2020..
64. Zoom Interview, first generation participant 1, December 7, 2020.

growth. One of the respondents says, "Our first pastor, Haile Woldemichael, moved back to Ethiopia for ministry, and then after some years, our second pastor, Badeg, moved back to Ethiopia to help with humanitarian work in Ethiopia. Then, we had another pastor who was left to face many challenges, including church splitting."[65] The participant adds, "In fact, the main reason for the church splitting in our church was because there were church members who were unhappy when Badeg left."[66] This clearly shows how ministry focus on their home country can have a negative effect upon the diaspora church.

Secondly, Ethiopian diaspora churches which overemphasize mission to their home country can distract from their missional endeavor of reaching out to communities beyond their own in the US In explaining this danger, one respondent says, "Any American churches had never invited our pastor to speak in their churches, or our Pastor never made any effort to reach out to them. His ministry was focused on Ethiopians here in America and back home."[67]

Thirdly, an overemphasis on ministry focus to Ethiopia may also detract from an Ethiopian diaspora church's ability to foster second-generation ministry. One of the second-generation participants said,

> Those of us in the second generation have a strong attachment with America while our parents have more attachment with their home country. The first generation tends to go back home in their elderly age, while America is a permanent home for the second generation. This strong tendency to go back home may lead to neglecting the second generation.[68]

Diverse Socioeconomic Status

Those Ethiopian immigrants who arrived in the US before the 1980s largely benefitted from strong educational backgrounds that led to stable lives in the US Solomon noted that "the pre-1980s migrants represent the largest number of Ethiopians educated abroad, while migrants who came in the 1980s and after are a mixture of highly educated professionals, high school students, and

---

65. Zoom Interview, first generation participant 1, December 7, 2020.
66. Zoom Interview, first generation participant 1, December 7, 2020.
67. Zoom Interview, first generation participant 1, December 7, 2020.
68. Zoom Interview, Second generation participant 1, December 8, 2020.

even illiterate peasants."⁶⁹ This means that currently one can find Ethiopians in the US ranging from highly professional people with good income to people who are working as unskilled laborers with low income.

When one of the respondents explains the diverse socioeconomic status among Ethiopians in the US, he says:

> The pre-1980s Ethiopian migrants are different from those who came after, both academically and economically. All of us who came prior to 1980s were people that have educational ambition. We were professional teachers, doctors, engineers. Most of us were in a good position financially and we have our own homes in the suburbs. However, the status was changed once refugees started coming in 1980s. They were not as educated. Consequently, their financial status was lower, and they live in apartments.⁷⁰

This socioeconomic diversity among its members has had an impact on the Ethiopian diaspora churches since the second wave of Ethiopian migration to the US One of the participants who is a lead pastor at one of the oldest and biggest Ethiopian evangelical churches in the US states, "Ministering to believing Ethiopian immigrants, particularly those who have jobs like driving, nursing home, and airport service are challenging because they do not get Sundays off."⁷¹ This respondent added "They even work extra time to provide for their family which affects their church attendance and availability for ministry in the church."⁷²

Another distinct social feature of the second wave of Ethiopian migrants in the US is marital status. Most of the arrivals during this time were single males. A participant stated,

> Most of us who came prior to 1974 were young students, very few that were married and many of them did not have children. Even though the marital status was a little bit different when some married refugees started to arrive with their families in

---

69. Solomon, *The History of Ethiopian Immigrants*, 42, 111.
70. Zoom Interview, first generation participant 1, December 7, 2020.
71. Zoom Interview, first generation participant 3, December 12, 2020.
72. Zoom Interview, first generation participant 3, December 12, 2020.

the 1980s, the dominance of the single male demography even among the refugees was apparent.[73]

In line with this argument, Solomon notes, "unlike the Vietnamese and Cuban refugees who had come as families, most Ethiopian refugees to the USA in the 1980s were single males."[74] For instance, Solomon noted that "in 1980 the Washington, D.C. Refugee Center recorded that more than 50 percent of Ethiopians in the city were single men in their early twenties."[75]

The absence of a strong conception of family among the believing Ethiopian migrants has greatly impeded their ability to form ministry which can be beneficial and ultimately bequeathed to their children who were born and raised in the US Ministry developed with the future generation in mind was not an urgent issue for these migrants, as most were single at the time of their arrival. One of participants says,

> At that time the situation in Ethiopia was so harsh. I did not have any option but to flee from the country leaving my family behind. I came to the USA alone and it was so tough to bring my wife and children over here. So, survival was the primary concern for me at that time.[76]

Another participant says,

> As a pastor I had a privilege to marry many couples in our church. When we started our church most of them were young and there was only one pregnant woman in our congregation. So, our entire focus was on how the first generation could serve in America. Second-generation ministry was not an important agenda for us back then.[77]

Another pastor confesses that Ethiopian evangelical churches in the US, including his church which was established in 1981, were not initially prepared to foster second-generation ministry. He states: "It is very sad that we lost the second generation between 1981 to 2017. It has been just three

---

73. Interview, first generation participant 1, December 7, 2020.
74. Solomon, *The History of Ethiopian Immigrants*, 119.
75. Solomon, *The History of Ethiopian Immigrants*, 119.
76. Zoom Interview, first generation participant 3, December 17, 2020.
77. Zoom Interview, first generation participant 4, December 15, 2020.

years since we have a formal church setting for the second generation, after 37 years."[78]

The Third Wave of Ethiopian Migration to the US (1991–Present)

The third wave of Ethiopian immigrants to the US (1991 to the present) is a current phenomenon. Immigration during this time has enjoyed the restoration of diplomatic relations between Ethiopia and the US, thanks to the overthrow of the Communist government (which was called "Derg") by the Ethiopian People's Republic Democratic Front (EPRDF) in 1991.

During this period, Ethiopians have arrived in the US in one of four ways. First, through the Diversity Visa Lottery program, which was established by the Immigration Act of 1990 to increase immigrants' diversity to the US starting in the fiscal year 1995.[79] Under the lottery program, "Ethiopia has ranked among the top five countries responsible for sending immigrants to the US from 1997 to 2000, and in 2004 and 2009, Ethiopia ranked first."[80] The advantage of the Diversity Visa Program for Ethiopian migrants is that it enables them to migrate as a family, and later to attract the rest of their family members to the US in various ways. For example, once settled in the US, Ethiopian migrants will frequently invite their parents to the US to help with newborn children. Some will invite family members to attend events like graduations and weddings, while some will connect family members with someone who lives in the US for marriage, and so on.

Another benefit of the DV Program is that it fosters family reunification. The predominantly male demography, which was a defining feature of Ethiopian migration to the US in the 1980s, started to change after 1991. The single men who left behind their families in Ethiopia were able to reunite with their spouses and children in the US Also, the single men and women were able to go back to Ethiopia to get married and then begin the process for their spouses to join them in the US.

---

78. Zoom Interview, first generation participant 2, December 12, 2020.

79. The Diversity Visa Lottery, Just the Facts: Boundless Immigration, accessed October 20, 2020, https://www.boundless.com/immigration-resources/diversity-visa-lottery/

80. Solomon, *The History of Ethiopian Immigrants*, 8.

Second, during this period, Ethiopians came to the US as political refugees. According to Solomon, "these refugees include those who disbanded from the national army of the communist "Derg" regime, members of political parties like the Oromo Liberation Front (OLF) who faced significant opposition from the ethnic-based policies of the EPRDF regime, and Ethiopians who fled from the contested Ethiopian election of 2005 that resulted in extrajudicial killing and detention of demonstrators."[81] Many of these refugees fled to Kenya and eventually came to the US.

Third, during the third wave Ethiopian migrants came to the US as international students, either sent by a specific institution or self-sponsored. Western organizations and institutions were allowed back into Ethiopia after the communist government was overthrown in 1991. The renewed presence of Westerners in Ethiopia and the growing access to the internet has helped Ethiopians increase their awareness about the possible opportunities of furthering their education abroad, specifically in the US Unlike the pre-1974 Ethiopian students in the US who were sent by the government, Ethiopian students during the third wave have not exclusively relied upon the government to provide the opportunity for study abroad. Therefore, those who wish to come as self-sponsored students have the freedom to explore and apply for further education at their own discretion.

Among the above-mentioned means of migration, the DV Lottery and student visa programs are the main reasons for the growing number of 1.5 generation Ethiopian immigrants who arrived in the US at a young age, with or without their parents. Currently, this 1.5 generation is contributing to the growth of Ethiopian evangelical churches in the US in three ways. First, these young adults account for the growing number of the second generation in the Ethiopian diaspora churches across the US This growth is still continuing, as most of these young adults are recent arrivals who are settling and building their own families in the US.

Second, 1.5 generation Ethiopian immigrants have contributed significantly to the growth of the Ethiopian diaspora church in the US since most of them are spiritually ardent and have a profound sense of calling for ministry. As part of the 1.5 generation group, this writer has a first-hand observation that many 1.5 generation young adults complain about the limited

---

81. Solomon, *The History of Ethiopian Immigrants*, 107–108.

ministry platform of the current Ethiopian evangelical churches in the US. Consequently, the gap between the higher number of those young adults who are interested in doing ministry and the limited platforms available to them has unfortunately led to much conflict and church splitting among Ethiopian evangelical churches in the US since 1991.

Thirdly, 1.5 generation Ethiopian immigrants are also contributing to the growth of the Ethiopian diaspora church financially. One of the participants points out:

> Those who arrived since 1991 have both sides of the coin in their economic status. Some of them are doing well and some of them are not. Those who are doing well are owners of restaurants, different shops, and real estate agents. For instance, I know an Ethiopian fellow man whose English is good enough to communicate but does not have a college degree. He owns four apartment complexes, and now he is a millionaire.[82]

This indicates that Ethiopian immigrants during this migration wave, particularly the 1.5 generation, are engaging in jobs and business opportunities which boost the financial capacity of their respective churches.

Features of Ethiopian Evangelical Churches in the US During the Third Wave of Ethiopian Immigrants to the US

During this period, Ethiopian evangelical churches in the US reflect one of the following features.

Second Generation Crisis

The massive arrival of believing Ethiopian immigrants during this third wave of migration has created a sizeable second generation, born and raised in the US. This researcher had visited most Ethiopian diaspora churches across the US and observed that the second generation has shown exponential growth because most Ethiopian parents (b
oth those from first and 1.5 generations) have up to four children on average. This makes the number of the second generation two or three times higher than the number of their parents, which in turn has created a second

---

82. Zoom Interview, first generation participant 1, December 7, 2020.

generation growth crisis in Ethiopian diaspora churches. These churches do not have the material or human resources to disciple the second generation in their new context. One participant says:

> We only have Amharic service, and our children do not speak our language. They never had a chance to connect with the church, so it is tough for many second generations to continue church after they graduate high school. It is very sad that we are losing many second generation because we failed to provide the necessary platform for them.[83]

Another participant states, "We have volunteers in our church to teach our children until they finish high school. But once they finish high school, some go to American churches, and, sadly, others renounce their faith."[84] One of the pastors also said, "We just woke up late, and it is too late to bring back those who left the church in 2017 and before. It has been only three years since our youth have begun to have their own church."[85]

Second-generation pastors planting Ethiopian diaspora churches is a relatively recent phenomenon. Such churches, planted within the last three years, include Pathway Church in Dallas, Overflow City Church in Washington, D.C., Paradigm Church in Los Angeles, and Perazim Church in Saint Paul. Avenue Church in Denver was an exemplary second-generation church established before 2017; unfortunately, it has since been dissolved.

Movement to Purchase Church Building

The rapid growth of Ethiopian evangelical diaspora churches means more meeting space is needed. Many Ethiopian churches began in the 1980s by renting space from US mainstream churches. However, it has become more challenging for Ethiopians to continue their services in the US churches because the spaces available have not been able to accommodate both their first and second generations neatly. Many of these Ethiopian diaspora churches are considering buying their own church buildings. One participant commented,

---

83. Zoom Interview, first generation participant 2, December 12, 2020.
84. Zoom Interview, first generation participant 2, December 12, 2020.
85. Zoom Interview, first generation participant 2, December 12, 2020.

> You know that things may get messy if you have children at home. Our kids want to play at the church, and things may not be in a place where they were before. We get many complaints from our renters (local American churches), and we will decide to move. It was challenging for us to keep moving from place to place, and that is why we consider buying our own facility.[86]

Today, almost all Ethiopian evangelical churches planted in the US between the 1980s and beginning of 1990s have their own facilities. The need to have their own dedicated facilities has been a new focus for Ethiopian evangelical diaspora churches in the US since 2000.

Over the past two decades, owing to a continuous growth in attendance, Ethiopian evangelical churches have not only bought their own church buildings, but have also moved from smaller buildings into larger ones. Ethiopian Christians Fellowship Church in Houston, Ethiopian Evangelical Baptist Church in Dallas, Ethiopian Evangelical Church in Denver, and Ethiopian Evangelical church in Atlanta have all moved into larger facilities.

Partnership and Collaboration with Local US Churches

While some Ethiopian diaspora churches became members of US church denominations, many of them still follow an isolation policy where they have zero relationship with US mainstream churches. Among Ethiopian churches in the US, the Ethiopian Evangelical Baptist Church in Dallas is remarkable because they were able to develop a mutual partnership and collaboration with the Baptist General Convention of Texas (BGCT). The relationship between these two bodies began when the Ethiopian Evangelical Baptist Church was planted in 1983. Notably, their relationship achieved its highest point when Bedilu Yirga of the Ethiopian Evangelical Baptist Church was nominated and elected as a second vice president of BGTC in 2014, and later as their first vice president in 2015.

Such remarkable willingness by certain US mainstream churches to involve ethnic participants from outside the US context in leadership roles is evidence of genuine, cross-cultural, mutual partnership. In other words, Bedilu has been both benefactor and beneficiary in this two-way relationship.

---

86. Zoom Interview, first generation participant 2, December 12, 2020.

On the giving end, by bringing Bedilu into a leadership position, the BGCT did so in the belief that he would help them expand their ministry to accommodate the state's increasing diversity.[87] The one who nominated Bedilu states, "the number one priority we should be engaging in this season is to pursue the ethnic church involvement in church planting as we are receiving more and more refugees and immigrants in Texas."[88] Explaining his focus during his time in leadership, Bedilu noted that his desire was to help Texas Baptists to involve more of its ethnic congregations in foreign missions endeavors.[89] He also "advocated pairing a predominantly Anglo congregation with an ethnic congregation to participate in overseas projects."[90]

On the receiving end, Bedilu was assisted by the BGCT in planting a church for second-generation Ethiopian immigrants. "Pathway Church, which was established by the second generation of Ethiopian Evangelical Baptist Church, is a start-up church supported by the BGCT."[91]

Leadership Crisis

The leadership crisis during this period was caused by two factors. First, Ethiopian diaspora churches did not properly understand the US context. Ethiopian pastors in the US continue to employ the same ministry strategy that they found to be effective in their home country. In other words, they are perpetuating the ministry approach they brought from Ethiopia without asking themselves if that would fit their new context or not. Consequently, they fail to effectively serve their own community in the diaspora and maximize their opportunities to spread the gospel in a new land. One of the participants remarks, "Pastors need a platform where they would encourage one another, be equipped to better understand their new context and strategize together."[92] When he stated his concern the participant added, "Ethiopian evangelical

---

87. "Yirga to be Nominated for BGCT First Vice President," *Baptist Standard*, accessed October 20, 2020, https://www.baptiststandard.com/news/texas/yirga-to-be-nominated-for-bgct-1st-vice-president/

88. Baptist Standard, "Yirga to be Nominated."

89. Baptist Standard, "Yirga to be Nominated."

90. Baptist Standard, "Yirga to be Nominated."

91. Kelile Nominee for BGCT Second Vice President, *Baptist* Standard, accessed October 20, 2020, https://www.baptiststandard.com/news/texas/kelile-nominee-for-bgct-second-vice-president/

92. Interview, first generation participant 5, December 20, 2020.

church pastors have overlooked the leadership development agenda, including the learning, strategizing and striving together for a higher goal."[93]

The second factor is that Ethiopian diaspora churches maintain a club mentality. One of the participants states, "It looks like the pastors' fellowship has missed its purpose and fallen into club mentality."[94] The participant adds, "Pastors are gathering with other pastors who are like them, and this has led them to became more inward-looking instead of missionally outward-looking."[95] To the researcher's knowledge, today there are at least four "Ethiopian pastors clubs," namely North America Ethiopian Evangelical Churches Fellowship, Ethiopian Pastors Fellowship, Ethiopian Pastors Congress, and Emerging Leaders Accountability Network (ELAN). The club mentality poses a challenge to the unity of Ethiopian evangelical church leaders, and arguably results in a diminished commitment to missions. All participants in this study have pointed out that the missions agenda among the Ethiopian evangelical church is either weak or completely overlooked.

Church Splitting

Lack of available ministry platforms for the young adults is one of the causes of church splitting among the Ethiopian evangelical churches in the US In the 1980s, few Ethiopian migrants to the US possessed both the calling and the capacity to engage in ministry. However, currently, the number of believing Ethiopian immigrants who claim to have the calling and the capacity to engage in church ministry is much higher than the number of platforms available. This is particularly true among the 1.5 generation young adult groups. One of the church pastors who participated in this study says, "I want to admit that we fail in providing platforms for those who came after us. Most of them were pastors and church ministers back in Ethiopia, but they did not get the opportunity here, because the platform is limited."[96] Another participant puts it like this:

> Because of the limited platform in the church, many new arrival Ethiopian pastors and young adults decided to create their own

---

93. Interview, first generation participant 5, December 20, 2020.
94. Interview, first generation participant 5, December 20, 2020.
95. Interview, first generation participant 5, December 20, 2020.
96. Interview, first generation participant 6, December 18, 2020.

platform by "planting" a church but not with a clear and distinct vision from the already existing Ethiopian evangelical churches in America. Churches that have been started out of such mindset are not really church planting or church multiplying, they are simply church splitting.[97]

When one of the participants explains this situation, he said,

Those people who say that they could not get a ministry platform in the church would stay in the church for some time until they get to know some people, and they would invite them to a spiritual conference they have organized, and finally those people would remain with them as their members.[98]

All participants in this study noted that their churches have experienced church splitting, not just once, but multiple times during this period. In contrast, the Ethiopian Evangelical Baptist Church in Dallas has done an exemplary job in protecting itself from splitting by engaging its members in ministry and following a church multiplication model in Texas. Church multiplication provides increased opportunity for ministry engagement for congregants and relieves the pressure of churches which have become unmanageably large. "The Ethiopian Evangelical Baptist Church in Dallas has multiplied throughout the Dallas area, including opening the Ethiopian Evangelical Baptist Church in the Allen area and Ethiopian Evangelical Baptist Church in the Irving area."[99]

Chapter Summary

The history and features of Ethiopian evangelical churches in the US are a reflection of the three waves of Ethiopian migration to the US No Ethiopian church was established in the US during the first wave of Ethiopian migration to the US between 1920 to 1974. However, the establishment of Ethiopian Evangelical Churches Association, commonly known as the Chicago

---

97. Interview, first generation participant 6, December 18, 2020.

98. Interview, first generation participant 2, December 12, 2020.

99. "Pastor of Ethiopian Church Nominated to Major BGCT Post," *Baptist News Global*, accessed October 20, 2020, https://baptistnews.com/article/pastor-of-ethiopian-church-nominated-to-major-bgct-post/#.X-M4IthKjIU

Conference, was a major accomplishment that facilitated the fruitful church planting initiatives in different states during the second wave of Ethiopian migration to the United States.

Many Ethiopian Evangelical churches were planted in the US during the second wave of Ethiopian migration to the US between 1974–1991. The main purpose of the Ethiopian diaspora church during this period was to provide spiritual and community services as churches began with home fellowships, prayers, and spiritual conferences. Since most Ethiopian migrants during this period, particularly in the 1980s, were predominantly single male refugees, a pervasive survival mentality among these refugees significantly negatively affected the Ethiopian diaspora's missions endeavor (reaching out to communities beyond their own), as well as the focus on fostering second generation ministry (preparing the necessary platforms to disciple their own children who were born and raised in the US). Partnerships between Ethiopian evangelical churches and local US mainstream churches during this period most closely resembled the relationship between landlords and tenants. Consequently, there was no noteworthy relationship between the two that developed around doctrine or resource exchange. Instead, the relationship was mainly utilitarian: US churches offering their facilities for Ethiopian churches to meet.

Ethiopian evangelical churches grew exponentially during the third wave of Ethiopian migration to the US, from 1991 to the present. During this period, the DV Lottery, student visa, and family reunification programs have been largely responsible for the influx of Ethiopians to the US Owing to this explosion, Ethiopian diaspora churches during this period have required their own spaces and have therefore begun the practice of buying their own church buildings. They have done this while facing challenges such as the above-described second-generation crisis, a leadership crisis, and widespread church splitting. In some instances, partnership between Ethiopian evangelical churches and local US mainstream churches has developed as certain Ethiopian churches became members of US mainstream church denominations. Particularly, the Ethiopian Evangelical Baptist Church in Dallas is exemplary in terms of their engagement with the Dallas Baptist Convention at a leadership level. However, a quandary remains at the heart of the current partnership between these two parties. On one hand, this relationship has enabled many Ethiopian churches to buy their own church buildings. On the other hand, those churches that have bought their own buildings exhibit less interest in forging partnership with US mainstream churches and find themselves in a position of sterile isolationism within the diaspora.

CHAPTER 3

Intergenerational Dynamics of the Ethiopian Diaspora Churches in the US

The intergenerational aspect of the diaspora is a complex issue because the generational differences within the immigrant community has a multiculturalism layer. Migrants are people on the move who settle in the country of destination as a diaspora within multilingualism and multiculturalism settings. The ways diaspora communities process their movement and resettlement vary from one generation to the other. In other words, the experience of carrying on their cultures and values, and the process and challenges of adjusting to the new culture differ across the generational lines within the diaspora community.

This chapter seeks to develop an understanding of the contextual dynamics of the three generations (first, second, and 1.5 generation) within the Ethiopian evangelical churches in the US. It is also the aim of this chapter to delve into the nature of interaction across these generational lines.

To meet the purpose of this chapter, the researcher answers the following three questions. First, who are the first, second, and 1.5 generation immigrants? This question discusses the definition and description of each generation in detail and offers biblical examples of each. Second, how does each generation adjust themselves in the diaspora? In this question the researcher discusses the nature and challenges of cultural adjustment of each generation in the diaspora. Third, what is the trend among Ethiopian diaspora churches regarding interactions across generational lines? This question is intended to highlight how the current structure and practices of Ethiopian diaspora churches handle its generational dynamics.

Description of the First, Second and 1.5 Generation Ethiopians in the US

Two factors can help us define and describe who the first, second and 1.5 generations are: age and cultural resonation.

First, Second and 1.5 Generation Age Factor

According to Immigration Initiative at Harvard "A person who is a first-generation immigrant is defined as one who is born outside of the United States. 1.5 generation immigrants are individuals who came to the United States as children. Second-generation immigrants are born in the United States but have parents who are born abroad."[1] This definition is helpful to understand each generation, but it lacks identifying specific age range for each generational group. The Tab noted that, "The term 1.5 Generation was coined in the 1960's by Ruben Rumbaut, a sociology professor at the UC Irvine and a Cuban American who immigrated to the United States as a child. Rumbaut defined 1.5 Generation immigrants as "stuck in-between" cultures as they are not quite first generation but not quite second generation citizens."[2] Here, one can notice that this is more of the description of the cultural situation of the 1.5 generation at the hosting country than defining 1.5 generation.

On the other hand, the United States Census Bureau explains the generational differences based on where the parents were born. "The first generation is composed of individuals who are foreign-born. The second generation refers to those with at least one foreign-born parent. The third-and-higher generation includes individuals with two U.S. native parents."[3]

The age and cultural exposure of an immigrant at the time of arrival at the country of destination are the two determining factors that this researcher used to distinguish one generation from other. As such, this researcher utilizes his lived experience as an immigrant to identify the age range that helps to define each generation along with the cultural exposures that each generation will have in those age ranges in the hosting country. Those who come to the

---

1. "First and Second Generation," *Immigration Initiative at Harvard*, Accessed November 7, 2024, https://immigrationinitiative.harvard.edu/topic/first-and-second-generation/

2. "What it's like to belong to the 1.5 Generation," Accessed November 7, 2024, https://archive.thetab.com/us/2016/07/11/what-its-like-generation-29952

3. "United States Census Bureau," Accessed November 7, 2024, https://www.census.gov/topics/population/foreign-born/about.html

host country at the age of 22 and older are considered the first generation. Immigrants who are coming in this age range will not have much exposure of the hosting culture because they never had the chance to enroll in the American schools where they can learn about the hosting culture the most. Joining college at the age of 22 and older in America could help this generation to learn a bit about the hosting culture, but their worldview remains primarily shaped by their home culture as they completed their formation back home. Those who come between the age of 11–21 are the 1.5 generation. Unlike the first generation, 1.5 generation have a better exposure to the hosting culture as they have the opportunity to enroll from middle school to college in the hosting country. Those who arrive in the host nation younger than 10 years old, or those who were born and raised in the diaspora, are the second generation. In this case, the second generation have much exposure to the hosting culture to the point where their worldview will primarily be shaped by the cultural lens of the hosting country. As the migrants continue to live in the diaspora, they may have a third generation who are born of the second generation and a fourth generation who are born of the third generation and so on.

First, Second and 1.5 Generation Cultural Resonation Factor

A cultural resonation to the home, host, or both cultures while living in diaspora is another factor that helps us to understand the distinction between the different generations within the diaspora community.

First-Generation Cultural Resonation Factor

Culturally, first generation Ethiopian migrants are known for their high commitment to preserve their Ethiopian culture in the diaspora. This means that the cultural resonation of the first generation tends toward the home culture. In this case, first-generation Ethiopians want to uphold their home culture and show less openness to the hosting culture while living in diaspora. For them, losing their culture means losing everything. Therefore, they work hard to preserve and teach their children to follow their culture in the diaspora.

As an Ethiopian immigrant himself, this researcher has had the opportunity to closely observe how first-generation Ethiopians preserve their culture while living in the US First-generation Ethiopians preserve their culture in two ways. First, they do this by strengthening their attachment with their home country. Family members and friends in Ethiopia as well as media are the main contributors in fostering the strong connection between the first generation and their home country. The worldviews and social values of first-generation Ethiopians are mostly shaped by their home culture because of their ties to their home country. First generation migrants are also highly impacted by the socioeconomic, political, and family matters in Ethiopia, which fosters their continued relationship with their home country.

Economically, the relationship with the home country has a direct impact on the first generation as they want to invest in different sectors in their home country and support their friends and family members in Ethiopia financially. In this case, the economic impact is significant on the first generation as they are responsible for supporting their family members back in their home country as well as their immediate family here in the US.

Regarding the social and political impact, first-generation Ethiopians have a high awareness of the sociopolitical atmosphere of their home country as they follow up and engage in the political and social affairs of their country, to the degree that it shapes their lifestyle in the US For instance, according to the researcher's close observation among the Ethiopian diaspora in the US, many first-generation Ethiopians are so impacted by the ethnic based politics in Ethiopia that they experience divisions along the lines of their different ethnic backgrounds. It is mainly the technological advancement in media that transports the sociopolitical atmosphere in Ethiopia to Ethiopians in the US That is what the researcher witnesses as he visits different Ethiopian homes in the US Instead of watching US news channels and talk shows, and listening to US music, first-generation Ethiopians prefer to watch Ethiopian TV programs and use social media to follow Ethiopian news and broadcasts. Thus the first generation has higher awareness about what is going on in their home country than in their current host country. In other words, first-generation migrants have a weak attachment with the host country while fostering a strong attachment with their home county, creating a sojourner mentality. This means that they consider the US to be a temporary residence and intend to return to their home country in their older age.

Since many Ethiopian evangelical churches in the US are led by the first generation, their ties to their home country affect the church in the diaspora. In other words, the preservation mentality of the first generation has highly influenced the way Ethiopian evangelical churches in the US operate. They have their services in Amharic and their Sunday service structure is like the one they had in Ethiopia, including the service length and worship style. It is common among Ethiopian evangelical churches in the US to invite guest speakers and singers from Ethiopia to speak and sing in their conferences. This practice nurtures the tie that Ethiopian diaspora churches in the US have with churches back in their home country. Thereby, such ties help Ethiopian diaspora churches in the US to preserve their worship style and other church practices while living in the US.

The first generation's strong connection with their home country also makes the church susceptible to the impact of the sociopolitical conditions in Ethiopia. In other words, the ethnic-based political situation and heretical teachings and practices in Ethiopia have high impact on the Ethiopian evangelical churches in the US For instance, according to the researcher's observation, the prophets and faith teacher's movements are one of the top issues that Ethiopian churches in the US are currently discussing. Members of Ethiopian diaspora churches are impacted by "prophets" who have unbiblical practices and "teachers" who teach heresy. Social media plays a major role in facilitating the connection between these prophets and teachers and their followers in the US as they stream their programs from Ethiopia.

The 2020 to 2022 conflict between Tigray and the central government of Ethiopia is one of the examples showing how politics can affect Ethiopian churches in the US In the conversation the researcher had with one of the Ethiopian church pastors, the pastor noted that there are members of his congregation who left the church because of the political conflict in Ethiopia that makes them feel their ethnic group is targeted in the church.

The primary means by which first generation migrants preserve their culture is by strengthening their attachment with their home country. The second means is by strengthening their community in the diaspora. Forming their own community is very crucial for the first-generation migrants because it helps them to preserve their culture and create a sense of security. In other words, community life is very important for first-generation Ethiopians as it enables them to support each other in the needs they may have and continue their Ethiopian lifestyle in the US First generation Ethiopian migrants prefer to use their language not only at home, but also when shopping and in other business areas. That is why they look for Ethiopian shops and businesses that can provide services in their language. They attend Amharic-speaking churches, dress in their traditional clothing, listen to their own cultural music, eat their traditional food, and attend community gatherings with their fellow Ethiopians. These practices nurture the cultural preservation of the first-generations Ethiopians in the US

The community-building process is backed by the settlement pattern of Ethiopians in the US First-generation Ethiopians tend to follow the migration and settlement patterns of their fellow Ethiopians. This is an important element that they want to keep in mind before or at their arrival in the country of destination. "Where do I find my community?" is one of the questions that helps them to set a goal for their migration journey. They first want to answer this question for themselves and then they labor to meet their goal. This means either they develop their own little Ethiopian community in the places where they find themselves, or they move to a different state with a strong Ethiopian community. Therefore, finding their community (Ethiopian churches, friends, or family members in the diaspora) is an essential factor that compels them to move from place to place even within the host nation.

Second-Generation Cultural Resonation Factor

Culturally, second-generation migrants, who were born and raised in the diaspora or who came to the host culture in their early childhood, are more open to the host culture than the homeland culture. In fact, the second-generation are born and raised between two distinct and solid cultures: their parents' culture and the host culture. The atmosphere at home is dominated by their parent's culture while the outside world is completely filled by a culture that is foreign to their parents. Born into the host culture, the second generation takes on more of its traits than their parents' home culture. Their parents' culture is functional only at home while the host culture is widely used in the country where the second generation is growing up. In other words, the second generation cannot shelter themselves in their parents' culture as it is mandatory for them to engage in the larger context of the host culture.

1.5- Generation Cultural Resonation Factor

The term "1.5 generation" is used to describe immigrants who fall somewhere between the first and second generations. Unlike the first and second generations, who culturally resonate to one culture or the other, 1.5 generation migrants tend to be open to both their home and the host culture. Lee noted that "1.5-generation refers to young-adult immigrants born in their country of origin but who have grown up in the US and are thus usually bilingual and bicultural."[4]

The bilingual and bicultural proficiency of 1.5 generation migrants varies depending on two aspects: age and community. When it comes to the age aspect, 1.5 generation migrants may arrive at the host country with their families or independently, depending on how old they were at the time of their arrival. Those who came with their parents as teenagers have a high possibility of being acquainted with the host culture due to the opportunity to enroll in middle and high schools in the country of destination. Therefore, 1.5 generation immigrants in this category are bilingual and bicultural, but more proficient in the host culture and language.

On the other hand, those who came to the hosting country independently in their 20s are bilingual and bicultural, but more proficient with their home culture as initially they have limited exposure to the host culture. This means that, compared to those who came with their parents as teens, 1.5 generation migrants who came independently in their 20s lacked the opportunity to enroll in middle and high school in the host country. Therefore, their cultural adjustment is not reinforced by the school system but is dependent on their choice to join college or seek employment in the host community.

Regarding the community aspect, the kind of community that 1.5 generation immigrants join at their initial settlement affects their language and cultural proficiency in relation to their home or host culture. For instance, the host culture would have a minimal impact on 1.5 generation migrants who have settled in a place where there are many migrants from their country of origin. This does not mean that these 1.5 generation migrants are ignorant of the host culture. However, because they have their community, they do not have much pressure to polish their accent or adjust their cultural disposition toward the host community. Consequently, their level of cultural and linguistic proficiency tends more toward their home culture. For instance, this researcher's wife came to the US as a sophomore in high school. As a high school student, she had exposure to the host culture, but since there were many Ethiopians in Seattle where she lived, she preferred to socialize more with Ethiopians. In this case, she is bicultural and bilingual as a 1.5

---

4. K. Samuel Lee, "Navigating Between Cultures: A New Paradigm for South Korean American Cultural Identification," *Pastoral Psychology* 54, no. 4 (2006): 293.

generation. However, her cultural disposition and language preference is influenced more by Ethiopian communities than US ones.

The 1.5 generation migrants who have encountered few or no fellow migrant communities other than their own in their initial settlement are more influenced by the host culture. In other words, 1.5 generation immigrants in this category do not have their fellow migrant communities as an option to engage with in the diaspora. Thus, their cultural and linguistic proficiencies are more inclined toward the hosting culture. For instance, an Ethiopian friend who came to the US at the same time as my wife, was more influenced by the hosting culture because she settled in a place with few Ethiopians. She had no option but to associate with friends from the hosting community, and consequently, she has a cultural and linguistic proficiency that is more fluent toward the hosting culture.

Below is a table that summarizes the impact of age and community on the cultural and linguistic proficiency of the 1.5 generation immigrants.

Table 3.1 Age and Community Factors Affecting Bilingual Competency of 1.5 Generation Migrants

Age Factors		Initially settle among the hosting community in the diaspora	Initially settle among the country-of-origin community in the diaspora
	Young adult at the time of entering the hosting country	Quadrant 1 Bi-cultural: though they arrive in the hosting country at a young adult age, they experience high influence of the hosting culture	Quadrant 3 Bi-cultural with high influence of home culture
	Teenage at the time of entering the hosting country	Quadrant 2 Bi-cultural with high influence of hosting culture	Quadrant 4 Bi-cultural: though they arrive in the hosting nation in their teenage, they experience the high influence of home culture.
Community Factors			

The above diagram shows that 1.5 generation immigrants in Quadrants 1 and 2 have a promising journey toward bicultural fluency because they are open to the hosting culture in addition to the home culture they already have. By contrast, 1.5 generation immigrants in quadrants 3 and 4 have limited bicultural competency as they have less openness to the host culture on top of the home culture they already have.

Some Exceptions in Each Generation

It is true that majority of migrants in each generation can be defined and described based on their age and cultural resonation factors. However, it is important to note that some migrants in each section prove to be exceptions. Particularly, this happens when some migrants who are classified as first, second, or 1.5 generation do not fit in their respective generation's cultural resonation. For instance, there are migrants who are classified as first generation according to their age at their arrival in the diaspora, but they are quite open to the hosting culture. Likewise, there are second generation migrants who were born and raised in the diaspora, yet they are open to their parents' home culture. Thereby, such first and second generation migrants are growing toward bicultural and bilingual competencies in the diaspora. On the other hand, there are migrants who are classified as 1.5 generations who would normally be open to both cultures, but are primarily open to either their home or the hosting culture. In this case, such 1.5 generation migrants are growing away from bicultural and bilingual proficiencies in the diaspora.

The following diagram illustrates the process of growing toward or away from the bilingual and bicultural fluency in the diaspora.

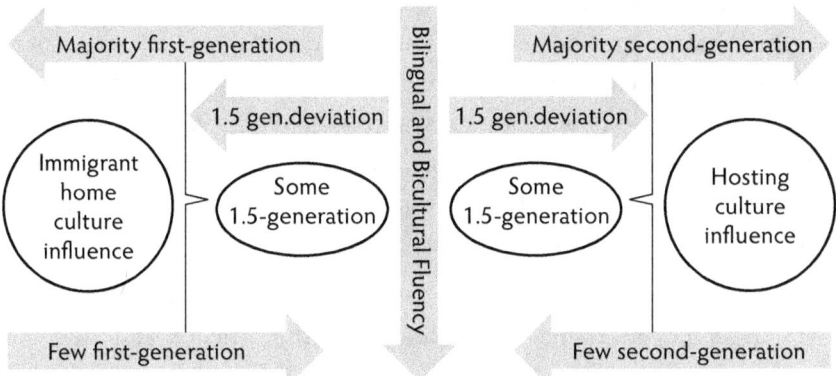

Figure 3.1 Process of Growing Toward or Away from Bilingual and Bicultural Fluency

From the diagram above, one can draw a conclusion that there is a wide cultural gap between the majority of the first generation (parents' generation) and their children (the second generation). There could be several reasons for the gap between these two generations, but lack of openness to learn from each other's context is the major one. In other words, it is rare to find first or second generation migrants who are working toward narrowing the cultural gap by growing in their bicultural and bilingual skills.

When it comes to 1.5 generation migrants, this diagram shows that they have a tremendous opportunity to attain bicultural and bilingual fluency as they are positioned in a place where they get enough cultural exposure from both the home and hosting sides. However, the diagram also shows us that 1.5 generation migrants can lose this opportunity when they deviate to one or the other side.

Biblical Examples of First, Second and 1.5 Generations

There are many examples of first, second and, 1.5 generation migrants in the Bible. This section highlights the lives of three such persons: Nehemiah as a first generation migrant, Joseph as 1.5 generation migrant, and Paul as a second generation migrant.

Nehemiah: First-Generation Example

Nehemiah was an exile in Persia. There are three parallels that can be drawn from the life of Nehemiah that resonate with first-generation migrants. Nehemiah's attachment to his home country is one of the parallels with first-generation migrants. Like Nehemiah, first generation migrants follow news from their homeland; they have great sorrow about the suffering that their people and country are going through, and they observe prayer and fasting for their country.[5] A second generation immigrant explained her parents' attachment to their country of origin:

> My parents live in America, but their heart is in Ethiopia. The news they hear, their conversation with their friends, and the

---

5. Nehemiah 1.

prayer and fasting are all about Ethiopia. Even the dream they have is to go back to Ethiopia eventually. Everything is about Ethiopia. I sometimes wonder, how about us and how about America? So many things are happening here too. We want them to pay attention to what is happening here and to pray for us too.[6]

Another common feature between first generation immigrants and Nehemiah is their passion for returning to their home country to engage in the nation rebuilding process. Upon his return, Nehemiah rebuilt the wall, restored justice to the poor, and brought a right order to the temple.[7] Like Nehemiah, first generation migrants want to contribute to their home country in areas of social and economic justice.

Joseph: 1.5 Generation Example

Joseph's story is found in Genesis chapters 37–50. Joseph migrated to Egypt because his brothers hated him and conspired to kill him; ultimately selling him as a slave to Egyptians.[8] In Egypt, Joseph eventually rose from slavery and imprisonment to the highest position after the king. When his brothers fled from the famine in their land and came to Egypt, Joseph chose to forgive and welcome them because he realized that God sent him to Egypt ahead of his family to rescue them.

Just like Joseph, many 1.5 generation migrants had dreams earlier on in their lives. However, they went through many trials both in their country of origin and in the diaspora. Many 1.5 generation migrants lose their dreams and find themselves in the diaspora doing unskilled jobs when they have higher education degrees from their country of origin. Like Joseph, they suffer in the host country until they are accepted in positions that fit them. Some flee their home country at a young age, betrayed by their brothers. Their dreams may have been crushed by corruption and a bureaucratic system that conspired against them. For instance, this writer's friend was one of the victims who was unfairly disqualified from the college education that she had dreamed of. Amid that despair, she obtained a Diversity Visa Lottery to

---

6. Amare, in person interview by author, 2019.
7. Nehemiah 3–6.
8. Genesis 37:19–20.

come to the US as a permanent resident. Now she is an accountant, working for one of the government offices in the US and she is a blessing to her family. Just like Joseph's family was welcomed in Egypt because of Joseph, all her family were welcomed to the US because of her.

Paul: Second-Generation Example

Paul's story is found in the book of Acts. Paul was a Greek-speaking Jew from Asia Minor. Paul's parents were migrant Jews living in the diaspora, and Paul was a Roman citizen by birth.[9] His upbringing in the major city Tarsus, Greek education, and Roman citizenship made him multilingual.[10] Consequently, Paul was successful on a global scale because he maximized the opportunity presented in his multicultural context.

Like Paul, some second generation immigrants maximize their opportunities as they grow up in a multicultural community. The multicultural context of the second generation immigrants includes their parents' culture, the hosting culture, and other cultures due to the presence of other immigrants and nationals in the hosting culture. Caleb Nyanni pointed out that "second-generation immigrants are an integral part of the global shift to the multicultural society or multiculturalism in our world today."[11] For instance, the rapid pace of globalization and migration is impacting Europe and America's social, political, and religious landscape as these second-generation immigrants engage in this multicultural context.[12]

Paul had a strong identification with both Jews and Hellenistic Jews. In other words, he navigated between his two primary cultures: Hebrew, his parents' culture, and Graeco-Roman, his hosting culture in the diaspora. Paul held on to his bicultural life, which helped him effectively fulfill his calling to preach the gospel to both Jews and Gentiles. Kwiyani notes,

> Paul's great work was shaped by the fact that he was conversant in two cultures – Jewish and Roman – at the same time. When among Jews, he could be wholly Jewish, and his Roman citizenship was also helpful when needed. The Pauline letters

---

9. Acts 22:3.
10. Acts 22:2.
11. Nyanni, "The Spirits and Transition," 254.
12. Nyanni, 254.

indicate that Paul thinks, speaks, and writes in the international language, Greek."[13]

Neuhaus stated, "Acts 17 shows how Paul was knowledgeable in Greek philosophy as he applied rhetorical methods in his conversation with local philosophers in Athens."[14] Neuhaus added, "Paul was a Greek-speaking Jew, but he was no less Jewish for that as he was a highly devout Jew and the strictest Pharisee of his generation."[15] In the same way, there are some second-generation immigrants who are strongly bicultural because they have maximized their opportunity to navigate in their multicultural context.

Cultural Adjustment of the First, Second, and 1.5 Generation Ethiopians in the US

Under this topic the author seeks to discuss the nature and challenges of the cultural adjustments of each generation in the diaspora. This includes studying how their cultural disposition affects the adjustment of each generation in the US Immigrant and refugee communities take their cultures and stories with them as they move from place to place, and Ethiopian diaspora communities in the US are no exception. Taking their cultures and stories from the country of origin all the way to the country of destination is a challenging process. However, it is more challenging to adjust to a country with a different culture.

Culture change is inevitable when two or more cultures come into contact. Two factors determine the extent of cultural change. First, the degree of cultural change is affected by whether the two or more cultures are contacted in a casual or formal way. Second, cultural change is affected by the migrants' reaction to the cross-cultural contact, whether more toward preserving or risking their culture. These factors help us to determine which culture (home or hosting) will change more, how long the change will take, and which cultural markers will change the most. Here, it is important to note that

---

13. Kwiyani Harvey, *Our Children Need Roots and Wings: Equipping and Empowering Young Diaspora Africans for Life and Mission* (UK, CreateSpace Independent Publishing Platform, 2018), 38.

14. David Neuhaus SJ. "Getting to Know Saint Paul Today: A Change in Paradigm?" *Thinking Faith*, accessed April 19, 2021, https://www.thinkingfaith.org/articles/20081027_1.htm.

15. Neuhaus, "Getting to Know." Philippians 3:4--6; Galatians 1:13--14.

migration impacts both the lives of migrants and the hosting communities. This means that migrant's lifestyle will be influenced by the hosting culture and the cultural disposition of the hosting communities will be altered as migrants bring their home culture into the hosting culture. Cultural adjustment of each generation and its challenges are discussed as follows.

First-Generation Cultural Adjustment

First generation migrants are characterized by their high commitment to conserve their home culture in the diaspora, which leads them to two lifestyle options: survival/isolation, or sojourner. The first option is a survival and isolation lifestyle. In this case, immigrants tend to uphold their culture against the hosting culture, particularly those that directly oppose their cultural values. This "validates the first-generation's minority group separatist attitude to seek its own community, and to build parallel social institutions to survive in such an antagonistic environment."[16]

To put it in a sociological perspective, first generation migrants follow a separation strategy of acculturation. Sam and Berry pointed out that "the separation strategy is defined by individuals who place a high value on holding on to their original culture and avoid interaction with members of the new society."[17] First generation migrants are classified in this acculturation strategy simply because they have a low sense of belonging with the hosting culture but are highly involved with their own community in the diaspora. Building their community helps the first generation to preserve their culture in the diaspora as it fosters the sheltering approach. In other words, the first-generation shelter themselves in their community to the point where they have minimal or no contact with people in the hosting culture. Mussa stated,

> First-generation Ethiopian immigrants are happy to have a Western education. They are happy to be accepted and granted resident status in America. However, they still want to keep their ethnic traditions, culture, and language because that gives them strength and hope by allowing them to spend time with

---

16. Tesema, "Global Nomads," 44.
17. Sam and Berry, "Acculturation," 476.

other Ethiopians to share past experiences and future dreams for themselves and their children.[18]

The cross-cultural competence of first-generation immigrants is low as they are mostly home culture-dominant monolinguals. Based on the author's observation, because of the sheltering approach, it is common to see first-generation Ethiopians who have lived in the US for decades but speak very little English and have no social contact with Americans. Consequently, life is not easy for them due a lack of fluency in the dominant language and little knowledge of the host culture. However, their social capital in their community offers significant support for their socioeconomic and psychological wellbeing.

Secondly, the high commitment to cultural preservation leads the first generation to a sojourner lifestyle. Their cultural preservation and attachment to their home country makes them retain the sojourner mentality because most of them eventually plan to return to their home country in their old age. Based on his close observation among the first-generation Ethiopians, this researcher developed the diagram below to illustrate the cultural adjustment process of the first-generation in the diaspora.

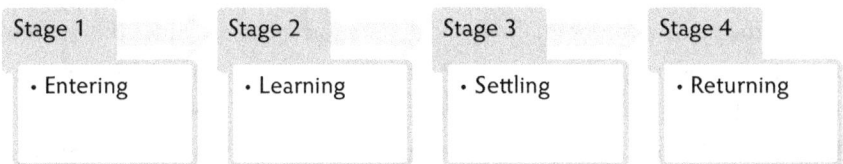

Figure 3.2 Adjustment Process of First Generation Migrants

Stage One: Entering the Host Nation

This is just a point of entry until first generation migrants get connected with their own community in the diaspora. They may take a few days to two years to move to their own community. Once they get connected with their own community, they minimize their connection with the host community. Or, if they find their own community in a different city, then they no longer

---

18. Mussa, "Sociocultural Problems," 34.

want to stay in the city they initially entered. Therefore, this is a stage of exploration where first generation migrants search for a strong community of their own in the diaspora. For instance, there is a strong Somali community in Minnesota. A first generation migrant from Somalia may initially enter the host nation via Denver. However, he could move to Minnesota within a short period of time as he connects with Somalis there. In this case, those who have a heart for welcoming migrants need to understand this feature of first generation migrants. First generation migrants at this stage are in an exploring mentality. Therefore, it is good to ask what they are exploring and build relationships with them around that. This helps both the welcomer, and the migrant have an effective connecting point in the brief time they may have before the migrant moves to a different place.

Stage Two: Learning the Host Culture

In this case first generation migrants are not open to the learning process until they get connected with their own communities. In other words, they prefer to learn about the host culture with their own community and in their language. This is a stage of building their comfort zone because they can get support from their community, which gives them a sense of security for their future life in the diaspora. They learn the hosting culture and lifestyle by following the patterns of their fellow first generation migrants. Since their fellow first generation migrants stay in their comfort zone for a long time, they only have limited experiences to share with the newcomers. Therefore, improving language skills to acquire a better job, and getting a wider perspective on how to raise their children in the diaspora continue to be challenging aspects in the lives of first generation migrants. In this case, if the host communities want to reach out to first generation migrants at this stage, they need to learn the movement patterns of migrants. Moreover, host communities need to know how to bring their programs into the migrants' context instead of expecting migrants to come to them.

Stage Three: Settling in the Host Country

The more first generation immigrants stay in their comfort zone, the more they develop a separatist attitude and a sojourner mentality. Because of the limited experience they have with the host community, first generation migrants prefer to go to shops and business centers where they can get services in their language. Religious institutions and cultural events are other aspects that foster the separatist lifestyle. In short, such first generation migrants are living outside their country physically, but their country is here in the diaspora as they create an island with the strong community they build. At this stage, host communities need to approach migrants as partners who can contribute to the community because they have well-established communities and institutions. For instance, at this stage, immigrant communities from Christian backgrounds have well-established churches that can benefit the host community with possible partnerships.

Stage Four: Returning to their Home Country

Returning is the final stage that is mostly practiced among the first generation migrants. It is easy for this group of people to move back to their home country because of their close attachment with their home country while living in the diaspora. This enables them to finally enjoy their life in their homeland after a long time of hard work in the diaspora. The beauty of this returning process is that it is not limited to a self-serving goal. This group of people also long to contribute to their home country by taking the necessary resources with them. In this case, the host communities can still partner with them in supporting their initiative to contribute to their home country.

Challenges of the First-Generation in Cultural Adjustment

There are two challenges that first generation immigrants face in the process of adjusting themselves in the diaspora. The first challenge has to do with the change in the social order. For instance, Halche noted that "upon their arrival to the United States, Ethiopian immigrants face an ethnically differentiated society where those who come from the upper social class in their homeland experience downward social mobility in their new host country."[19] Solomon also highlighted that "it is common to see both the educated and uneducated Ethiopian immigrants hold similar jobs and that education does not help secure better jobs."[20]

The downward socioeconomic mobility happens particularly among the first generation because their age and family responsibilities do not allow

---

19. Halche, "*A Socio-Cultural Analysis of Leadership*," 16.
20. Solomon, *The History of Ethiopian Immigrants*, 147.

them to upgrade themselves to the standard of the hosting system. The lack of connections and language proficiency also contribute to this downward socioeconomic movement. Solomon stated that "the skills of immigrants do not translate into higher-paying jobs in the hosting county due to the lack of job opportunity networks and nontransferable professional credentials."[21] The language barrier also negatively affects employment opportunities among the diaspora communities. Answering interview questions and carrying out jobs in the host country's language makes first generation migrants' entrance and performance very challenging. Therefore, immigrants tend to work in unskilled labor, with little chance of a better-paying job.

The second challenge that first generation immigrants face in the diaspora is raising their children in a different culture. In his study, Mussa noted that "problems between immigrant children and their parents rise when children want to adapt to the American culture and parents seek to impose the Ethiopian way of life on their children."[22] Mussa added, "conflicts between Ethiopian parents and their children in the US surface around freedom, friendship, dating, and cultural understanding."[23] In this case, parents are not prepared for the social and cultural difficulties, but that is what they face while dealing with the economic challenges in the diaspora. The language barrier intensifies the problem. Language barrier affects first-generation parents' communication with their children in the same way it affects their job opportunities in the diaspora. Most immigrant children use the host culture's language, English, as their means of communication, while parents have difficulty understanding it. Therefore, the language barrier creates a communication gap between parents and children, resulting in conflict.

1.5 Generation Cultural Adjustment

The 1.5 generation migrants are positioned to bridge the gap between the first generation immigrants who have a stronger attachment to their country of origin and second generation immigrants who have a stronger attachment to the hosting country. Though the cultural and linguistic proficiency of 1.5 generation immigrants varies depending on age and community factors, they

---

21 Solomon, *The History of Ethiopian Immigrants*, 147.

22. Mussa, "*Sociocultural Problems*," 178.

23. Tesema "Ethiopian Immigrant Children," 118.

are generally bicultural and bilingual. Their bicultural skills allow 1.5 generation immigrants to play a strategic role between the two generations. These 1.5 generation immigrants need to grow toward fluent bicultural competency. It is the "add-on" strategy that helps them increase their bicultural competency. The 1.5 generation migrants are already established in their home culture before they encounter the hosting culture, which helps them retain their homeland heritage and add the hosting culture onto their cultural experience without losing their background. Therefore, what determines their growth toward bicultural fluency is their openness to adding the hosting cultuo their solid home culture.

To put it in a sociological perspective, most 1.5 generation immigrants follow what Sam and Berry call an integration acculturation strategy.[24] Integration happens when immigrants engage in both the country of origin and the host culture. Sam and Berry stated,

> Individuals use the integration strategy with interest in maintaining one's original culture while having daily interactions with other groups. Thus, there is some degree of cultural integrity maintained, while at the same time they seek, as a member of an ethnocultural group, to participate as an integral part of the larger social network.[25]

Those who pursue this acculturation strategy are characterized by a high sense of belonging to their diaspora and hosting communities. Both sides support these migrants, and they experience less or no discrimination in the process of acculturation. Sam and Berry added,

> Integration results in better adaptation outcomes because it entails a form of double competence and the availability of double resources. These competencies come from one's own ethnic and cultural group and the new and larger society, and these resources double an individual's ability to cope with cultural transitions.[26]

---

24. Sam and Berry, "Acculturation," 472.
25. Sam and Berry, 472.
26. Sam and Berry, "Acculturation," 472.

The integration model is mostly adopted by 1.5 generation immigrants who arrive in the hosting country at a young age, and some second-generation who are open to their parents' cultural heritage and the hosting culture. Maria Garcia noted that "an individual who identifies strongly with both cultures is referred to as having a "bicultural" identity."[27] Those who choose the integration model tend to have high cultural competence and psychological wellbeing as they can engage in both cultures with their bilingual and bicultural skills.

Members of 1.5 generation who are not willing to "add-on" the hosting culture face cultural adjustment challenges in the diaspora. Such 1.5 generation migrants have a surface level connection with the hosting culture, or they may reject it altogether. Consequently, they have limited language and cultural knowledge of the hosting nation, which makes it challenging for them to culturally adjust to the hosting country.

Second-Generation Cultural Adjustment

Cultural adjustment of second generation migrants is determined by three cultural influences around them: the hosting culture, their parents' home culture, and the multicultural context in their areas of settlement.

The Hosting Culture

Second generation migrants have a stronger attachment to the hosting culture than to their parents' culture, simply because they were born and raised in it. In other words, the hosting nation is home to the second generation whereby its culture takes a primary role in shaping the cultures and worldviews of the second generation, including lifestyle, interest, and language.

Sociologically, most second-generation migrants follow the assimilation acculturation strategy.[28] According to Sam and Berry, "assimilation is one of the acculturation strategies pursued by individuals who tend to engage more with the hosting culture than their ethnic communities."[29] Sam and Berry added that "assimilation is a strategy used when individuals do not wish to maintain their cultural identity, and instead seek close interaction with other

---

27. Garcia, "Cross-cultural Identity," 2.
28. Sam and Berry, "Acculturation," 476.
29. Sam and Berry, "Acculturation," 476.

cultures (or, in some cases, adopt the new society's cultural values, norms, and traditions)."[30] Alba and Nee also remarked that "assimilation happens when individuals from two or more different backgrounds perceive themselves as more similar because the cultural marks of their ethnic origins are becoming less noticeable."[31]

There are two types of assimilation theories: classic straight-line assimilation and segmented assimilation.[32] Classic straight-line assimilation theory sees immigrants "and majority groups following a 'straight-line' convergence, becoming more similar over time in norms, values, behaviors, and characteristics."[33] In other words, this theory expects to see immigrants become more uniform with the hosting culture over the course of time.

Arguably, the classic straight-line assimilation theory works for the first wave of European immigrants to the US Their assimilation process can be summarized by the "melting pot" or "soup" metaphor that discourages diversity and promotes uniformity. This model was challenging for Europeans who came from outside of Northwestern Europe. Skin color matters a great deal in the US, even today. The subsequent immigrants to the US were largely people of color from Africa, Asia, and Latin America. "The 1965 Immigration Act greatly changed the demographic makeup of the American population as diverse immigrants entering into the USA under the new legislation from countries in Asia, Africa and Latin America, as opposed to Europe."[34] Even though these migrant groups have lived in the US for generations, it still is difficult for them to attain the classic straight-line assimilation toward the social and economic state of the White Anglo group, which tends to discriminate against those with darker and brown skins. In this case, children of immigrants may be able to speak the hosting language well, but they can do nothing about their appearance. Mussa noted that "the third-generation immigrants may overcome economic and educational problems but may not be able to overcome social problems due to the aforementioned discrimination."[35]

---

30. Sam and Berry, "Acculturation," 476.
31. Alba and Nee, *Remaking the American Mainstream*, 11.
32. Brown and Bean, "Assimilation Models."
33. Brown and Bean, "Assimilation Models."
34. "The Legacy of the 1965 Immigration Act," *Center for Immigration* Studies, accessed March 21, 2021, https://cis.org/Report/Legacy-1965-Immigration-Act
35. Mussa, "Sociocultural Problems," 38.

Here it can be asserted that attaining straight-line assimilation is challenging and even impossible in some cases. For instance, the second generation immigrants and the subsequent generations can talk and act just like the people of the hosting culture, yet they are still subjected to socio economic discrimination because of their appearance or skin color that will never be assimilated to become white.

Segmented assimilation theory was developed as an alternative to the classical straight-line assimilation model. This theory proposes that people from different cultural backgrounds will assimilate to different groups rather than to one dominant hosting culture or society. Yu Xie and Emily Greenman defined segmented assimilation as a "process by which new immigrants may take divergent assimilation paths to assimilate into different groups of communities in the hosting culture."[36] Brown and Bean pointed out,

> Segmented assimilation theory in America is constructed in the context of black-white models of racial/ethnic relations that apply much less forcefully to new arrivals from Latin America, Africa, and Asia, whose histories and contemporary experiences differ considerably from those of both blacks and European immigrants. For instance, even though Mexican immigration dates back many generations, and even though current Mexican immigrants are diverse in terms of their migration status and modes of entry into the United States, theorists envision the group's experiences in one of two ways — either as similar to that of European immigrants (i.e., as different from that of blacks) or as similar to that of African Americans.[37]

In this case, non-European immigrants to the United States are deemed in the Black or White category depending on how well they succeed in their assimilation into the White Anglo or Black socioeconomic status. In other words, 'non-European immigrants who manage to assimilate into the White Anglo socioeconomic status are perceived as immigrants like Europeans who achieve the upward social mobility, while others "perceived as nonwhite

---

36. Xie and Greenman, "Segmented Assimilation Theory," 1.
37. Brown and Bean, "Assimilation Models."

minorities who are subjected to discrimination in the manner of African Americans, downward social mobility."[38]

Both classic straight-line assimilation and segmented assimilation are difficult processes for immigrants to go through. Assimilation is a challenging path for two reasons. First, people who pursue assimilation strategy need to take critical steps like abandoning their cultural heritage and resisting the negative social mirroring of the hosting society. Taking responsibility for cultural adjustment and earning acceptance in the hosting culture is a very tough process even for the second generation who may feel like they are assimilated to the hosting culture as they have a high sense of "belonging" to the hosting culture and low "belonging" to their parents' culture.

Second, assimilation is a challenging path because it creates conflict between immigrant parents and their children. Hasanoviü et al. stated,

> When children of immigrant completely embrace a different culture, consciously or unconsciously, because they experience it as more prestigious and dominant, or they deem it to be opportune, this leads to a breakdown in the relationship with their parents and conflict, or at the very least it disturbs the harmonious family structure.[39]

The assimilation approach that substitutes the "old culture" (their parents' heritage) with the "new culture" (hosting culture) may lead the second generation into conflict with their parents (the first generation). Looney noted that from a cultural perspective, "assimilation represents the death of one's heritage and identity."[40] It is not easy for immigrant parents to see their children abandoning their heritage.

There are many reasons why the second generation loses interest in embracing their heritage and are drawn more to the hosting culture. One is what this researcher defines as an imposition approach. Instead of helping them be rooted in their parents' culture, this approach may cause the second generation to resist learning their parents' culture. In line with this argument, Mussa noted that "conflict between immigrant children and their parents is caused

---

38. Brown and Bean, "Assimilation Models."
39. Hasanoviü et.al, "Migration and Acculturation," 388.
40. Looney, *Crossroads of the Nations*, 23.

by children wanting to adapt to the American culture and parents imposing the Ethiopian way of life on their children."[41] Mussa added,

> Ethiopian parents may want to raise their children according to a traditional Ethiopian value system, which emphasizes family, respect for elders, and honor; yet the children being raised in the American culture may prefer a lifestyle that encourages individualism, freedom, and self-expression, leading them to disagree with their parents.[42]

Here it is important to note that family dynamics are a crucial factor in the acculturation process. Garcia noted that "acculturation not only affects a person on an individual level, but it also affects the family as a unit as each family member may acculturate at a different pace, resulting in a growing discrepancy in cultural values or practices."[43]

The Parent's Home Culture

The fact that the hosting culture takes a greater role in influencing the second-generation does not mean that this generation is completely taken over by the hosting culture. In other words, their loose attachment to their parents' culture does not eliminate the fact that they are immigrant descendants. Different facts remain to signify them as children of immigrants. For instance, if they are children of immigrants to the US, they may feel like Americans inwardly, but remain outwardly African, Latino, or Asian. That is why most second generation immigrants prefer to be identified by their parents' continent or country and the hosting country, like Asian-American, African-American, Latino-American, South Korean-American, Ethiopian-American, or Chinese-American. In line with this argument, Habecker affirmed that "second-generation immigrants have no tribalism or ethnic attachment with their parent's ethnic background, such as Yoruba or Igbo in Nigeria."[44]

---

41. Mussa, "Sociocultural Problems," 178.

42. Ibid, 176.

43. Garcia, "Cross-cultural Identity of Second-Generation Immigrant Youth," 7.

44. Shelly Habecker, "Becoming African Americans: African Immigrant Youth in the United States and Hybrid Assimilation." *Africology: The Journal of Pan African Studies* 10, no. 1 (2017): 62.

However, the "national or continental identity played a more significant role in their self-identifications."[45]

Other indicators that the second generation immigrants are more than merely Americans include the cultural food they share with their parents, their parents' language that they grow up hearing, and cultural interaction between older and younger generations. For instance, several parents wear African clothing to church services, birthdays, and anniversaries. "Young people respectfully refer to their elders as 'auntie' or 'uncle' regardless of a biological relationship."[46] To share the researcher's own experience, an Indonesian second-generation who participates in our youth Bible study shows this cultural interaction as he bows his head to greet older people. That is a sign of respect that he learnt from his parents.

The Multicultural Setting

In addition to navigating between two cultures, second generation migrants grow up in a diverse community both online and in person. Second generation migrants grow up with other migrant children from diverse backgrounds, and they connect with people globally through social media like Facebook and Instagram. Looney pointed out that "the hosting and the parents' cultures are not the only influences that shape the second-generation behavior and values, however, it is the lens through which all of life is seen and interpreted."[47] This means that second generation migrants have a wider scope beyond their parents' and the hosting cultural perspectives. Their upbringing in these two cultures gives them the privilege of a "dual" citizenship where they can express themselves in those two contexts. In addition, growing up with their friends from many different ethnic backgrounds gives them a "global" citizen identity which makes their perspective wider than a person who grew up in a predominantly monocultural context. In this case it can be argued that second generation migrants are given wings to navigate and embrace many cultural experiences due to their broad exposure. The more they extend their wings to embrace those cultures around them, the higher they can fly and expand their sphere of influence around the globe.

---

45. Ibid.
46. Ibid.
47. Looney, *Crossroads of the Nations*, 35.

Challenges of the Second-Generation in Cultural Adjustment

As challenging as it is to grow up as second generation immigrants, it is also a unique privilege and opportunity that one can only be born into. It is an opportunity that people of the hosting nation could not acquire, their parents (the first generation) could not realize, and 1.5 generation immigrants could not maximize. Furthermore, because second generation immigrants grow up mainly between two cultures and possibly among diverse communities, they have a wider perspective than those who grew up in a predominantly monocultural context. This opportunity could lead the second generation to become multicultural and multilingual. Consequently, this enhances the realization and maximization of upward socioeconomic mobility locally in the hosting nation and as well as globally.

The issue of identity is one of the major challenges among second generation migrants. No culture is better than the other. Kim noted that "it is unfortunate when individuals find themselves in a society that perceives that one culture is better than the other."[48] It is common to believe that one's culture is the best simply because it works well for them. However, the truth is that all cultures equally work well for the people in that culture. It is challenging for second generation migrants to navigate all the cultural influences as they face challenges from both their parents and the hosting cultures who impose an ethnocentric, "mine is the best" approach. This approach is dangerous because it leads to forced assimilation that pressures the second-generation to be rooted in one category or the other, rather than allowing them to grasp both. It may be easier to associate the first and 1.5 generation migrants' identity with rootedness. First generation and 1.5 generation immigrants are rooted in their home culture because their identity formation is solidified before they encounter the hosting culture. The home culture shapes their cultures and worldviews. However, they may still be affected by the hosting culture, but nevertheless will have a frame of reference to accept or reject whatever they face in the country of destination.

In contrast, second generation immigrants do not have this option because their identity formation begins in the diaspora. Theirs is a different world that no one can understand unless they are born into it. In other words, life in the diaspora for second generation immigrants is challenging because they

---

48. Rebecca Y. Kim, "Second Generation South Korean American Evangelicals," 3.

continuously have to juggle the responsibilities of taking on their parents' tradition, fitting into the hosting culture, and engaging in their multicultural context. Lee highlighted,

> Individuals experiencing multiple cultures, especially those of minority status, feel caught between the dynamics of cultures. They report wrestling with self-identity, different values, attitudes, beliefs, and questions of loyalty to a particular cultural group. All of these are influential factors in shaping the overall pattern of their cultural adaptation. Whether voluntarily or involuntarily, consciously or unconsciously, these individuals choose ways to identify themselves with the cultures with which they come into contact. These ways to identify with cultures represent a stable personality trait that affects in significant ways individuals' attitude, behavior, and experience.[49]

Particularly, second generation immigrants feel pressured to meet people's expectations, mainly their parents and the hosting community. However, meeting requirements to be rooted in their parents' culture and to be entirely accepted by the hosting culture are challenging processes. In Habecker's words, "they often experience identity confusion while navigating other people's expectations for who they are."[50] In other words, "it is challenging for the second generation to find acceptance or meet the many and varied expectations of who they are and how they should act."[51] Consequently, they often are misunderstood by both their parents and the hosting communities. What makes the problem worse for the immigrant children is not when their parents misunderstand them, but when their attempt to fit into the hosting culture fails. Mussa noted that "by the time Ethiopians reach the third generation in the host culture, they could overcome spoken accent problems and perhaps educational and acculturation problems. However, there is one thing they cannot overcome, and that is their color."[52] African and Asian descendants remain African and Asian, at least by their appearance, which creates frustration when facing challenges because of their physical features or skin color.

---

49. Lee, "Navigating Between Cultures," 290.
50. Habecker, "Becoming African Americans," 59.
51. Habecker," 67.
52. Mussa, "Sociocultural Problems," 82.

There are some second generation immigrants who drop both cultures because they are frustrated by the challenges from both their parents' home culture and the hosting cultures. To put it sociologically, such second generation migrants are following a marginalization acculturation strategy. The marginalization strategy is defined by Sam and Berry as "a lack of interest in cultural maintenance because of an enforced acculturation approach and little interest in having relations with others because of exclusion or discrimination."[53]

This strategy is mostly used by second generation immigrants who feel a low sense of belonging to both their parents' and the host societies. Hasanoviü et al noted that "children of migrants who engage in the marginalizing strategy feel entirely rejected by their host society as they are labeled as a subculture that the mark of 'foreigner' is stamped on even those who are best integrated."[54] In his study, Tesema also highlighted that "nineteen out of twenty-five interviewees reported derogatory treatments and put-downs because of their ethnic background."[55] Salerno et al. also suggested that such "immigrants are more likely to move away from immigrant enclaves into neighborhoods where they are exposed to higher levels of social stress like discrimination and prejudice, leading to reported higher levels of substance use."[56]

Second generation migrants who use the marginalization acculturation strategy also feel that they are not fully accepted in their parents' community. For example, Tesema remarked that "although the second generation self-identified as Ethiopian and appeared proud of their ethnicity, many said the Ethiopian community did not fully embrace them."[57]

Second generation immigrants who adapt this acculturation strategy may not like the way both the hosting nation and their parent's generation treat them. The feeling of not being understood by both their parents and the hosting culture may lead them to the question of self-identity. They ask themselves, "where do I belong?" and "who am I?" If these questions are not dealt with early, they may lead the children to many life crises. Nyanni highlighted, "children of immigrants who cannot embrace their own culture and had formulated their identities around rejecting aspects of mainstream

---

53. Sam and Berry, "Acculturation," 476.
54. Hasanoviü et.al., "Migration and Acculturation," 389.
55. Tesema "Ethiopian Immigrant Children," 114–121.
56. Salerno et al., "Immigrant Generation," 1–10.
57. Tesema, "Ethiopian Immigrant Children," 117.

society might be drawn to gangs."[58] Nyanni added, "for such youth who lack meaningful opportunities, gangs offer a sense of belonging, solidarity, protection, support, discipline, and warmth."[59] Moreover, marginalized second generation immigrants face other crises such as mental health, substance abuse/addiction, gang/criminal acts, and suicide. For instance, based on this researcher's close observation, suicide rates, substance abuse or addiction of any sort, and mental health issues are increasing among Ethiopian second generation migrants in the US.

The four sociological acculturation strategies—separation, integration, assimilation, and marginalization—are summarized in the following diagram.

Table 3.2 Summary of the Four Acculturation Strategies

Immigrants Home Culture		Low ← Hosting Culture → High	
	High	**Separation** Acculturation strategy that exclusively incline to the hosting culture. Mostly used by the first-generation and some 1.5 generation who fail to grow in their bicultural skills. Monocultural - parent's home culture and language dominant	**Integration** Acculturation strategy that embraces both hosting and parent's home culture. Mostly used by 1.5 generation and some second-generation. Bicultural and bilingual It is a recommended acculturation strategy.
	Low	**Marginalization** Acculturation strategy that rejects both hosting and parent's home culture. Mostly used by second-generation. Anomie -they have no desire for both cultures; so, they tend to create their own like gang group. It is a dangerous acculturation strategy that leads to identity crisis, substance abuse, criminal activities and mental health issues including suicide.	**Assimilation** Acculturation strategy that exclusively incline to the hosting culture. Mostly used by second-generation. Monocultural - hosting culture and language dominant.
		Low	High
		Hosting Culture	

---

58. Nyanni, "The Spirits and Transition," 108.
59. Nyanni, 108.

Based on the above diagram, those who engage in both their heritage culture and in the larger society (by way of integration) are better in their adaption to the new culture and psychological wellbeing than those who acculturate by orienting themselves to one or the other culture (by way of assimilation or separation) or neither culture (by way of marginalization).

Current Intergenerational Trends of the Ethiopian Diaspora Churches in the US

Ethiopian migrants are recent diaspora communities in the US, compared to other migrant communities, such as the Hispanics, Chinese and South Koreans. Migration Policy Institute noted that "many Ethiopian immigrants to the United States (87 percent) arrived during or after 2000, thereby making the community as a whole quite young."[60] Accordingly, it can be asserted that Ethiopian diaspora communities in the US largely consist of the first, second, and 1.5 generations, meaning that it is uncommon to encounter a third generation.

The emerging and growing number of second generation immigrants is one of the realities we see in our world today. "In 2020, the number of international migrants reached 281 million; 36 million of them were children."[61] This number could increase exponentially because of two main reasons: first, the continuing phenomenon of immigrant and refugee movements across the world; and second, most immigrants and refugees are of the working-age population who could produce more children in the diaspora. In the previous chapter we discussed how Ethiopian evangelical churches in the US have grown rapidly since their establishment in 1981. Particularly, the DV Lottery program, family reunification, and marriage among 1.5 generation Ethiopians were the main reasons for the increase in the number of second-generation Ethiopian migrants in the US.

This section discusses trends in Ethiopian evangelical churches in the US as regards their practices among their first-, 1.5-, and second-generation migrants. Since resources are limited, the author utilized different internal

---

60. *Ethiopian Diaspora*, 5

61. "Migration" accessed March 12, 2021, https://data.unicef.org/topic/child-migration-and-displacement/migration/

church documents, and his own close observation as an Ethiopian immigrant working among the Ethiopian diaspora churches across the United States.

First Generation Trends

First generation Ethiopian migrants arrived in the US in the 1980s as political refugees, after 1991 as Diversity Visa holders, and a few as international students. Trends among members of the first generation in Ethiopian diaspora churches reflect the following features.

First, they have a culture-driven church. Ethiopian diaspora churches in the US use their ethnic language such as Amharic and Oromifa for their church service; their worship style reflects their style in Ethiopia; and they use examples in their sermons related to Ethiopian traditions. These all indicate that they are inwardly locked and their ministry is exclusively relevant for themselves. Such separatist models lead Ethiopian churches to form their own island in the diaspora. In this case, one can argue that the missional dimension of Ethiopian churches established by the first generation is weak. This means that the first generation lacks intentionality for crossing cultural boundaries to reach out to communities beyond their own and their children who are highly influenced by the hosting culture. In other words, because of their lack of a missional mindset, Ethiopian churches in the US are struggling to pass their faith to their own children because of the language and cultural gaps with their children and the hosting communities in general.

This challenge is not only a challenge in Ethiopian diaspora churches. For example, in Nyanni's study when one of the second generation reflected on the situation in his Ghanaian church, he said that the church services are catered to exclusively address the needs of their parents and not his generation.[62] More specifically, the participant noted that there is no attempt by the first generation to embrace the second generation as "they kept singing Twi songs and the preacher speaks in Twi" knowing that the second generation are there with them in the congregation.[63] In the same study, another second generation participant said, "I do not mind being called a Ghana church, but the point is that they literally did everything like we are in Ghana."[64] Here one can

---

62. Nyanni, "The Spirits and Transition," 180.
63. Nyanni, "The Spirits and Transition," 180.
64. Nyanni, "The Spirits and Transition," 179.

note that when first-generation pastors plant a church, their goal is strictly to have an ethnic church that targets the first generation. These ethnic churches are not intended to serve the whole family in their congregation, including the second generation, who are culturally different from their parents. For instance, none of the first-generation Ethiopian pastors that the researcher knows of at the time of this study have plans to start an English service to reach their children and their hosting society in the US.

Another feature of the first generation immigrants is that they are highly influenced by the socioeconomic and political situations in their country of origin. These factors have considerable impact on the members of the first generation immigrants in the Ethiopian diaspora churches. The situation in their country of origin has a great deal of contribution in shaping their sermons and prayer items. Ethiopian diaspora churches in the US pray a lot for the economic and political situation in their homeland. Members of the first generation in the Ethiopian diaspora churches of the US are from different ethnic backgrounds. Problems arise because the ethnic-based politics in Ethiopia can directly impact the congregation. Consequently, the subject of unity is one of the areas that the first-generation pastors give emphasis to in their sermons, and it is also a big prayer topic.

First generation migrants have a strong tie with their families in their country of origin. Most of them take on the responsibility of supporting their families financially. That is even one of the main reasons for some migrants leaving their country. The concern they have for their country and family members in their homeland causes them to focus solely on their country of origin. They send their money and other resources, they travel back and forth to engage in church ministry and nation-building, and eventually they will likely move back to their homeland. This researcher has observed first generation migrants in the Ethiopian diaspora churches, including some pastors traveling back and forth, transnationally exchanging resources with churches and other organizations in Ethiopia, and running mission projects in their homeland. Focusing on their homeland is not wrong. However, they should not do so at the expense of neglecting the God-given opportunity to reach out to the hosting community and their children in the diaspora. To sum it up, the survival mentality that leads the first generation to focus on their family members in the country of origin and direct their ministry activities to their home country may prohibit their missional endeavor among their children here in the United States and beyond.

1.5 Generation Trends

We find two groups of 1.5 generation in the Ethiopian diaspora churches. The first group consists of those who want to replicate what the first generation is doing. The 1.5 generation in this category want to continue an ethnic church in the manner of the first generation migrants who are distancing themselves from the second generation and the hosting culture. It is common to see young adult services organized by young adult leaders among Ethiopian diaspora churches in the US Based on the researcher's close observation, many young adults have a sense of calling for ministry, which creates both an opportunity and a challenge. It is an opportunity as the ethnic church can continue because of the 1.5 generation young adults. It is a challenge because if members in the 1.5 generation feel that they are not given an appropriate platform for ministry, the church may face conflict that leads to church splitting.

The second group of 1.5 generation in the Ethiopian diaspora church consists of those who tend more toward the preferences of the second generation. This group of people are concerned for the second generation who are not privileged to take part in their parents' church for cultural and language reasons. The 1.5 generation people in this category put their energy and time into filling the gap by helping in the second-generation children and youth ministry. Consequently, the nature of their ministry leads to loneliness and burnout. Since they are ministering to the second generation separated from the church community, they are detached from the church community as well. They are always in the classrooms at the back of the church tackling the difficult task of ministering to the second generation, while losing community support from those in the main sanctuary. This leads to frustration and burnout, which makes many 1.5 generation young adults leave ministry. Consequently, this leaves the church in a vicious cycle of constantly asking for volunteers from 1.5 young adults to teach the second generation in English.

Second Generation Trends

Tesema highlighted that "the passing of the Christian faith to the American-born and -raised children of Ethiopian descent is an arduous task due to the cultural and linguistic differences between the first and second generations."⁶⁵ When Tesema further explains this challenge using the conversation between his son and his wife as an example, he writes:

> "Are you ready for church?" Abby (his wife) asked Abel (his son) that particular Sunday morning. "Which church?" Abel said. "Your church or my church?" Abby was horrified. How can you say, 'your church'? Your father is the pastor!" "So what?" Abel said. "I do not understand what my father preaches. How can it be my church?⁶⁶

In the light of the conversation between his wife and his son, Tesema realized that "the first-generation immigrants were happy because they built a congregation of Ethiopians in America, unfortunately, their kids were not."⁶⁷

Now the question is, how do children of immigrants get to the point where they say, "that is not my church"? It is important to pull our discussion back to where it all begins to answer this question. Beginning from the first day when parents bring their children to church, they send their children to the classrooms at the back of the church where they have their Sunday schools, while parents go to the main sanctuary for a service in their ethnic language. This creates a huge gap between parents (first generation) and their children (second generation).

In this system, the second generation are not only removed from the "big church" (which is what they call their parents' congregation), but also segregated based on age and school grades as the ministry at the back of the church for the second generation follows the school system. Consequently, relationships among older and younger second generation migrants at church is weak, with each knowing only their age clusters. This system continues until they finish high school and then, for many second-generation students, graduation from high school is also graduation from the church. That means that once they graduate from high school, they will not have an interest in coming back to their parents' church anymore.

Kim noted that "South Korean churches in America use the term 'silent exodus' to predict or indicate the drastic drop in second-generation South

---

65. Tesema, "Global Nomads," 6.
66. Tesema, "Ethiopian Immigrant Children," 114.
67. Tesema, 114.

Korean American adults' participation in ethnic churches."[68] There are many reasons for this "silent exodus," but lack of platforms for the second generation to grow, as well as miscommunication with older leaders, are the main ones. When it comes to the lack of platforms, the pattern in the Ethiopian diaspora churches discussed above clearly shows that the second generation immigrants have no platform that fits them as adults after they complete high school. At this point, they neither want to come back to the "backyard" ministry because it still is more like a daycare, nor to their parents' ethnic congregation because there are cultural and language barriers. Nyanni states,

> One of the themes that came up in most of the conversations with the second-generation who left the church was culture. Unlike the first-generation members who started the church as a response to a need, including maintaining cultural identity, the second-generation members are more integrated into the hosting culture and do not necessarily share the same needs as their parents. The second generation is more open to other cultures, while their parents are very loyal to the Ghanaian way of life, culture, and practices."[69]

The same is true among members of first generation immigrants in Ethiopian diaspora churches. Their children leave their culture-driven church because it does not provide the necessary platform for them.

Miscommunication is another reason for the "silent exodus" of the second generation. Nyanni pointed out that the "first-generation leaders did not understand the second generation and were not given the opportunity to grow."[70] When one of the second-generation participants in Nyanni's study shared his experience, he said, "what is the point of going to a place where your voice cannot be heard? The second-generation was frustrated because leaders did not listen to their suggestions concerning what they thought might work for the second generation."[71] This researcher also had a similar conversation with one of the second-generation members in the Ethiopian diaspora church in Colorado who reflected the same truth. She said, "We had several meetings

---

68. Kim, "Second-generation South Korean American Evangelicals," 267.
69. Nyanni, "The Spirits and Transition," 179.
70. Nyanni, "The Spirits and Transition," 181.
71. Ibid,182.

with the first-generation leaders; it feels like we were heard at the meeting, but the reality on the ground is still the same." She added, "unfortunately, we do not have any option other than functioning with what they have given us because the financial and leadership power is with them."[72]

Another reason for the "silent exodus" of the second generation is lack of providing appropriate resources. The space provided for the second generation at the back of the church is not convenient. In many Ethiopian diaspora churches of the US, I have observed second-generation youth gathering in small, inconvenient rooms or in extra spaces like indoor basketball courts. Moreover, second generation ministry in most Ethiopian churches are run by volunteers who are not passionate about their ministry. This tends to foster what this writer calls "a baby-sitting mentality." These volunteers are not well trained for children's ministry. Some are there to merely fill a gap. Others are there just because they speak good English. These volunteers take care of the second generation until their parents finish their ethnic congregation service.

Second generation migrants who have decided to exit their parents' church could become churchless or be absorbed in the US mainstream churches or establish their own church. From these options, it is obvious that becoming churchless cannot be a good option by any means. However, according to the researcher's observation among Ethiopian churches in the US, it is sad that many in the second generation are making that choice. In this case it is important to note that second-generation persons are mission fields that need to be addressed with the gospel of Jesus Christ.

A more recent phenomenon among Ethiopian second generation believers in the US is the establishing of their own churches. This has both pros and cons. On one hand, it is good for the second generation to establish their own church because US mainstream churches would be an unfamiliar environment. According to the author's observation, there are second generation Ethiopian Christians in the US who have joined mainstream U.S churches. However, after a while, some returned to churches established by their second generation peers because they felt that the mainstream churches did not embrace their otherness, including their stories, heritage, and skin color.

On the other hand, the option of having their own church has the following challenges. First, second-generation Christians lack the concept of church

---

72. Zoom Interview, second generation participant 2, December 12, 2020.

mainly because they have been denied the opportunity to see what the church looks like. They were removed from the church platform in childhood, and they were subjected to growing up in a church system that felt more like their school system, or like having a babysitter. The school system that is offered in their classrooms may have a great curriculum that can provide good head knowledge. However, the second generation will be deprived of the church concept until they are given the opportunity to develop relationships and experience sharing with their parents in the church setting. In other words, there is an absence of the church concept among the second generation because relationships are broken, and experience sharing is missed. Therefore, the church should not wait until their children finish high school to have church. The church should stop the "daycare system" and find a way to engage the second generation in the church from childhood.

Another challenge that comes with establishing their own church is that it tends to make the second generation remain an ethnic church. Generally, second generation migrants desire to be open to other communities outside of their own. In reality, however, they still have a long way to go in terms of diversifying their congregation. For instance, there are five Ethiopian churches established by the second generation that this researcher knows of across the United States. Their congregations are still predominantly (98 percent) Ethiopian descendants. In this case, they are replicating another form of ethnic church in the manner of the first generation that is weak in its missional dimension. Once again, we see that because the second generation has never observed a healthy, multi-generational church, they do not have a pattern to follow in their own church planting.

Lack of finances and other resources is another challenge that the second generation could face as they decide to establish their own churches. Kim noted that "it is challenging for English speaking South Korean congregations to become fully independent from South Korean immigrant churches because they cannot yet become financially self-sufficient."[73] Kim added that "all English-language congregations within South Korean immigrant churches were financially dependent upon immigrant congregations but independent in worship services and other sociocultural activities."[74] The same is true

---

73. Kim, "Second-generation South Korean American Evangelicals," 271
74. Kim, "Second-generation South Korean American Evangelicals," 273.

among second-generation Ethiopian believers in the US For instance, based on this researcher's knowledge, Avenue Church, planted in 2017, was the first Ethiopian second-generation led church that was launched in Colorado. This church was using the first-generation facility for their Sunday afternoon service until it was dissolved in 2019. Other churches led by second generation Ethiopian pastors like Pathway and Perazim are independent churches, but they are still working hard to generate their own resources.

Chapter Summary

This chapter develops an understanding of the intergenerational dynamics of Ethiopian evangelical churches in the US The chapter contains three sections. The first section focused on defining, describing, and offering Biblical examples of the first, second, and 1.5 generation migrants. Age and cultural resonation are the main determining factors for the distinction between these three generations.

The second section highlighted the cultural adjustment of the first, second and 1.5 generation Ethiopian evangelical Christians in the US The nature and challenges of each generation's cultural adjustment was explained using the different sociological acculturation methods, including separation, integration, assimilation, and marginalization. Moreover, the cultural adjustment of each generation was also characterized by the different processes they undertake in the diaspora. We noted that first generation migrants follow four stages of cultural adjustment process: entry, learning, settlement, and return. The 1.5 generation migrants take on the added process for their cultural adjustment toward bicultural and bilingual proficiency. Second generation migrants have three cultural influences in their cultural adjustment, including hosting culture, parent's home culture, and their own multicultural setting. Navigating these cultural influences is challenging. However, if they can manage to do so, it can lead them to a high cultural competency in our globalized era.

The third section discussed current trends in the Ethiopian evangelical churches in the US regarding their practices among the first, 1.5, and second generation migrants. Particularly, this section focused on describing the nature and structure of each generation as well as challenges of interactions across the lines of generations.

CHAPTER 4

Research Findings on Participants' Demography, Church Features and Interaction Across Generational Lines

The first chapter of this study focused on the need for research on the intergenerational perspective of missions from Ethiopian diaspora churches in the US In chapter two, the historical background of Ethiopian diaspora churches in the US was discussed in light of the three waves of Ethiopian migration to the US Chapter three developed an understanding of the intergenerational dynamics and identity of Ethiopian diaspora churches in the US, including the definition, description, and biblical examples of the first, 1.5, and second generations. Moreover, cultural adjustment of each generation in the diaspora and the current trend of Ethiopian churches regarding handling their generational dynamics in the US context was a focus of the previous chapter.

In this current chapter and the next one, this author will analyze the aforementioned findings. How does the historical background and its implication discussed in chapter two affect the current reality of Ethiopian diaspora churches in the US? How do the opportunities and challenges of the intergenerational dynamics discussed in chapter three contribute to the current missions endeavor of Ethiopian diaspora churches in the US?

The focus of this chapter is to offer research findings on participants' demography, church features, and interaction across generational lines. The practical realities on the ground concerning how missions is understood and practiced among Ethiopian diaspora churches in the US is the focus of the next chapter.

Understanding the Research

This researcher conducted original research to assess missions from the Ethiopian diaspora churches in the US from an intergenerational perspective. This study anticipates developing a comprehensive missions strategy to help Ethiopian evangelical churches in the US effectively mobilize their intergenerational context for missions. Prior to discussing results of the research, it is important to explain the research methods utilized, the nature of participants in this study, and the tools used to gather and analyze data.

As a case study, this researcher conducted qualitative and quantitative surveys to describe the phenomenon and sort out patterns that can be replicated if they are positive or improved if they are negative. An online survey was distributed to first, 1.5, and second generations who are actively involved in the Ethiopian diaspora churches as pastors, young adult leaders, children ministers, youth ministers, worship leaders, media team, and church members. This author's hope was to draw helpful perspectives from these groups of people by exposing them to the same survey questions, including exploring their personal understanding of missions and how that is practiced in their churches. What challenges and opportunities are involved in their intergenerational dynamics for missions?

This researcher also conducted interviews with selected groups of people. One of these groups were those who have independent ministries with both Ethiopians and non-Ethiopians. The second group includes second-generation church planters who are pastoring second-generation-led churches. The third group consists of some first and 1.5 generations who are believed to be influential among the Ethiopian church communities in the US This researcher conducted interviews with these three groups to get further insights on missions from Ethiopian diaspora churches and their intergenerational dynamics.

Tools used in this study include a general survey (see Appendix 1) and interview questions (see Appendix 2 and 3). Participants were asked to complete an online survey that was developed on Google Forms. The survey link was shared with participants through regular text, WhatsApp, Viber, Facebook Messenger, and email. The advantage of using Google Forms for data collection is that it automatically compiles results, which is helpful for creating reports. Participants were given the option of responding orally to the open-ended questions. It was necessary to give this option to participants, particularly to the first and some 1.5 generations, because they may prefer verbal communication to communicate their responses more effectively.

The interview was conducted through telephone and Zoom conversations. Most of the interview questions comprised of the same questions as the online survey, with the exception of a few questions that were geared toward respondents, such as participants from independent ministries, and second-generation church planters. Responses were carefully recorded with the Voice Memos app. The record was securely saved on an additional device in case this researcher lost the original record.

It was easy for this researcher to connect with participants since he himself is an Ethiopian immigrant who closely works with Ethiopian evangelical churches in the US This researcher obtained participants for this study from ministry visits to Ethiopian evangelical churches across the United States, and the annual pastors' conferences he has attended.

Participants were given the freedom to complete any or all the questionnaires. All participants chose to remain in the study and most of them fully completed the survey and the interview. However, seven participants left some of the questions unanswered, particularly in the open-ended questions section of the survey. Many respondents chose to remain anonymous, but some were willing to give their contact number in the event that this researcher needed further discussion with them to get clarity on their responses.

The online survey and the interview questions covered six issues: participants' demographics, description of participants' churches, participants' definition of missions, mission practices among Ethiopian diaspora churches in the US, missions to future generations, and challenges of and participants' recommendations for Ethiopian diaspora churches in missions. Each issue is analyzed and discussed as follows.

Demography of Participants

Demography of participants presents the age, gender, ministry role, full-time and voluntary correlations, as well as participants' motivation to join their current ministry in the church.

Age Demography

Two categories describe the age demographics of participants who were interviewed. Of the twelve participants, eight are between the ages of twenty-five and thirty-five, and four participants are between the ages of fifty-five and seventy. This age demographics indicates that 1.5 generation young adult leaders, second-generation church planters, first-generation pastors, and those with independent ministries are represented well in the study.

When it comes to online survey participants, the youngest was twenty-one years of age while the oldest was seventy years of age. All thirty-seven online survey participants willingly gave their response to the questionnaire. The survey results indicated that 62 percent of them were between twenty-one and forty years of age. This age group consists mostly of second generation and some 1.5 generation participants. From the total participants, those aged between twenty-one and thirty were the largest ten-year demographic, accounting for over 35 percent. Survey results also show that more than 37 percent of the participants were between forty and seventy years of age. This age group consists of a few 1.5 generation, with most being first-generation participants. Meanwhile, those in the age group between sixty and seventy were fewest in number, only accounting for about 5 percent of those surveyed.

Gender Demography

Out of the twelve participants in the interview, two were female, and the rest were male. Not all of the survey participants responded to this question. In other words, out of the total number of participants (thirty-seven), only twenty-four respondents indicated their gender. Of the survey participants who indicated their gender twenty two were male, while two participants were female. Hence, both the online and interview survey results showed that most participants in the study are male.

Ministry Role

Since the ministry roles of interview participants have already been described, this section is focused on online survey results. Online survey results showed that participants were taken from a wide range of responsibilities in the church, including pastors, youth and young adult leaders, children's ministry, worship and media, teachers, mentors, and church members. Results of the survey reveal that most participants in this study are pastors and youth/young adult ministry leaders. Out of the total thirty-five respondents, twenty-one participants indicated that they are part of these two ministry roles. This means that those who are pastors and youth/young adult ministry leaders account for about 60 percent, while the remaining 40 percent were divided among children's ministry, teachers, worship and media and church members. In this survey, a fair number (14 percent) of church members are represented. In this case, their voice is important in getting views of members compared with opinions of pastors and others who are serving in a leadership capacity.

Survey results on gender distribution and ministry roles discussed above indicated that most participants in this study are male and church leaders in different capacities. This implies that majority of Ethiopian evangelical churches in the US have male leaders.

Full-time and Voluntary Correlations

This section also describes an online survey result. To further understand the nature of their ministry, online survey participants were asked to record the status of their ministry role as either full time (paid) or voluntary. The survey result showed that there is a slight difference in ministry role status. About 52 percent of participants self-identified as volunteers, while about 47 percent participants indicated that they work as full-time paid ministers in the church.

Ministry Motivation

Again, data results in this section reflect only responses to the online survey. Online survey participants were asked to give their initial motivation for joining their current ministry in the church. All thirty-seven participants gave a response to this question. It was possible for respondents to select more than one option. About twenty-one participants indicated that a desire to help fill the gap in the church is the main initial motivation for them participating in their current ministry. Another seventeen participants indicated that ministry calling is the second major motivation for joining their current ministry in the church. None of the participants chose the option that their motivation was job seeking. However, about eleven participants indicated that their personal life experience was a driving factor for them to join their current ministry in the church. Participants' desire to help fill the needed gap in the church and their personal life experience together account for 81 percent. Perhaps these two data points indicate that more church work is accomplished by volunteers than full-time ministers.

Features of Ethiopian Evangelical Churches in the US

This section offers the online survey results that illustrate features of both the Amharic and English-speaking congregations of the Ethiopian diaspora churches in the US Participants were asked to reflect on the year of establishment, size, operation, and structure of their Amharic and English-speaking congregations.

Year of Amharic and English-Speaking Churches' Establishment

Participants were asked to record the year the Amharic and English-speaking church congregations were established. Survey results displayed the comparison between the establishment of Amharic and English-speaking congregations of Ethiopian churches in the US Ethiopian evangelical churches in the US need to establish English-speaking congregations to reach out to their children who were born and raised in the US Survey results revealed that most Ethiopian evangelical churches in the US still do not have English-speaking churches planted by or for their children. About sixteen participants indicated that they do not have English-speaking churches planted by or for the second generation. Only four participants said that they have planted English-speaking churches in the last one to five years.

By contrast, two participants indicated that there were Amharic congregations established in the US over forty years ago. Seven participants indicated that their Amharic-speaking church congregation was established between thirty and forty years ago. Fourteen participants revealed that their church was established between twenty and thirty years ago. This clearly shows that most Amharic-speaking church congregations have experienced a steady growth over the last twenty to forty years. Here, one can see that the establishment of English-speaking church congregations are very recent phenomenon compared with the establishment of Amharic congregations.[1] This corresponds with what has been discussed in chapter two.

The majority of Ethiopian migrants arrived in the US beginning in 1991, during the third wave of migration. Consequently, the few churches that had been planted in the mid-1980s were expanded during this period. Six survey participants noted that their Amharic-speaking churches were planted between ten and twenty years ago. This indicates that the number of Ethiopian churches planted during this period showed a significant drop compared to the prior decade. Perhaps this is because most Ethiopian diaspora believers were absorbed into the existing Ethiopian churches in the US However, participants indicated that this decline has changed in the last 5 years and shown a slight increase. In this case, the recent increase in church establishment could be the result of church splitting during this period as discussed in chapter two.

Size of Amharic and English-Speaking Congregations

Participants were asked to give responses on the current size of their congregations, both in terms of membership and Sunday service attendance. Survey result revealed that most participants, 36 percent or thirteen participants, have Amharic-speaking members between three-hundred and five-hundred. A fair number of participants (16 percent) also recorded that they have over five-hundred members. Respondents who indicated that they have fewer than fifty members account for only 8 percent.

Regarding church attendance of Amharic-speaking congregations, 33 percent (twelve) participants recorded that they have church attendance of between 150–300 in their Sunday services. Only 8 percent of participants (three) revealed that they have the highest attendance (over five-hundred) in their Sunday services. On the other hand, 13 percent of respondents (five) indicated that they have the smallest number of church attendance (< fifty). From the survey results, one can conclude that the average size of Ethiopian churches in the US ranges between three-hundred and five-hundred.

---

1. For further information on the second-generation church planting initiatives in North America, refer to a recent groundbreaking work by Tesfai Tesema, *Hope for the Second Generation: How Children of Immigrants Can Rekindle Christianity in the West* (N.p: Tenth Power Publishing, 2022).

When it comes to membership size of the second-generation, English-speaking congregation, survey results indicated that over 23 percent of participants (eight) have English-speaking members ranging between fifty and150. The same number of participants also indicated that their English-speaking congregations is less than fifty members. When it comes to church attendance of the English-speaking groups, over 36 percent of participants (twelve) reflected that every Sunday they have fewer than fifty attendants. Only 6 percent of respondents (two) stated that Sunday attendance at their English-speaking congregations is between 150 and three-hundred.

It is difficult to trust the above estimation because most participants did not submit their responses to this question, and those that gave their answers did not have the independent English-speaking churches in mind. Rather, what is on their mind are the different forms of second-generation gatherings under the first-generation Amharic-speaking churches. For instance, one of the respondents stated, "We have children ministry all the way up to eighteen years of age who are having their program in English."[2] Another respondent said, "There is no church established for the second-generation, but we have youth ministry, and they have youth pastor who teaches them in English."[3] The nature of the second generation, English-speaking congregation is discussed further in the next section.

Church Growth Since Establishment

Participants were asked another question concerning the size of the Amharic and English congregations: whether their churches had grown since being established. They were also asked to explain the factors that contribute to their church's growth, or lack thereof.

Over 80 percent of participants answered "yes" to the question, "Is your church growing since establishment?" Participants explained that their church has grown numerically since being established, for four reasons. First, most participants indicated that migration played a major role in the numerical growth of Ethiopian evangelical churches in the US One of the participants stated, "Yes, our church is growing, and migration is the sole reason for the

---

2. Zoom Interview, first generation participant 1, December 7, 2020.
3. Zoom Interview, first generation participant 3, December 17, 2020.

growth."⁴ Another participant said, "Our church is growing since establishment because Ethiopian communities in our city grew throughout the last 10–20 years."⁵ The migration refers to both Ethiopians who immigrate from Ethiopia or those who move from one city to another within the US. A participant writes, "The primary cause for our church growth is the migration of Ethiopian Christians who came from Ethiopia or moved to our city from other cities within America."⁶

The second reason for the numerical growth of Ethiopian diaspora churches in the US is fervent prayer and evangelism. One of the participants said, "Our church is growing because of prayer and evangelism outreaches in our city. We invite friends to church and to our different events so that they would hear the gospel."⁷ Another participant stated, "Our church is growing because non-believers are added, and our youth are getting baptized."⁸

The third reason for the numerical growth of Ethiopian evangelical churches in the US is a strong community. Ethiopian migrants could join the mainstream churches in the US, but one of the participants stated a desire to worship in their own language drew them to Ethiopian churches in the US One of the participants said, "I believe the family oriented and strong children ministry in the church has drawn many members to our church."⁹ Another participant added, "Members have great fellowships that attract others to the church. Particularly we have a ministry called 'Barnabas' that focuses on welcoming newcomers and help them with the settlement process in America."¹⁰

The fourth and final reason for numerical growth among Ethiopian churches is, as one respondent indicated, that their church is open to the diverse community in their city: "Yes, our church is growing because we are open to a diversity of people within our city, not just Ethiopians."¹¹ This answer is given from a second-generation respondent as their church tends to grow toward a multi-ethnic context.

---

4. Zoom Interview, first generation participant 4, December 15, 2020.
5. Zoom Interview, first generation participant 1, December 7, 2020.
6. Zoom Interview, first generation participant 3, December 17, 2020.
7. Zoom Interview, first generation participant 2, December 12, 2020.
8. Zoom Interview, first generation participant 5, December 20, 2020.
9. Zoom Interview, first generation participant 3, December 17, 2020.
10. Zoom Interview, 1.5 generation participant 1, December 16, 2020.
11. Zoom Interview, Second generation participant 1, December 8, 2020.

Survey results demonstrated that from the total thirty-two respondents, four participants (over 12 percent) indicated that their church's growth is slow. Some of the reasons participants gave for the slow church growth included church division, a small population of Ethiopians in their city, and many Ethiopians moving to a different city. One of the participants stated, "Our church has faced church division multiple times and each church split resulted in church decline. That is why our church growth declined over time."[12] Another participant added, "Our church is currently experiencing a very slow growth because of high moving turn over due to job and costly living expense."[13]

Survey results also revealed that one respondent (3 percent of participants) gave the answer "yes and no." The participant elaborated:

> My answer to this question is yes and no. Yes, because I have started to notice several new faces at our church, especially young adults/adults between the ages of 20–35. There has been growth in this age group, however, around the same time, several people who have been members of the church for ten plus years, have left the church or attend occasionally. I would attribute these trends in growth/decline to more resources and support being catered towards those in the age group of 20–35, conflict of interest within leadership, lack of follow-ups with those who were active at one point, just to name a few. Also, a lack of reinforcing the vision of the church through practical means such as church organized mission-centered projects and community integration/involvement.[14]

One participant (3 percent) replied no to this question. Another participant stated, "our church is not growing because the church culture is not participatory. It does not let most people to serve or participate with their calling."[15]

---

12. Survey participant 1, November 13, 2020.
13. Survey participant 2, November 14, 2020.
14. Survey participant 3, November 17, 2020.
15. Survey participant 4, November 14, 2020.

Features of First, Second and 1.5 Generation Ministries

In this section participants were asked to reflect on the features of different ministries in their churches that are geared toward the first, second, and 1.5 generations. Regarding features of first-generation ministry, all thirty-seven participants responded to the question, "How do you describe the first-generation Amharic speaking congregation"? Over 75 percent (thirty participants) revealed that the first-generation service is designed just for the Amharic-speaking groups. From the options provided, this response was selected by most participants. This indicates that most Ethiopian first-generation-led churches have ministries that solely serve their own people.

In other words, their ministry in the diaspora is not extended to other ethnic communities or even to their children who are living in a different culture than their parents. A participant who chose the "other" option stated,

> I want to emphasize that the first-generation church service is designed for the Amharic-speaking group, to the point the children and youth ministry within the church have trouble integrating to the main congregation themselves, let alone non-Ethiopians. This can have significant impact on the integration of Ethiopians within the church and non-Ethiopians. The youth/young adults in the church to some extent serve as the bridge when it comes to integrating non-Ethiopians into the church.[16]

In this case, the above respondent suggested that the inward-looking ministry approach of the first generation can be improved with the help of 1.5 generation young adults who can act as liaisons between the hosting culture, which has a strong influence on the second generation, and the first-generation culture.

Survey results showed that over 10 percent (four participants) indicated that the first-generation service is designed in a way that allows parents to worship with their children. To the best of this researcher's knowledge, none of the first generation-led Ethiopian churches in the US have services in English. Perhaps, these respondents are referring to the corporate worship times that occur two or three times a year, mostly during holy days. Another participant who chose the "other" option reinforces this by saying,

---

16. Survey participant 5, November 13, 2020.

"The first-generation service is mainly designed for the Amharic-speaking congregation, but sometimes we have English worship so that parents and children can worship together."[17] In this respect, it can be asserted that there are no permanent platforms among Ethiopian churches in the US that bring parents and children together for worship and ministry.

Over 5 percent (two participants) reflected that the first-generation service is designed to allow other ethnic groups to worship with them. As another participant who selected the "other" option pointed out: "The first generation-service is primarily for the Amharic speaking group, but translation is available if other ethnic people want to join the service."[18] It is good that Ethiopian churches have the option of hosting other ethnic people in their church services through translation. However, as churches planted in the diaspora, Ethiopian churches in the US can be missional churches that maximize their opportunity of reaching out to non-Ethiopian communities by opening more platforms that fit them.

When it comes to features of the second-generation ministry among Ethiopian diaspora churches in the US, twenty-three participants specified that the second-generation service is more like youth ministry, sixteen participants indicated that the second-generation service is more like children's ministry, and fourteen participants said that members are predominantly Ethiopian descendants. In this case, it can be asserted that the current Ethiopian second generation context mainly consists of ethnic Ethiopian children and youth. Therefore, the second generation appears to follow the separationist approach of the first generation. This approach is opposite of the diverse second-generation context in schools and their day-to-day lives in the broader community. In other words, just like the first-generation ministry is mainly designed to serve Ethiopian communities solely, the second generation seems to follow the same pattern. Particularly, if children and youth ministry teachers do not have enough exposure to the hosting culture, the second generation would only get the Ethiopian perspective that makes the discipleship process in the diaspora less effective.

Only three respondents revealed that the second generation had its independent church planted by the second generation. This survey result shows

---

17. Survey participant 6, November 14, 2020.
18. Survey participant 7, November 12, 2020.

that only a few second-generation Ethiopians are privileged to have church services in a church setting. Another eight participants described the second-generation service as more like Sunday school ministry, while twelve participants indicated it is more like college ministry. This feature shows that the second-generation ministry in most Ethiopian diaspora churches in the US has not gone beyond fellowships in a classroom setting.

Concerning features of ministry catered to the 1.5 generation, nineteen participants indicated that it is designed just for Amharic-speaking young adults. In this survey, ten participants recorded that 1.5 generation members have services that have a similar framework as the Amharic-speaking Sunday services, except that young adult leaders run them. Another seven participants also indicated that 1.5 generation young adult services allow them to worship with English-speaking second-generation groups. For instance, one of the participants who selected the "other" option said, "Yes, young adult service is like the Amharic-speaking Sunday service, but most of the teachings have topics that pertain to the 1.5-genration age group."[19] Another participant added, "Our young adult congregation is currently serving only the Amharic-speaking young adults, but it is designed to address the English speaking second generation as well."[20]

Interactions Across Generational Lines

In this section this researcher discusses the interaction of the first, second, and 1.5 generations across the lines of their generational circles. This includes exploring how open they are to each other's context, the challenges they face when they want to communicate across the boundaries of their generational circle, and what church structure can bring all the generations together for effective missions.

---

19. Survey participant 8, November 15, 2020.
20. Survey participant 9, November 14, 2020.

Openness of the First, Second, and 1.5 Generations Across Each Other's Context

Openness to each other's context is very important. An interview participant stated, "Most parents do not know their children and vice versa."[21] To explain his point, the participant shared his experience with his parents. He said,

> It was not until I was an adult, I learned how my mom and dad met. I did not know what my dad work for living when he was in Ethiopia. I found out recently that he worked at a gas station when he moved to America. I did not know that my mom and dad went to jail in Ethiopia because of their faith during the communist government regime. The reason I can never relate to them, and they never understand me is because I did not know their stories.[22]

An online survey participant also noted, "I do not believe the first generation understands the cultural viewpoint their children may have. Essentially, they do not know that their children are not believers at all."[23]

How First Generation Migrants are Open to Their Children's Cultural Context

Most participants (eighteen) noted that first generation migrants are open to learning English and twelve are open to learning American culture in order to better understand their children. On the other hand, thirteen participants specified that the first generation is not open to any of the second generation's cultural context. Based on these survey results, one can say that there is willingness among the majority of the first generation to learn the English language but not necessarily the cultural context of the second generation, as a significant number of participants indicated their unwillingness to have practical engagements with the second generation's cultural context.

---

21. Zoom Interview, second generation participant 2, December 11, 2020.
22. Zoom Interview, second generation participant 2, December 11, 2020.
23. Survey participant 3, November 17, 2020.

How The Second Generation is Open to Their Parents' Cultural Context

About seventeen participants indicated that the second generation is open to learning their parents' language. Another seventeen participants, however, said that the second generation is not open to any aspect of the first generation's culture. In other words, members of the second generation are either open to learning their parents' language or they neglect their parents' culture altogether. Based on the survey results, nine participants indicated that there are second generation immigrants who want to go back to their home country to contribute transnationally, and five participants said that there are second generation immigrants who want to participate in the Amharic service with their parents. However, only one person specified that the second generation is willing to take over and continue their parents' ethnic church. In this case, one can note that the second generation may be interested in learning their parents' language, attending Amharic service with their parents, and going back to their home country. However, almost none of them are willing to take over and continue their parents' ethnic church in the US.

How Open 1.5 Generation is to Both First and Second Generation Context

Most participants (nineteen) indicated that the 1.5 generation is more open to the first-generation context. Another nineteen participants also recorded that the 1.5 generation are not properly playing their bridging role between the first and second generations. It is only nine participants who indicated that the 1.5 generation support the idea that the first generation need to have a church service in English with their children and that the 1.5 generation themselves are willing to engage in an English-speaking service. In this case, even though the 1.5 generation likes to do church in the manner of the first generation, it is encouraging to see that there is openness among them to cross the cultural barrier to engage in ministry with the second generation.

Challenges of Interaction Across Generational Boundaries

The focus of this section is to identify challenges that influence the relationship between the first and second generations. Identifying these challenges is important because it could help identify the source of the generational gap. As one of the second-generation interview participants pointed out:

The worldview of the first generation is different from the second generation. Even, how the gospel informed our views on the issues of culture, justice, race is another dynamic where Ethiopian diaspora churches in America are struggling in their ability to reach the next generation. In this case, they are behind the game, because as a diaspora church they have lots of things to navigate, not only the generational gap but also the cultural gaps between parents and their children.[24]

Challenges of the First Generation in Their Relationship with the Second Generation

About thirty-one participants indicated that the relationship between the first and second generations is negatively affected because the first generation is mostly focused on the Amharic-speaking ministries. The survey result also agrees with the finding in the previous section that the first generation congregation is exclusively designed for the Amharic-speaking groups. Twenty participants identified the language barrier as the second factor that affects the relationship between the first and second generations. However, it is interesting to note that interview results showed that the language barrier is not the major factor that affects the relationship between the first and second generations.

Participants acknowledged it is true that language barrier can cause challenges in the relationship between the first and second generation. However, they highlighted that the tendency of the first generation to solely focus on themselves and exclude the second generation plays a more significant role in creating the gap between the first and second generations. For instance, one of the participants elaborated:

> One of the misconceptions among the second generation is that they do not want to hear their parents, or they cannot understand their parents because of the language barrier. That is not true at all. For me, my parents are always speaking to me in Amharic. I do not speak the language fluently, but I understand what they want to say. I have friends who do not understand

---

24. Zoom Interview, second generation participant 3, December 11, 2020.

Amharic that well, so their parents primarily speak to them in English. As a second generation we do not only understand our parents' language, but we also understand broken English as well. We understand the message our parents want to convey. For instance, there are parents who say that they are not qualified to teach their children the Bible because of language barrier. However, I know a lot of them, when their children get bad grades at school, regardless of whether they qualify or not they challenge their children on their education. So, for me it is a question of priority, and it is not about language barrier.[25]

Here, when the participant said, "as a second generation," he is communicating the nature of the second generation. They understand their parents' ethnic language and their parents' nonstandard English. That is part of being raised as a second generation immigrant.

This section also examines if challenges of the first generation in relationship to the second generation arise from the lack of willingness by the second generation to listen to their parents. According to survey results, only two participants suggested that the second generation are not willing to listen to their parents. In this case, unwillingness to obey their parents is the least factor in its contribution to the relational challenges between the first and second generations.

Simply put, the main factor that is responsible for causing challenges to the first generation in their relationship with the second generation is not language barrier or lack of willingness from the second generation to listen to their parents, but it is the first generations' tendency to exclusively design anything they do for themselves while neglecting the second generation. In other words, everything they do centers on themselves, and they are unwilling to compromise that approach to relate better with the second generation.

Challenges of Second Generation in Their Relationship with the First Generation

Survey results highlighted that the top challenges of the second generation in their relationship with the first generation are threefold. Not being well

---

25. Zoom Interview, second generation participant 2, December 11, 2020.

understood by the first generation is the first challenge. Twenty-seven participants indicated that the second generation is not well understood by the first generation. In other words, most participants believe that the second generation faces challenges mostly because the first generation do not understand them or their context. In the previous section, survey results suggested that the first generation is open to the context of the second generation. However, this section disproved the first generation's claim as participants strongly suggested that the second generation being misunderstood by the first generation is the biggest problem.

Lack of a platform to bring the two generations together is the second factor that causes a challenge for the second generation as they wish to relate with the first generation. For instance, eighteen participants indicated that the second generation has not had a chance to do church with the first generation.

The second generation's third challenge in relating to the first generation has to do with the second generation being always labeled as youth. A significant number of participants (sixteen) stated that the second generation being always considered as youth is another factor that contributes to the gap between the first and second generations. In other words, to always be labeled as "youth" is a huge challenge among the second generation that casts a negative shadow on their relationship with the first generation.

Other Challenges Across Generational Lines

Other challenges such as mental health, addiction, substance abuse, lack of economic opportunities, and social prejudices are discussed in this section. This researcher wanted to investigate all these factors to have a better sense of the context of each generation, and their interaction across their generational lines, by identifying common challenges particular to each generation.

Survey results indicate that economic opportunity, or lack of access to decent jobs, is one of the challenges shared by the first and 1.5 generations. That is why most 1.5 generation immigrants take college courses while working to generate their income for a living. Consequently, most 1.5 generation have a busy life to the point they do not have much time left for church. The researcher's close observation among Ethiopians confirms this. As a 1.5 generation immigrant himself, this researcher knows many friends who are working hard for a better future for themselves and their families.

The issue gets even worse with the first generation. It is difficult for the first generation to raise their children well in the diaspora. Compared to 1.5 generation groups, the first generation do not have the linguistic ability to go to school to upgrade themselves. They are left with the option of staying in unskilled jobs where they work for many hours, but for lower compensation. As a result, most first generation immigrants have less time to spend with their children and when they get a chance to be around their children they have poor communication with their children because of the language barrier. Most of these parents are focused on tackling their economic challenges, but there are lots of other issues they need to address in their children's life. Cultural, spiritual, and mental issues are crucial issues among the second generation, who are born and raised in the US In the previous chapter we discussed how the first generation can shelter themselves in their community while living in diaspora. Only breadwinning, or providing for their family, gets them out of their comfort zone. Otherwise, they do not have much exposure to the hosting culture. One of the participants from the second generation stated:

> The first-generation assumes that they know what life is like in America. That is why they say to their children, "If I were you," "if I had your opportunity," "if I had been raised in America." However, the truth is that they do not really know what life is like in America until they carve out a time to sit down with their children, ask them how they are doing and if there is anything they are struggling with and listen without judging them.[26]

Another common challenge that both first and 1.5 generations face is social prejudices, or discrimination based on their skin color or accent. These social prejudices present real barriers to decent jobs. Unlike the first and 1.5 generations, lack of economic opportunity is the least challenge for the second generation. Growing up in the US gives them the ability to maximize their economic opportunity through education and employment. However, spiritual issues remain a challenge. As an interview participant stated, "Many second-generation face faith crises related to the secular culture of America.

---

26. Zoom Interview, second generation participant 1, December 8, 2020.

For instance, the concept of deconstruction is one of the new age movements that is challenging the Christian life of the second-generation."[27]

Meanwhile, survey results indicate that other factors, such as mental health, addiction, substance abuse and social prejudices, are also significant challenges among the second generation. Another second generation interview participant noted,

> The existence of God is obvious for our parents because they came from a religious community. However, the second-generation need apologetics that deals with issues of culture, social justice, and mental health. We have to exegete the culture that we inhabit. What is the time, culture, and the generation that we are living in look like? Being able to maneuver through it is crucial for all of us but particularly in the second-generation ministry.[28]

Church Structure

So far, this researcher has discussed the openness and interaction challenges across generational boundaries of the first, 1.5, and second generations. This current section takes the discussion one step further and explores how Ethiopian churches are attempting to bring these three generations together for effective missions. Keeping this goal in mind, this section first discusses the perception of the second generation toward their parents' ethnic churches. By taking participants' responses on the first issue into consideration, this researcher will further discuss how that leads the second generation to withdraw from their parents' ethnic churh. Finally, this researcher focuses on participants' responses about the church structure that helps to bring all the generations together for effective missions work.

Perceptions of Second Generation Toward Their Parents' Ethnic Church

The survey results indicate that most second generation immigrants are not interested in taking over their parents' ethnic church. Thirty-two participants

---

27. Zoom Interview, second generation participant 1, December 8, 2020.
28. Zoom Interview, second generation participant 3, December 8, 2020.

disagreed with the statement "second-generation are interested in learning Amharic because they want to continue their parent's ethnic church." This response aligns with what we have discussed in the previous section. In the previous section we discussed how the continuation and expansion of the first-generation ethnic church is not through the second generation, but largely depends on Christian immigrants who keep coming to the US, and the 1.5 generation who tend to follow the pattern of the first generation.

Exodus and Destiny of the Second Generation

The second generation are neither interested in taking over and continuing their parents' ethnic church, nor do they feel a sense of belonging to the first generation church. Consequently, the second generation is forced to exit their parents' ethnic church and end up in different places including abandoning their Christian faith altogether.

Twenty-five participants disagreed with the statement, "Second-generation feel a sense of belonging in their parents' ethnic church." This implies that the first-generation ethnic churches do not have space for the second generation to engage and contribute. Survey results also revealed that most participants (thirty-two) agreed with the statement, "Second-generation leave their parents' ethnic church when they finish high school." In other words, for most second generation immigrants, graduation from high school is also graduation from the church. By this time, they are on their own, they leave their parents' ethnic churches, and they are not interested in coming back. This confirms what was discussed in the previous chapter, where South Korean churches in the US use the term "silent exodus" to indicate the drastic drop in second generation South Korean American adults' participation in ethnic churches.

This researcher asked participants to indicate some of the reasons that the second generation leave their parents' ethnic church. One of the reasons participants indicated is the gap between the first generation and their children that occurs early on in the children's lives. An interview participant stated,

> I was responsible for the children and youth ministry in our church for more than six years. When parents come to the church they separate with their children at the door. The children go to

their classrooms and the parents go directly to their service in the main sanctuary.[29]

This separation creates a big disconnect between parents and children, which causes the second generation to feel less belonging with their parents' ethnic church, and eventually leave the church altogether.

Most participants (thirty) also recorded that one of the reasons for the second generation's departure from their parents' ethnic church is the lack of platforms that fit them as adults. This survey result conforms with findings in an earlier section of this chapter and the researcher's observation discussed in the previous chapter. According to these discussions, the platform provided for the second generation is more like children's ministry or youth ministry. Neither context is viable for the second generation because they do not reflect a church nature that fits second-generation adults. Consequently, these groups of second-generation adults are left with no other option but to leave their parents' ethnic church.

Now, the question is, where do they go after leaving their parents' ethnic church? This question is the focus of the next discussion. According to survey results, most participants indicated that those in the second generation who left their parents' ethnic churches either join US mainstream churches or stop going to church altogether. Other participants indicated some second generation immigrants either join college ministries in their church or go to churches planted by the second generation themselves. However, none of the participants indicated that these second generation immigrants joined their parents' ethnic church after they finish high school.

In this case, the second generation is looking for mainstream churches that are ready to embrace their stories, heritage, and skin color. If they do not find such platforms in the US mainstream churches, they either come back to churches planted by their second-generation peers, or they may stop going to church altogether.

---

29. Zoom Interview, 1.5 generation participant 1, December 16, 2020.

What Model of Church Structure Brings the Three Generations Together?

This researcher posed three related questions to explore possible church structures that can bring the three generations together for missions. The first question probes participants' views on the three generations, whether doing church together is possible or not. Next, this researcher asked participants to share their opinion on a suggested strategy. That is, if Ethiopian evangelical churches in the US would be willing to have two services on Sundays, one in Amharic and the other in English. Finally, this researcher asked participants to indicate whose responsibility it is to establish an English-speaking church: the first, second, or 1.5 generation?

Can The First and Second Generations Do Church Together?

In this question, this researcher wanted to know if participants realize the need and possibility of doing church together. Most participants (twenty-seven) agreed about the need for corporate church, but their churches do not have a structure that brings the first and second generations together. Three participants recorded that it is impossible for the first generation to do church with the second generation. On the other hand, another three participants indicated that it is possible to have a corporate church and their churches are working toward that structural adjustment.

Simply put, survey results show that most participants agreed on the need and possibility of having a church that can help the first and second generations worship and do ministry together. However, they do not know how to develop that structure because it is a new practice among Ethiopian evangelical churches in the US.

Participants who selected the "other" option gave diverse responses to the question. One of them said, "Yes, it is possible to have a church that consists of parents and children together, but it takes prayer and hard work on the details."[30] Another participant also stated, "I agree that we need a church structure that brings the first and second generations together. This can happen if parents teach their kids Amharic at home so that the gap would not be there as we can worship together in Amharic."[31]

---

30. Survey participant 8, November 15, 2020.
31. Survey participant 13, November 14, 2020.

Another suggestion by participants reflected that it is possible to have church service together occasionally. For instance, one of the participants stated, "I agree that we need to have church together and our church is trying to include English service at least once a month where both the first and second generation can worship together."[32] Likewise, another participant pointed out, "It may not work if we do it together all the time, but it is possible to come together for worship occasionally."[33] Unlike most participants however, there were a few participants who did not see the need to have church together. For instance, one of the participants noted, "No need to have joint service. I think we can still be effective with the separate services we already have."[34]

Most participants do not question the need to have church together; instead, they question how to do so. In the next question, this researcher explored whether participants agree or disagree on a suggested strategy that could help on the how question. This researcher calls the strategy a "two-service strategy."

A Two-Church Service Strategy

Participants were asked whether their church would be willing to have two services, one in English, where parents can worship together with their children, and one in Amharic for the first generation to worship in their heart language. Most participants (twenty-three) recorded that their church would be willing to have two services, but they do not have that structure at the moment. Six participants indicated that their churches are already practicing two services, one in Amharic and another one in English. Based on the researcher's close observation among the Ethiopian diaspora churches in the US, none of the Ethiopian churches have such a structure. It is possible that these participants have the two separate services (English and Amharic) in mind as they respond to this question. Three participants disagreed with the suggested strategy. One of them disagreed with the two-services strategy because they do not have the capacity to manage the two services. An additional

---

32. Survey participant 14, November 14, 2020.
33. Survey participant 11, November 19, 2020.
34. Survey participant 15, November 14, 2020.

two participants disagreed with the suggested strategy because their churches already have two services, but both services are in Amharic.

Four participants selected the "other" option. One of them stated, "I do not see the suggested strategy as a working strategy that can bring solution to the gap between the first and second generations."[35] Another participant added, "In my context, there is not a desire from the second-generation for such strategy."[36] Meanwhile, another participant noted, "I will not say never, but it does not seem practical at all. We have to consider that both the children and the parents need to be fed by the church based on their spiritual level."[37] Another participant said, "I disagree with the suggested strategy because our children can learn Amharic and join us in the Amharic service. It is easier to teach Amharic to the second generation than teaching English to the first generation."[38]

From these survey results, one can conclude that most Ethiopian diaspora churches prefer to have two services (one in English and one in Amharic), but the "how" question is still unresolved. A significant number of participants said that their churches do not have such a structure and they doubted the practicality of the suggested strategy for several reasons, including: they already have two services (in Amharic), they do not have enough space, they believe that their children can learn Amharic and join them in the Amharic service, the second generation is not interested in it, and their pastor does not have the capacity to manage two services in different languages.

Does the First Generation Need to Establish an English-Speaking Church?

Most participants (twenty-two) responded "yes" to this question. The first generation is responsible for establishing an English-speaking church service because they are in charge of discipling their children in the US context. Another five participants also said "yes," but most in the first generation would not be willing to worship with their children in English. Four participants

---

35. Survey participant 16,17,18, and 19, November 19, 2020.
36. Survey participant 20, November 17, 2020.
37. Survey participant 5, November 14, 2020.
38. Survey participant 20, November 17, 2020.

gave a "yes" response but said that most in the second generation would not be willing to worship with their parents in English.

These survey results show that most participants agreed that it is the responsibility of the first generation to establish an English-speaking church along with their Amharic-speaking congregation. However, these survey results also indicated that the first generation would face challenges in the process of establishing the English-speaking congregation. Participants clearly showed that these challenges would come from both the first and second-generation members who are not willing to do church together.

Five participants gave a "no" response to this question for several reasons. For instance, two of them said "no" because they felt it is the responsibility of the second generation to establish an English-speaking church, as they know the language better. Meanwhile, another two participants said "no" because this will never happen, and one participant said "no" because their children can learn Amharic and join the first generation in their Amharic-speaking church congregation.

To further understand the responsibility of planting English-speaking churches among Ethiopian diaspora churches in the US, this researcher explores the potential of each generation in missions. Regarding the first generation, all thirty-seven participants agreed that the first generation needs to have a missional mindset to reach their children in the US The first generation needs to cross linguistic and cultural barriers to reach out to their children who hold different cultural worldviews.

Most participants also indicated that the first generation has the potential to provide resources for missions. According to participants, finances and life experience are some of the resources that the first generation can offer. One of the interview participants from the second generation noted,

> The first generation is a lot wealthier and far more resourceful than the second-generation in terms of age, seniority, experience, wisdom, beliefs, being established and finances. They have been in the church for a lot longer than the second-generation. The second-generation are just eating out of the blocks of the first-generation as they begin to take ownership recently in the last three to five years. The first-generation can consider doing missions with the second-generation but at the same time,

they need to realize that the second-generation are their mission fields as well. ... As a second-generation church planter, I was helped by the first-generation. I have received not only prayer supports but also financial assistance in the resourcefulness of the first-generation.[39]

Another online survey participant stated, "Most first-generation have lived in America for fifteen plus years and therefore they are well established in the US which can be foundational in helping navigate through local areas and providing more funds for missions."[40] Based on these survey results, one can see two reasons for the first generation to take the responsibility of establishing an English-speaking church along with their Amharic-speaking congregation, or assist in planting second-generation churches. They should do that first because they are expected to disciple their children in the US context, and second, because they have the financial resources and life experience to support the second generation.

When it comes to the role of the 1.5 generation in establishing English-speaking churches, most participants indicated that the 1.5 generation could play a bridging role between the first and second generation, as well as between the Ethiopian and US communities. The 1.5 generation faces challenges in this role. One of the participants stated, "The 1.5 generation know both sides of the world but may not have a full exposure of either."[41] Another participant said, "The challenge with 1.5 generation is that they often feel they are not enough Americanized to function well in the American context."[42]

Despite these challenges, the 1.5 generation is resourceful in providing a platform where the first and second generation can come together to strategize. One participant said, "The 1.5-generation are good bridges between the two generations and are able to offer wider understanding of missional strategies that are helpful to reach out to the diverse communities in America."[43] Another participant added, "The 1.5 generation can play an instrumental role in helping mentor the second-generation for missions and organizing events

---

39. Zoom Interview, second generation participant 1, December 8, 2020.
40. Survey participant 20, November 17, 2020.
41. Survey participant 21, November 17, 2020.
42. Survey participant 22, November 18, 2020.
43. Survey participant 23, November 17, 2020.

where all generations can come together and learn about as well as implement strategies for missions."⁴⁴ Yet another participant noted, "The 1.5 generation understand the differences between both generations better because they have one foot in the first generation and another foot in the second-generation. They are probably the best resources when it comes to contextualizing and connecting cross culturally."⁴⁵

From these survey results, one can conclude that the 1.5 generation can play their bridging role between the first and second generation, as well as between Ethiopian and US communities, by maximizing their cultural exposure in all these groups. Some of the practical bridging roles they can offer include mentoring the second generation, organizing platforms where the first and second generation can come together to have ongoing dialogue, and developing missions strategies that can help Ethiopian diaspora churches to be more missional in the US.

Regarding the potential among the second generation, participants indicated that the second generation has the zeal, energy, and passion to share the gospel among their second-generation peers and to Americans. Compared to the first and 1.5 generations, the second generation is uniquely positioned for missions due to their versatility and ability to identify with others. One of the interview participants from the second generation said,

> As a second-generation, we are forced to grow up in two different cultures. We are never Ethiopian enough for Ethiopians and we are never American enough for Americans. However, we are well versed in both communities and that gave us a gift of versatility. We know how to navigate between cultures in general. We are ministering to the diverse community here in our city including our second-generation peers from Hispanic and Asian communities as we have a common challenge and opportunity of between two cultures.⁴⁶

---

44. Survey participant 24, November 18, 2020.
45. Survey participant 20, November 17, 2020.
46. Survey participant 25, November 17, 2020.

The second generation is also uniquely positioned for missions in their ability to identify themselves with people who feel like they have not made it in this life. As one participant stated,

> A lot of people are trying to make it in this life. As a second-generation we have the ability to identify ourselves with such people because growing up in the Ethiopian family we understand that struggle as our parents work very hard to provide for us. We know what it is like to fight for your purpose and destiny.[47]

The ability to use social media for missions is also another element that makes the second generation uniquely positioned for missions today. An interview participant stated,

> We are digital natives in this digital era. We utilize social media for missions. Our online presence is playing a huge role in drawing people to our church. Every Sunday we have two to three people who visit our church and when we ask them how they find us, they said it was through our social media like Instagram.[48]

Also, second generation immigrants are uniquely positioned for missions because they do not have the cultural and language barriers compared to the first and 1.5 generations. An interview participant from the second generation noted,

> I have observed the first-generation, whenever they have evangelism campaigns they specifically go to where lots of Ethiopians congregate rather than going to anybody. However, for the second-generation, going beyond the Ethiopian community is not a problem because they have no language and cultural barriers. They know the context of America and the people. They even have the potential to plant churches that can accommodate a multi-ethnic congregation.[49]

---

47. Zoom Interview, second generation participant 3, December 11, 2020.
48. Zoom Interview, second generation participant 1, December 8, 2020.
49. Zoom Interview, second generation participant 3, December 11, 2020.

From these survey results, one can note that the second generation immigrants have a wider sphere of influence for the gospel than the first and 1.5 generations. They know the context because they have lived in it. There is staggering potential among the second generation that can be maximized through financial support from the first generation immigrants in their church-planting initiatives and by mentorship support from the 1.5 generation who would be willing to come walk alongside the second generation.

Chapter Summary

This chapter discussed findings on participants' demography, features of Ethiopian diaspora churches in the US, and their interactions across generational lines both at a personal and church level.

Participants of this study consisted of pastors, youth, young adults, and children's ministry leaders between the ages of twenty-one and seventy. Most of them serve as volunteers and their initial motivation to join their current ministry was to help fill the gap in the church. In other words, participants' motivation to join their current ministry is inward focused, and not outward focused or missional in nature. Most first-generation Ethiopian diaspora churches in the US were established between twenty and thirty years ago and very few over forty years ago. The current average membership size of Ethiopian diaspora churches is between 300–350, and caters largely to the first and 1.5 generation, solely designed for the Amharic-speaking groups.

It is a recent phenomenon to find English-speaking churches planted by the second generation. They were planted between one and five years ago and their current average size is between fifty and 150 members. The ministries that cater to the second generation bear closer resemblance to children, youth, and college ministries than to adult ministries, and predominantly consist of Ethiopian descendants. All these survey results imply that Ethiopian diaspora churches in the US have a good size in terms of number. However, they are more self-focused in their establishment and ministry approach, which could negatively impact their missions work to communities beyond their own.

Concerning interactions across generational lines, survey results indicated that it is a misconception to see language barrier as the primary problem affecting the relationship between the first and second generations. Rather, it is the first generation's focus on themselves that leads them to neglect the second generation. Consequently, the feeling of not being understood by their parents is the primary challenge of the second generation in their relationship with the first generation. When it comes to the 1.5 generation, the challenges that affect their relationship with the first and second generations include their busy schedule to achieve the American dream, and their tendency of following the first generation Amharic-speaking congregation.

Three factors contribute to the generational gap. First, there is lack of a platform in the Ethiopian diaspora churches. For instance, the second generation does not have a chance to do church with their parents. Second, the second generation is always regarded as youth. Third, the focus of the first and 1.5 generations is on tackling the economic challenge, while lacking the time and knowledge to address the cultural, spiritual, and mental issues in their children's lives.

Moreover, not only does the second generation feel that they are not well understood by their parents, but they also feel that they do not belong to their parents' ethnic churches and therefore, they have no interest to take over and continue their parents' ethnic church. Consequently, most second generation immigrants tend to leave their parents' ethnic churches once they finish high school, and they either join the US mainstream churches or stop going to church altogether. Some second generation immigrants also consider going to churches planted by second generation pastors, if there are any in their area.

This researcher explored whether the Ethiopian diaspora churches can narrow down the generational gap through church structure adjustment. Most participants agreed that the first, second, and 1.5 generations need to do church together for effective missions. However, they do not know if that is practical since most of them do not have such structure. Again, most participants agreed on the need to implement the "two church service" approach, one in English where parents can worship with their children, and the other one in Amharic for parents to worship in their heart language. However, they still doubt its practicality for several reasons.

One of the reasons is that there is a lack of interest among the first and the second generations in having joint church. Others added that it is not necessary to do church together because the second generation can join the first generation church occasionally. Still, others said instead of teaching parents English, it is easier for parents to teach their children Amharic so they can join the first generation church; and moreover, others indicated that there is no need to bring the first and second generations together because they should be ministered to according to differences in their spiritual and cultural experiences.

Despite all these challenges, survey results indicated that the first generation needs to have a missional mindset to carry out its responsibility of discipling second generation immigrants in the US Most participants agreed that the first generation is responsible for establishing English-speaking churches alongside their Amharic services or help second generation church planters who take the initiative to plant English-speaking churches. Participants said that the first generation can do this because they are well established in the US, and they have the financial resources and life experience to do so. The 1.5 generation can facilitate these church-planting initiatives by mentoring the second generation, organizing platforms where the first and second generations can come together to have constant dialogue, and developing missions strategies that can help Ethiopian diaspora churches to be more missional in the US There is also tremendous potential among the second generation for missions as they have a wider sphere of influence in the US compared to the first and 1.5 generations.

CHAPTER 5

Research Findings on Definition and Practices of Missions Among Ethiopian Diaspora Churches in the US

This chapter offers research findings on the definition and practices of missions among Ethiopian churches in the US, including their mobilization, recruitment, organizational structure, and transnationalism. This researcher explored what factors have shaped the respondent's definition of missions. Finally, the strengths, weaknesses, and challenges of Ethiopian diaspora churches in missions are presented in this chapter.

Factors That Shape Participants' Definition of Missions

This researcher needed to explore the definition of missions among Ethiopian diaspora churches in the US in order to identify the churches' perceptions on missions and how that affects their missions practice here in the US and beyond. Before discussing participants' definitions of missions, this researcher asked both online survey and interview participants to share their thoughts on the following four factors that could shape their definition of missions: missionary sending and recipient countries, missionaries' activities in the recipient countries, participants' own missions experience in the US, and participants' Biblical views on missions. Participants' responses on these factors are discussed in detail as follows.

Factor One: Participants' Views on Missionary Sending and Receiving Countries

Both online survey and interview participants were asked to share their views on which countries are known as missionary-sending nations and which are identified as recipients. Most participants (thirty-two) view the West (America and Europe) as the largest missionary-sending continents. According to participants' responses, South Korea and China are the second-largest missionary-sending countries, next to the Western nations. Participants did not perceive African and South American nations as mission-sending countries.

When it comes to online survey results on missionary-receiving countries, participants indicated that non-Western countries are the major recipient countries. Participants' response displayed that Africa takes the most significant share, as thirty-two participants perceived the continent as a missionary recipient. Fourteen participants noted Southeastern Asian countries as the second largest missionary recipients, after African countries. Still other participants specified the 10/40 window, South American countries, and Middle East countries as missionary recipients. On the other hand, none of the online survey participants perceived the West (North America and European countries) as missionary-receiving nations.

In short, the above online survey results indicates that most non-Western countries are missionary recipients and notably participants perceived Africa as a missionary recipient only. On the other hand, most participants said that the West (North American and European countries) are the most missionary-sending and none of the participants see those countries as missionary recipients.

As an African diaspora in the US, this perception could impact the Ethiopian diaspora churches' understanding and practices of missions here in the US and beyond. In other words, Ethiopian diaspora churches may lose the missional aspect of their movement to the US because they do not perceive the US as a mission field. In addition, this perception could make Ethiopian diaspora churches focus on their homeland or Africa in general because of their perception that missions work is needed only in Africa. Moreover, their perspective toward Africa as only recipients may cause Ethiopian diaspora churches to continue their recipient mentality even in the diaspora. This researcher has observed many Ethiopian Christians in the US who reflect a recipient mentality. When they want to do missions, they think less about mobilizing resources from their fellow Ethiopians. However, they tend to work with Americans simply because they identify missions as an American thing. It is not wrong to ask American Christians to support Ethiopians' initiatives in missions, but it should not be done with a dependency mentality that makes Ethiopians passive when they have the resources to do the missions work themselves.

Interview participants frame their responses on mission-sending countries in three ways. First, an East-West missions dynamic dominates mission-sending movements. An interview with a second-generation participant revealed that the current mission-sending trend is from the East to the West,

> Historically, missions movement began form the East (Middle East) to the West. It shifted and became from the West to the rest in recent history, as Islam and Buddhism took root in the East. Currently, the missions movement is on the decline in the West as secularism is taking root in the Western nations. Today, the tides are changing to the way before, from the East to the West, mainly through migrant Christians.[1]

Another participant added, "For instance, the Chinese resurgent missions movement through its migrants, all over the world, is a current phenomenon from the East."[2] In another instance, the participant said,

> Even as Ethiopian immigrants, we are here in America serving the West. Our church is not reaching out to just Ethiopian communities. We have Hispanics, Asians, African Americans, and White Caucasians. This all shows that the East is ministering to the West in this era.[3]

Second, the nineteenth and twentieth century missionary-sending movement was used to explain how the global majority joined the current missionary-sending trend. In the interview, a first-generation migrant pastor framed his response using the nineteenth century missions movement from England, which most Americans joined in the twentieth century. The participant stated,

---

1. Zoom Interview, second generation participant 2, December 11, 2020.
2. Zoom Interview, second generation participant 1, December 8, 2020.
3. Zoom Interview, second generation participant 1, December 8, 2020.

England took the early missions movement before and during David Livingstone and Hudson Taylor to Africa and China. Missionary sending movement from the West exploded in the beginning of the twentieth century as Americans joined the field by sending thousands of missionaries to almost all over the world.[4]

Daniel H. Bays supports the participant's statement: "By 1900, the expansion of the American mission was in full bloom, and would continue well into the twentieth century, with its presence on all continents of the globe characterized by a distinctive American mixture of religious and national or 'civilizing' purpose."[5] Another participant added, "Today, Europe and North America are still sending missionaries, but their number is in decline while other nations such as South Korea, China, Brazil, Nigeria, and South Africa are on the rise." Another interview participant echoed that many different nations are currently evangelizing the world. The participant remarked,

> Western nations are still well known for sending missionaries in the early twentieth century and before. In addition, many non-Western countries are on the rise to join them in sending out their missionaries to different parts of the world. For instance, Ethiopian Kale Hiwot Church has missionaries in different countries of which I am privileged to mentor one missionary family to Pakistan.[6]

Another participant also took the diaspora movement as an example to describe the involvement of all nations in the current mission-sending movement. The participant said: "Churches or mission organizations did not send Christian diaspora communities as missionaries to the countries where they migrated to, but diaspora missionaries from all nations are taking part in the missions work today."[7]

The third trend in missionary-sending practice is misplacement. When one interview participant shared his observation on mission-sending countries'

---

4. Zoom Interview, first generation participant 2, December 12, 2020.
5. Bays, "The Foreign Missionary Movement in the 19th and Early 20th Centuries."
6. Zoom Interview, independent ministry participant 1, December 10, 2020.
7. Zoom Interview, independent ministry participant 2, December 10, 2020.

trends, he noted that most missionaries do not go to the right place. The participant explained:

> Today, most missionaries are going to the already reached places. Biblically, nations refer to people groups, not countries, and so over 90% of missionary sending agencies are sending their missionaries to different countries but not necessarily to specific people groups that are least reached. For instance, when they go to Ethiopia, most people stay in Addis Ababa or go to Sidamo (Hawassa), where over 85% are Christian, and it is rare to find missionaries who go to least-reached places like Afar and Somali. In another instance, very few missionaries are going to the 10–40 widows compared to missionaries sent to the rest of the world. This implies a huge imbalance on where missionaries are going and where they are supposed to go.[8]

Interview participants indicated that Western and non-Western countries are missionary recipients. All over the world, missionaries are going either to countries within their continent, or beyond. A participant pointed out, "Geographical proximity is essential in missions because it is easier for missionaries to understand the cultural context to preach the gospel."[9] The participant added, "Africans send their missionaries to different countries within the continent of Africa and Romanian missionaries do their missions work in East Europe." Another interview participant indicated that missionaries relocate themselves beyond their continent. A participant remarked, "USA send its missionaries to almost all continents including the 10–40 window, Brazil to the USA, China to the Arab world, and Nigeria to Europe, particularly England."[10] Another interview participant added:

> In the Baptist convention where I am part, I have a relationship with missionaries from Latin America to the USA for missions. Most of them are involved in our Missionary Adoption Program (MAP) with the focus of evangelism, discipleship, and church

---

8. Zoom Interview, independent ministry participant 1, December 10, 2020.
9. Ibid.
10. Ibid.

planting by the Latin American missionaries here in America and back in their home country.[11]

It is essential to note that these interview participants have a broader understanding of global missions than the online survey participants. All interview participants indicated that most missionaries are still sent from Western nations because of their resources and missions experience. However, participants also listed non-Western missionary-sending nations from every continent such as Africa (Tanzania, Nigeria, and South Africa), Asia (South Korea, China, Mongolia), Latin America (Brazil), and Eastern Europe (Romania). On the other hand, online survey participants traditionally perceived missions as going from the West to the rest. In this case, online survey participants reflected that the Western countries are not missionary recipients at all, while online survey participants perceived most non-Western countries, mainly African countries, as only missionary recipients.

While the tide of traditional missions (from the West to the rest) is continuing, the resurgence of mission-sending movements from believers in all other continents indicates that the current mission-sending trend has become from everywhere to everywhere, and by all believers in the global body of Christ. Consequently, this implies that both Western and non-Western countries are missionary recipients today. Therefore, Ethiopian diaspora believers in the US need to examine their view toward Africa as the only missionary recipient continent and see the missional aspect of their movement as African missionaries to America.

Factor Two: Participants' View on Missions Activities in the Recipient Countries

This researcher explores both online survey and interview participants' observations on how missionaries carry out missions in the recipient countries. This researcher wants to know if this factor shapes the definition of missions among Ethiopian diaspora churches.

When the online survey participants were asked to share their observations on the nature of missionaries' activities in the countries they went to, most of them indicated that Western missionaries do missions work that

---

11. Zoom Interview, independent ministry participant 2, December 10, 2020.

meets recipients' physical and spiritual needs. Participants stated that Western missionaries provide various humanitarian and community services, including clean water, nutrition, healthcare, and education.

On the spiritual side, they preach the gospel, plant churches, distribute Bibles, and provide biblical and theological training. Interview participants gave different responses to explain some of the missionaries' activities in the countries they went to. Interview participants' responses can be divided into three categories. First, participants offered a historical perspective to describe how missions activities changed over time and shaped today's missions practices toward compassion-oriented missions. When expounding this shift in missions practice, a participant remarked:

> Early missionaries had a real burden for the gospel. They were on missions sacrificially with high commitment because there were not enough funds backing them, there were no convenient roads in the places they went, and some even had the decision to go on missions knowing that they will be martyrs.[12]

The "Church History" section in *Christianity Today* supports the above point. The article noted,

> Missionaries who were part of Hudson Taylor's China Inland Mission (CIM) would not have guaranteed salaries, nor could they appeal for funds. They would simply trust God to supply their needs; furthermore, its missionaries would adopt Chinese dress and then press the gospel into China's interior.[13]

One interview participant added, "These missionaries learned the language and culture of the communities they serve, and they identified themselves with them until they saw the fruit of their ministry. During that time, those who came to faith were not many. However, the missionaries knew how to expand the kingdom of God with and through those few indigenous converts."[14]

---

12. Zoom Interview, first generation participant 2, December 12, 2020.

13. "Hudson Taylor: Christian History," accessed on January 22, 2022, https://www.christianitytoday.com/history/people/missionaries/hudson-taylor.html

14. Zoom Interview, first generation participant 2, December 12, 2020.

Another participant presents the strengths and weaknesses of the missions practice during the twentieth century compared with the missions activity in the nineteenth century:

> One of the strengths of missions practice during the twentieth century was that going overseas for missions was relatively easier because of several reasons including the availability of modern transportation, and the provision of good financial support as industrialization elevated the living standard of Americans . . . one of the weaknesses of the missions movement during this period was the division among missionaries along the lines of denominations.[15]

In this participant's words, "During this time missionaries were working for their denominations, and little attention was given to the body of Christ. For instance, there is a strong denominational mark in the African churches as they share their denomination tradition with them."[16] Another weakness identified by participants was the result of a loose tie between missionaries and the recipient communities. A participant noted, "missionaries started to have their comfortable camps during this period instead of living with the indigenous community. Moreover, humanitarian work took on more emphasis during this era than gospel proclamation."[17] Based on his observation, the participant concludes that these weaknesses impacted the missions' work outcome in the twentieth century because:

> Even though more people were coming to faith compared to the missions movement in the nineteenth century, the depth of discipleship in this era was shallow. One of the reasons for this shallow outcome is the shift of missions practice from a more genuine gospel-centered mission to humanitarian work-driven missions.[18]

---

15. Zoom Interview, independent ministry participant 2, December 10, 2020.
16. Zoom Interview, independent ministry participant 2, December 10, 2020.
17. Zoom Interview, independent ministry participant 2, December 10, 2020.
18. Zoom Interview, independent ministry participant 2, December 10, 2020.

The participant shared his recent experience to explain how American Christians still have a compassionate ministry-oriented mindset toward missions. He said,

> Recently, I was trying to raise funds to go to Ethiopia for missions work. I had seen most Americans moved to give when I communicated the economic and social needs in my fundraising campaign rather than sharing my church planting programs. They are more committed to helping less fortunate communities than focusing on the gospel.[19]

Another participant added: "It is good that Western missionaries have a heart to respond to humanitarian crisis and poverty alleviation, but it should not be done at the expense of the gospel."[20]

Second, participants view a recipient country's situation as one factor in determining the kind of missions activity that needs to be done in the recipient country. One of the interview participants indicated that missionaries' activities vary depending on where the missionaries are going. He said:

> Missionaries are going as professionals in countries with limited or no access to enter as a traditional missionary. They study pedagogy, medicine, and other relevant fields to the recipient country, and they use their profession as a vehicle to preach the gospel.[21]

Another participant added,

> The need in the West is different from the non-Western countries. For instance, mental health, depression, and loneliness are big issues in America, therefore believing diaspora communities in America can use these needs as a vehicle to reach out to Americans with the gospel. On the other hand, economic needs are huge in non-Western countries. Therefore, missionaries can use this need to preach the gospel to them.[22]

---

19. Zoom Interview, independent ministry participant 2, December 10, 2020.
20. Zoom Interview, first generation participant 4, December 15, 2020.
21. Zoom Interview, independent ministry participant 1, December 10, 2020.
22. Zoom Interview, independent ministry participant 2, December 10, 2020.

Third, missions activity in the countries they go to is described using the traditional and diaspora missions approach. When explaining this factor, one of the participants noted,

> Intentionally sent missionaries are different from believers who relocate to a different country as diasporas. Intentionally sent missionaries practice missions using the sending mission agency or church framework. However, believers who find themselves in a different country as a diaspora do not have such framework, but they can be witnesses to the gospel by living their Christian life with their neighbors in the hosting country.[23]

Another participant added, "We have not been sent as missionaries out to different countries, but we are living on missions within our city. As a second-generation diaspora, we are reaching out to both the diaspora and American communities." A different participant said,

> It is common to see that inviting people to church is the popular way of doing missions. There is nothing wrong with that, but missions should be about going to them, not the other way around. For this reason, our church focuses on discipleship to give the necessary tools to our church members to love their neighbors and reach out to people in their workplaces and schools.[24]

Survey results regarding missionaries' activity in the recipient countries also displayed that those interview participants have a broader perspective than online survey participants. Interview participants pointed out that historically, missions have shifted from more genuinely gospel-centered missions to humanitarian work-driven missions and missionaries tend to go to mostly reached areas instead of going to the least-reached people groups. These issues are still controversial in the study of missiology today. Interview participants are not entirely against social work in missions. One of the participants stated, "the differences between any humanitarian organization and the church's mission lays on their motivation and purpose. The humanitarian organizations'

---

23. Zoom Interview, first generation participant 5, December 20, 2020.
24. Zoom Interview, first generation participant 2, December 12, 2020.

motivation and purpose are limited to the physical need alone. However, a Christian missions motivation and purpose is rooted primarily in the gospel."[25]

To summarize participants' responses on factor two, Christian missions have been actively involved in addressing the physical and spiritual needs of communities for the gospel. This includes utilizing the missionaries' professional skills and other resources that can benefit the community they want to serve. However, discipleship making, gospel proclamation, and church planting should be at the center of their mission work because that makes their practice a Christian mission.

Factor Three: Participants' Own Missions Experience in the US

Both survey and interview participants agreed that every believer could be a missionary. One of the online survey participants remarked, "All believers are called to engage in missions locally or globally in one or another way including in sending, giving or going." Another participant added,

> Those who stayed in their city should preach the gospel locally as they live their day-to-day lives. For instance, when I was in Ethiopia, I used to work for a government office as an agriculture professional, but at the same time, I was a missionary in that region where I planted many churches. In the same way, believers can be a witness for the gospel at their job place, in their apartment complex, or their schools.[26]

When one interview participant described the nature of calling for global missions, he said, "All believers are missionaries. Some do not need to be relocated geographically. However, others prepare themselves to commit going to different places where they would be required to cross geographical and cultural boundaries."[27] When explaining the commitment level of such missionaries, one participant said:

> Everyone is called to do missions, but not everyone is called in the same way for the same kind of missions work because

---

25. Zoom Interview, first generation participant 4, December 15, 2020.
26. Zoom Interview, second generation participant 2, December 11, 2020.
27. Zoom Interview, first generation participant 3, December 17, 2020.

the costs are different. Few believers are called to go and relocate geographically. If a church has 100 members, maybe 1 or 2 would be called for such purpose.[28]

When participants were asked if they specifically see themselves as missionaries in the US, most of them said "yes." From the total of thirty-four respondents, twenty-eight said "yes," and six participants responded "no."

The online survey participants were asked to discuss their responses further so that this researcher would better understand their missions experience in the US If they said "yes," they would explain what their missions activity looks like in the US, and if they said "no," they would elucidate why they said no. One of the explanations given by participants as to how they are conducting missions in the US was through living out their Christian life in the diaspora. One participant stated, "I do missions here through love-centered engagement in all aspects of my encounter with others; be it at the hospital I work, when I drive for Lyft, or when I get groceries or raise my children."[29] Another participant also said, "I do missions using my skills to support people around me while sharing the love of Jesus with them."[30]

Engaging in discipleship programs at their church was another explanation offered by most participants about how they are practicing missions in the US Most participants indicated that they engage in teaching and equipping church members, particularly the next generation, including children, youth, and college ministries. Mentoring and leading Bible studies are also among the mission activities mentioned by participants.

Another response given by participants indicated that partaking in the occasional evangelism outreach campaigns organized by their church is one of the ways they practice missions in the US. A participant stated, "I regularly attend the monthly evangelism outreach campaign organized by our church. Our evangelism outreach includes feeding homeless people, holding spiritual conversations with people on the street, and distributing gospel tracts."[31]

Other participants specified that they practice missions here in the US and back in their home country, Ethiopia. One of the participants said, "I

---

28. Zoom Interview, independent ministry participant 2, December 10, 2020.
29. Survey participant 31, November 22, 2020.
30. Survey participant 27, November 18, 2020.
31. Survey participant 33, November 22, 2020.

am praying for America. I am preaching the gospel to everyone who comes across my way. I help church revitalization and church planting initiatives to mitigate the current church decline in America."[32] Another participant also stated, "Refugees who come from unreached people groups to America and agnostic communities in America are my two evangelism target groups. I share the gospel with them."[33] Regarding missions back in their homeland, Ethiopia, one participant stated, "My heart is for Africa, more specifically for Ethiopia."[34] Another participant also specified, "In addition to helping various missionaries as a church, we are reaching out to the tribe called the Borana people. They live in northern Kenya and Southern Ethiopia."[35]

Some participants answered "yes" to this question because they believe they are missionaries in the US However, these participants are not sure how they practice missions in the US For instance, a participant noted, "Even if I believe I am a missionary in America, I am not doing anything. I do not know how to involve in missions here, or I do not get a chance to have the exposure."[36] Another participant added, "I do see myself as a missionary here though I have not been consistent in my activities carrying out the work of a missionary."[37]

When it comes to participants who answered "no" to this question, they explain why they do not see themselves as missionaries in the US One of them pointed out, "I hope to see myself as a missionary in America, but I have not participated in any missionary activities in a long time because Ethiopian churches are not open for missions work or they give less priority to it."[38] Another participant also said, "I did not engage in missions thus far because I have been focused on work and education. I have been trying to make it here."[39] Another participant added, "I do not see myself as a missionary here in America because I am not engaging other cultures with the gospel."[40]

---

32. Survey participant 32, November 22, 2020.
33. Survey participant 34, November 22, 2020.
34. Survey participant 33, November 21, 2020.
35. Survey participant 36, November 21, 2020.
36. Survey participant 20, November 17, 2020.
37. Survey participant 27, November 18, 2020.
38. Survey participant 37, November 21, 2020.
39. Survey participant 26, November 18, 2020.
40. Survey participant 30, November 20, 2020.

To summarize participants' response to factor three, all survey participants agreed that every believer can be a missionary, be it locally (without relocating to a different country) or globally (relocating to a different people group where they are expected to cross geographical and cultural barriers). While most online survey participants believe that they are missionaries in the US, a significant number of people do not know what that means or how they can practice missions in the US On the other hand, some participants do not see themselves as missionaries in the US Participants who indicated that they are practicing missions in the US stated that disciple-making is the crucial missions activity in their churches. They equip their members with the necessary tools to better love and reach out to their neighbors, coworkers, and friends at school as they live out their faith as salt and light. Occasional evangelism outreach campaigns in their city and missions work back in their home country, Ethiopia, are also other missions activities they practice.

Factor Four: Participants' Biblical Views on Missions

In this section, participants were asked to share their biblical views of missions. Mainly this researcher investigates what books and verses in the Bible have shaped their understanding of missions. When participants give their response about the Bible verses that shaped their view of missions, most online survey participants (93 percent) indicated that their understanding of missions is mainly shaped by New Testament verses, including Mathew 28:16–20; Acts 1:8; Romans 10:14, and other New Testament verses. From these verses, Mathew 28:16–20 was selected by most participants (34 percent). On the other hand, only a few online survey participants (7 percent) listed some Old Testament verses that shaped their view of missions.

Regarding books of the Bible, most online survey participants (40 percent) indicated that the book of Acts had shaped their understanding of missions. A comparison between Old and New Testament books showed that about 88 percent of participants' views on missions lean toward the New Testament, while few (12 percent) participants indicated that the Old Testament books had influenced their understanding of missions.

To better comprehend how the Bible verses and books shape the understanding of participants in mission, online survey participants were asked if they had an educational background in theology or missions. Most of them (over 57 percent) said no. Meanwhile, the rest (over 42 percent) replied yes.

This survey results show that a fair number of participants have theological and missions trainings. However, most of them do not reflect the whole counsel of the Scripture in their understanding of missions. Most participants indicated that the New Testament, particularly Mathew 28:16–20, has shaped their understanding of missions. In this case one can assert that the Biblical view of participants toward mission is shallow because it suggests that missions did not start until the Great Commission was given in Mathew 28:16–20.

Out of twelve interview participants, ten listed both Old and New Testament Bible verses that have shaped their perspectives on missions. These verses include Genesis 3:15, Genesis 12:1–3, Exodus 8:1, Psalm 96:3, Isaiah 6:8, Isaiah 12:4–6, Isaiah 52:7, Jeremiah 1:5–7, Matthew 28:16–20, Mark 16:15, Luke 10:2, John 17:4, John 20:21, Acts 1:8, Acts 13:1–3, and Romans 10:14–15. Interview participants were also asked to reflect on which books of the Bible have shaped their view of missions. Most interview participants indicated that the whole Bible is about God's mission to redeem lost humanity. One participant said, "Every book in the Bible deals with the mission of God."[41] Another participant noted,

> All books in the Bible have shaped my view on missions. In fact, from a missions standpoint, I see the Bible as one book, not as 66 books. The first two chapters show life before the fall, and the last two chapters reveal life after believers return to their original glory. However, the middle of the book is all about one love story. How the loving God is seeking and saving the lost humanity and how he invites his children to join Him in his redemption plan.[42]

Another participant added, "I believe that the whole Bible informed my view on missions. You find the sender (God), all nations, and messengers in all the books of the Bible."[43] Another participant also said, "The Bible has one message, and that is salvation to all nations as it unpacks the depth of its mystery from Jews to Gentiles and from Peter to Paul."[44] Here, it is essential to note that interview participants have a broader Biblical perspective

---

41. Zoom Interview, first generation participant 4, December 15, 2020.
42. Zoom Interview, independent ministry participant 1, December 10, 2020.
43. Zoom Interview, second generation participant 2, December 11, 2020.
44. Zoom Interview, first generation participant 1, December 7, 2020.

on missions than the online survey participants because they approach the Bible as one book from a missions standpoint. In other words, the missions understanding of interview participants is well informed by both the Old and New Testament verses and books of the Bible.

To summarize participants' response on factor four, online participants' view of missions is shaped mainly by New Testament books and verses, particularly Matthew 28:16–20. However, interview participants take the whole counsel of Scripture (Old and New Testaments) that portrays God as a missionary God who is on his mission of redeeming humanity and inviting all believers to join him on his mission.

Participants' Definitions of Missions

"Missions" is not a term found specifically in the Bible. According to Christopher Little, "the word 'mission' comes from the Latin word *mittere*, which means 'to send.'"[45] In line with the understanding of missions as *mittere* (send), and the context of the believer's community, William Larkin described missions as the divine activity of sending. Larkin noted that "God sends His supernatural or human messengers to speak or do God's will so that God's purposes for judgment or redemption are furthered."[46] However, Korcho pointed out that "historically, the terms 'missions' and 'missionary' have been understood in association with Western Christians and their service of helping the poor in the Global South."[47] According to Jonathan Bonk, "since the beginning of the modern missionary era, the material and economic advantage of the West remains deeply embedded for good and ill, at the very core of Western missionary thinking, strategy, and policy."[48] In other words, Korcho stated,

> The historical understanding of missions as an activity from the "haves" (Westerners) to the "have-nots" (poor non-Westerners) is the norm even today. Breaking the norm of this trend is the

---

45. Little, "Biblical Theology of Missions," 2.
46. Larkin, "Introduction," 3.
47. Korcho, "The Case for Missions," 237.
48. Bonk, *Missions and Money*, xx.

assignment of Christians in the diaspora and others coming up as missionaries from the Global South.[49]

That is the reason why in the previous section, this researcher examined factors that affect definitions of missions among Ethiopian diaspora churches in the US.

This section offers participants' definitions of missions. According to participants' responses, missions should involve the following elements: partnering with God in his mission, prioritizing the gospel proclamation over humanitarian work, going to all nations, and disciple-making. These elements are discussed in detail as follows.

Missions is Partnering with God in His Mission

God invited his people to join him in his mission of seeking and saving the lost. Both online survey and interview participants reflect this definition. One of the points to note in this definition is that it acknowledges God as a missionary God. One of the participants stated, "Missions finds its origin in the character and activity of God. God is the one on missions, and we are joining him in his work."[50] Another participant said, "God is a missionary God who initiated the plan of redeeming humanity through love. Love motivated him to create us, and that same love motivated him to redeem us."[51] Another participant still remarked, "Mission begins with our Lord who himself is on missions. According to John 20:21, he commissioned his people to the same mission saying, 'as the father has sent me so I send you.'"[52]

The other point about this definition is that it holds the whole counsel of Scripture to inform its view on missions. This definition traces the Great Commission in Scripture from Genesis 3 in the Old Testament to Matthew 28:16–28 in the New Testament. God began his plan of redemption right after the fall of humanity in Genesis 3, and began to call his people to join him on his missions more openly starting from Genesis 12. In other words, this definition suggests that missions did not start with the Great Commission given in Matthew 28:16–28.

---

49. Korcho, "The Case for Missions," 237.
50. Zoom Interview, independent ministry participant 2, December 10, 2020.
51. Zoom Interview, independent ministry participant 1, December 10, 2020.
52. Zoom Interview, second generation participant 3, December 11, 2020.

Moreover, this definition indicates that believers are required to respond to the call of God. Throughout Scripture, we find God calling his people for missions. For instance, God called Abraham in Genesis 12:1–3, the Israelites in Exodus 8:1, David in 2 Samuel 7, all prophets until John the Baptist, and Jesus' disciples and the Church in Matthew 28:16–28. In this regard, a participant stated, "Missions is a believer's response to God's call of his mission (Missio Dei) to all (Imago Dei)."[53] Another participant also said, "Missions is God's task in saving the world where believers are called to proclaim the gospel and make disciples of all nations." Still another participant remarked, "Missions is the calling on believer's life to glorify or hallow the name of God in and through the gospel primarily through holiness and preaching of the gospel of God about his son Jesus Christ."[54]

Ethiopian diaspora believers in the US need to view missions as a task that begins with God, and all believers are invited to join him. Their ethnic and educational background or socioeconomic status do not matter. All the people in Scripture have different backgrounds and life statuses. However, they responded to God's calling to join him in his mission. Likewise, Ethiopian believers in the diaspora can respond to God's calling despite their background or status.

Missions Involves Both Gospel Proclamation and Humanitarian Work

Acts of mercy (humanitarian works) and good relationships (community engagement) are significant factors in the task of missions. These are essential tools for Christians to achieve their goal in missions. The goal of a Christian mission is to communicate the gospel of Jesus Christ in which human beings are freed from the bondage of sin. A participant stated, "The primary duty of missionaries is to preach the gospel of Christ. Having that in mind, they can look for opportunities to communicate their message through helping those who are in need, and do all this to bring glory to the Father."[55] Correspondingly, most participants in this study indicated that missions is reaching the world by being the hands and feet of Christ. In other words,

---

53. Zoom Interview, first generation participant 3, December 17, 2020.

54. Zoom Interview, 1.5 generation participant 2, December 16, 2020.

55. Zoom Interview, independent ministry participant 1, December 10, 2020.

missions is about delivering the gospel by serving people in their need. A participant stated, "Missions is engaging people groups with the gospel by providing humanitarian aid based on community needs."[56]

When one of the participants described such need-based missions, he pointed out, "In the traditional sense, missions usually mean going to poor countries to share the gospel."[57] It is not wrong to meet the physical needs of recipient communities. However, the problem arises when people tend to give a broad definition of missions that might sideline the proclamation of the gospel message as they put a great deal of emphasis on social or humanitarian work. Stephen Neill noted, "If missions is everything, missions is nothing."[58] Neill added, "If everything that the church does is to be classed as missions, we shall find another term for the church's particular responsibility of reaching out for those who have never yet heard the name of Christ."[59] Timothy Tennent also argued that "in recent years the word "mission" had broadened even further to mean "everything the church should be doing," which makes the term slowly migrate from a theocentric connotation to a more anthropocentric one."[60] In line with this argument, one of the interview participants set the defining marks for a Christian mission. He stated:

> Everything cannot be missions. The great commission (go and make disciples of all nations) narrows down the task of missions. If "all nations" is not in the picture, you missed the mark. Again, if "making disciples" is not, you missed the mark. You could do everything, including providing schools, clinics, food, and clean water, but if you missed those two marks, then you are not doing missions.[61]

Here one can note that these two defining marks – "all nations" and "making disciples" – help Ethiopian diaspora churches in the US revise the traditional, needs-based, and from the rich to the poor concepts of missions. These

---

56. Zoom Interview, first generation participant 5, December 20, 2020.
57. Zoom Interview, 1.5 generation participant 1, December 16, 2020.
58. Neill, *Creative Tension*, 81.
59. Neill, 81.
60. Tennent, *Invitation to World Missions*, 54.
61. Zoom Interview, 1.5 generation participant 1, December 16, 2020.

two factors are discussed further in the section below as they are reflected in the missions definition of most participants.

Missions Involve Going to All Nations

The term "all nations" does not only refer to developing countries alone. Instead, it refers to all nations, including one's own nation and wealthy countries in the West. Therefore, Ethiopian believers can see themselves as missionaries here in the US For instance, one of the participants stated, "Missions for me is to share the good news of Jesus Christ in word and deed with everyone the Lord brings me in contact with irrespective of their country of origin /location, age, language, and culture."[62]

Also, it is essential to note that "all nations" refers to engaging other cultures in missions and focusing on unreached people groups. Regarding engaging other cultures, one of the participants stated, "Missions is the call to spread the gospel to all nations, establishing churches, and showing the love of Jesus for people across all cultures, languages, and ethnicity."[63] Another participant also added, "A Christian mission would be any organized effort to spread Christianity that involves sending individuals or groups, but they are sent to preach the gospel across some sort of boundaries most commonly geographical and cultural."[64] Crossing cultural barriers is not an easy process. Yet another participant stated, "Missions demands us to take a sacrificial step of compromising our comfort zone for the sake of the gospel. It truly is about taking up our cross that requires high commitment and following Jesus' example of loving us by giving his life."[65]

Another participant shared his experience in his church,

> Our church has a monthly evangelism outreach campaign which I attend regularly. I do not call this evangelism campaign as missions mainly because we are not engaging with other cultures. We come out of our Ethiopian church community once a month and return to where we are after finishing the campaign. We are not willing to live with them. The evangelism outreach is just one

---

62. Zoom Interview, 1.5 generation participant 2, December 16, 2020.
63. Zoom Interview, independent ministry participant 1, December 10, 2020.
64. Zoom Interview, first generation participant 3, December 17, 2020.
65. Zoom Interview, 1.5 generation participant 2, December 16, 2020.

encounter with a person we are evangelizing, and we may not see that person again. This is not missions. Missions requires going beyond our culture and living among the community we want to serve. This takes time and more intentionality as it involves knowing the community you serve and their culture.[66]

To further explain his point, the participant gave this researcher's ministry experience with Americans as an example. The participant said, "For example, I can say that you are a missionary among Americans because you are living among them, learning their culture, and engaging in church revitalization with them."[67] In another instance, a participant pointed out, "For instance, an Ethiopian Christian in Minnesota is a missionary without leaving the city, if he is willing to cross the culture to reach out to Somalis in the city. This includes building relationships, eating with them, and planting a Somali church."[68]

When it comes to the term "all nations," referring to focusing on unreached people groups, a participant said, "For me, missions is proclaiming the gospel for those who have not heard it and planting churches for the edification of believers."[69] Another participant argued:

> Many Ethiopian churches in America say that they are doing missions, but they are doing evangelism. Evangelism is preaching the gospel where the church is, and missions is preaching the gospel where the church is not. Therefore, missions require identifying and going to the unreached people groups.[70]

Missions Involves Disciple-Making

Disciple-making is another concept that stood out in the participants' definitions of missions. One of the participants noted, "Biblically, I see missions as disciples making disciples. That is why I believe that every mission has to do church planting at the end."[71] This disciple-making in the church focuses

---

66. Zoom Interview, 1.5 generation participant 1, December 16, 2020.
67. Zoom Interview, 1.5 generation participant 1, December 16, 2020.
68. Zoom Interview, second generation participant 2, December 11, 2020.
69. Zoom Interview, independent ministry participant 1, December 10, 2020.
70 Zoom Interview, independent ministry participant 1, December 10, 2020.
71. Zoom Interview, second generation participant 3, December 11, 2020.

on equipping believers to play their salt and light role in their day-to-day life, in their sphere of influence. One of the participants noted,

> Missions is carrying the burden of the gospel and letting everything that I do about the gospel. That is how we equip our church members. We encourage them to see their lives from getting married to making money, to spending their time, using their gifts and skills, their relationships, and opportunities as a platform to spread the gospel.[72]

For instance, said the participant, "I am a psychologist by profession, and I see many people struggling with depression and anxiety, which is a huge hindrance for the gospel. So, I use my profession to help them in their needs and preach the gospel in a way."

Another participant also stated, "Missions for me is using any platform, resources, skills, and opportunities God has given me to fulfill the Great Commission. Primarily I preach the gospel of Christ, help those who are in need with all the resources I have and do all these to bring glory to the father."[73] Still another participant remarked, "Missions is to carry out our priestly responsibility in all the skills and professions we have, in all places we find ourselves."[74]

To summarize, participants' definitions of missions are shaped by the four factors discussed in the previous section, including their views on missionary sending and receiving countries, their observations on missions activities in the recipient countries, their own missions experience in the US, and their biblical views on missions. Interview participants have a broader understanding of historical, global, and biblical missions views than online survey participants. In other words, interview participants, including those who have independent ministries and second-generation church planters, can share their more profound understanding of missions with most online survey participants, including first-generation immigrant pastors and others who serve in different ministries. Based on the definitions given above, it is encouraging that most participants view missions as God's call to all

---

72. Zoom Interview, second generation participant 2, December 11, 2020.
73. Ibid
74. Zoom Interview, second generation participant 1, December 11, 2020.

believers, and that most of them are focused on disciple-making to join God on his mission. However, participants' responses indicated that Ethiopian Christians in the US need to revise their views on the connection between gospel proclamation and humanitarian work. Also, they need to grow from missions through occasional evangelism outreach campaigns to engaging in the missions work by going to all nations beyond their own.

The Practice of Missions Among Ethiopian Diaspora Churches in the US

This section explores missions practices of Ethiopian diaspora churches in the US, including their mobilization and recruitment, organizational structure, and transnationalism in missions.

Mobilization and Recruitment for Missions

Under this topic, this researcher discusses what resources are available in the Ethiopian evangelical churches and how they are mobilizing these resources for missions.

Available Resources for Missions Mobilization

Of the thirty-seven online survey participants, thirty-six shared the resources available in their churches for missions mobilization and recruitment. Survey results revealed that the top three resources available in the Ethiopian diaspora churches for missions include human resources (members who have a passion for missions; selected by twenty-seven participants), experience (members who have experience in missions; indicated by seventeen participants), and finances (regular budget for missions work; specified by sixteen participants). Only six participants indicated that their church has training materials and trainers.

Participants were also asked to reflect on the percentage of funds their churches invested in missions. Most of them said they are unsure how much their church is budgeting for missions. Meanwhile, other responses revealed that their churches' budget for missions ranges between a minimum of 1 percent and a maximum of 20 percent.

Based on the survey results above, one can note that Ethiopian diaspora churches in the US desire to be involved in missions yet lack practical actions. The financial resource allocation to missions is still minimal. The experience-sharing is limited to the Ethiopian context, not a cross-cultural ministry practice. Moreover, a lack of training affects those who desire to engage in missions.

Methods of Mobilization for Missions

Participants were asked how their churches mobilize their members for missions. Out of a total of thirty-five participants who responded to this question, eighteen recorded that their churches support members who take personal initiatives to do mission work mostly in Ethiopia, ten indicated that their churches offer mission-focused training, and nine participants noted that they preach mission-focused sermons during Sunday services. Meanwhile, five participants revealed that their churches have no mobilization methods for missions. Some participants who selected the "other" option pointed out that experience-sharing with guest speakers from the mission field is another way to encourage and mobilize their congregations.

Based on the above survey results, it can be asserted that Ethiopian churches have no intentional programs designed to mobilize their members for missions. However, they mobilize resources for missions from their members, mainly using sermons and testimonies that motivate the church to give.

Church Organizational Structure for Missions

Participants were asked to indicate their church's organizational structure concerning missions. Twenty-eight participants recorded that their churches have occasional outreach campaigns in their city, while six participants indicated that their churches have short-term mission programs. Meanwhile, another six participants showed that their churches have long-term mission programs. Only four participants revealed that their churches have a missions department with a full-time worker.

In this case, one can note that most Ethiopian diaspora churches in the US do not have a missions department run by full-time staff. Instead, they mostly organize occasional evangelism outreach campaigns run by volunteers.

Transnationalism in Missions

This section examines Ethiopian diaspora churches' missionary sending and cross-cultural ministry practices in the US and beyond. This researcher sought to study the transnational missions activity of Ethiopian diaspora churches in light of the following three elements: strategies utilized by Ethiopian diaspora churches to function in the US context effectively, gospel-sharing practices of Ethiopian diaspora churches in US cities, and Ethiopian diaspora churches' global missionary sending activity in the US.

Strategies Utilized to Effectively Function in the US Context

When participants were asked to share their strategies to help them function effectively in the US context, twenty-two participants specified that assisting their church members settle in the US is the most helpful strategy. Also, seventeen participants revealed that partnerships with US churches is another helpful strategy for Ethiopian diaspora churches to effectively function in the US Only five participants showed that they have English services, and one participant signified that their church offers cross-cultural training to function well in the US context. In this case, survey results clearly showed that the primary focus of Ethiopian churches in the US is their own communities, and that establishing English-speaking churches and equipping their church members with cross-cultural tools receives the least attention.

There were participants who indicated that Ethiopian diaspora churches partner with local US mainstream churches for effective ministry in the US context. To further understand the kind of partnership that Ethiopian diaspora churches have with local US mainstream churches, this researcher asked participants to describe their churches' experiences on the matter. In their response, most (thirteen) participants indicated that their churches do not have any partnership with US churches or mission organizations. Meanwhile, another twelve participants specified that their churches are part of US church denominations. Also, eight participants noted that their churches rent space at US churches, five revealed that their churches support US missionaries financially, and two showed that their churches had sent missionaries through US mission organizations.

Based on the above survey results, one could say that Ethiopian diaspora churches have partnerships with US churches or missions organizations mainly through denominational affiliation or by renting space at US church facilities. Neither kind of relationship reflects a mutual partnership between US mainstream churches and Ethiopian diaspora churches. In chapter two, this researcher discussed that the primary goal of most Ethiopian diaspora churches in affiliating with US churches is to share financial resources with the larger organization. It is rare to find Ethiopian diaspora churches contributing to the leadership and missions work in their affiliated denominations. The Ethiopian Evangelical Baptist Church in Dallas is the only exception because they actively engage in leadership and mission work together with the Dallas Baptist Convention.

Gospel Sharing in US Cities

Mission practices of Ethiopian diaspora churches within the US were explored in light of their gospel-sharing practices in US cities. Out of thirty-five participants, thirty indicated that their churches' gospel-sharing practices are solely focused on Ethiopians. Meanwhile, thirteen participants signified that their churches are more focused on sharing the gospel with non-Ethiopian communities in the city where they established their church. Only four participants noted that their gospel sharing practice is directed towards both Ethiopian and non-Ethiopian communities.

In this case, the survey result clearly shows that Ethiopian diaspora churches in the US have inwardly focused evangelism outreach strategies because they emphasize reaching out to their own communities in the US.

Global Missionary Sending Activity

Regarding cross-cultural missions activities outside the US, this researcher explores the missionary-sending experience of Ethiopian diaspora churches back in their home country and globally. Online survey results showed that only three participants said their churches send missionaries globally. By contrast, thirty-four participants indicated that their churches have no global missionary-sending experience, and twenty-nine participants revealed that Ethiopian churches in the US send their missionaries back to Ethiopia. Meanwhile, only ten participants specified that their churches do not send missionaries back to Ethiopia.

Based on survey results, one can conclude that Ethiopian diaspora churches' missionary-sending practices in the US are also inwardly focused because they mainly send their missionaries back to Ethiopia. In other words, survey results indicated that it is rare to find Ethiopian churches in the US that send missionaries on a global scale, cross-culturally.

To further understand how Ethiopian evangelical churches in the US engage in missions with their home country, this researcher asked participants to describe who participated in the trip to Ethiopia for the mission work and what their missions practice reflects. Most participants (twenty-two) noted that their pastors usually go to Ethiopia for missions. About sixteen participants also specified that church members take the initiative to personally go to Ethiopia for a missions trip. Meanwhile, none of the participants indicated that second-generation young adults participate in missions work in Ethiopia. In this case, one can assert that it is pastors who primarily run missions initiatives among Ethiopian diaspora churches in the US.

This survey result confirmed this researcher's close observation within Ethiopian churches in the US Most first generation immigrant pastors have visions like "Ethiopians for Christ," "Compass Ethiopia Ministry," "Destination Ministry," "From Dallas to Addis Ministry," and "Vision Leadership Institute," to name a few. That is why most participants in this study indicated that their pastors mostly take missions trips to Ethiopia. Some of the mission activities in these initiatives include providing training to pastors and evangelists, engaging community supports such as health care and schools, financially supporting Bible schools, sponsoring local missionaries, and church-planting initiatives in the remote areas.

Interestingly, these survey results also revealed that a significant number of church members take the initiative to go back to their home country as missionaries. It is a remarkable attitude that members have such zeal for missions, but their effort needs to be coordinated with their pastors' vision in order to effectively utilize resources.

These survey results also showed that first generation immigrants tend to go back to their home country while the second generation does not show the same propensity. In other words, the second generation does not participate in the mission-sending practice, even to their parents' home country.

Strengths, Weaknesses, and Challenges of Ethiopian-Diaspora Churches in Missions

This section discusses participants' responses regarding their churches' strengths, weaknesses, and challenges in missions.

Strengths of Ethiopian Diaspora Churches and Lessons that Churches in the US Can Take

This researcher asked participants to share some of the strengths of Ethiopian diaspora churches and what US churches and mission organizations can learn from them. Interestingly, some online survey participants indicated that there is nothing that US churches can learn from Ethiopian churches in the US One participant said, "The immigrant churches have a lot of positive values to offer to the American churches if they could use their unique potential and opportunity but, unfortunately, the Ethiopian diaspora churches have a long way to go before being able to share their mission experiences."[75] In other words, some Ethiopian diaspora churches in the US do not think they have enough to share or are good only for themselves.

Other participants in this study reflected on several strengths of Ethiopian diaspora churches, including community, spiritual fervency, simplicity, and cultural skills. Most participants indicated that US Christians could learn about community building and engagement from Ethiopian Christians in the US One of the participants stated, "Ethiopian diaspora churches are a close-knit community, caring and hospitable people. Particularly, hospitality is one of the practices that American Christians can learn from Ethiopian Christians in America."[76] Another participant said:

> The Bible is written in a communal cultural context where God's people practice breaking bread together and washing each other's feet. However, Americans tend to reflect an individualistic culture. They may congregate at church, but they are not necessarily connected. They do not have a house-to-house connection. By contrast, the Ethiopian culture reflects a community life in the ways we invite each other for home coffee ceremonies, grieve together, and putting together different events like graduation and wedding.[77]

Another interview participant said, "American churches are more focused on church organization, but there is lack in practicing hospitality. Ethiopians

---

75. Zoom Interview, 1.5 generation participant 1, December 16, 2020.
76. Zoom Interview, first generation participant 3, December 17, 2020.
77. Zoom Interview, first generation participant 5, December 20, 2020.

know how to invite people to their homes. The way they grieve together, and their community events are so alive."[78]

The advantage of individualism is that it gives an individual the privilege of making decisions for himself/herself. The downside of individualism is that it may cause loneliness and other related mental health issues. Richard Weissbourd and Milena Batanova et al. pointed out:

> Thirty-six percent of all Americans—including 61% of young adults and 51% of mothers with young children—feel "serious loneliness." Not surprisingly, loneliness appears to have increased substantially since the global pandemic outbreak. Young adults suffer high rates of both loneliness and anxiety, and depression. According to a recent CDC survey, 63% of this age group are suffering significant symptoms of anxiety or depression.[79]

In other words, Americans can learn from Ethiopians' communal lifestyle to remedy the expanding problem of loneliness.

Paradoxically, the Ethiopian community life survey results in this study indicated that most Ethiopians in the US have an isolationist approach. Their ministry is designed exclusively for themselves. Therefore, Ethiopians need to extend their community life beyond their own. One participant stated, "Although the Ethiopian diaspora churches can be kind and hospitable, there is a sense of judgment that makes these churches intimidating and unapproachable to non-Ethiopians. The second-generation who grew up in America also face such judgmental attitude from the first-generation group."[80] To have a welcoming community, the Ethiopian diaspora churches need to avoid social prejudice based on their cultural lenses.

Spiritual fervency is another strength of Ethiopian diaspora churches in the US Ethiopian Christians in the US are devoted to their faith. Most participants of this study appreciated the spiritual zeal among Ethiopian Christians in the U.S, and the sense of calling for ministry among young adults. Christians in the US can learn from Ethiopian diaspora Christians regarding prayer life, holiness, giving, and passion for evangelism outreach.

---

78. Zoom Interview, second generation participant 2, December 11, 2020.
79. Weissbourd et al. "Loneliness in America."
80. Survey participant 33, November 21, 2020.

Regarding their prayer life, one of the online survey participants stated, "Ethiopian diaspora church in America is a praying church. We take time to pray the whole morning or overnight. It is rare to find such practice among American churches."[81] An interview participant added, "As a second-generation, I always appreciate the role and place that prayer has within the Ethiopian Christian diaspora communities."[82] Another participant stated:

> In the Ethiopian evangelical churches' context, prayer takes the highest portion of their ministry, while American churches focus on strategy. It is good to have good strategies, but it should not take the place of prayer. Ethiopian churches tend to pray for everything, and that is good because we cannot do much without prayer.[83]

As far as pursuing holiness is concerned, one participant said, "Most Ethiopian evangelical Christians practice holiness amid the secular culture of America. People get censured for their wrong deeds, which shows how unacceptable behaviors and practices do not have a place in the Ethiopian diaspora churches."[84] Another participant also said, "We are not that perfect, but relatively our church members are strict in practicing holiness because most Sunday sermons are good at challenging and encouraging the church to pursue a holy life."[85]

When explaining the giving practice among Ethiopian Christians in the US, one participant said, "Ethiopian Christians are determined to give sacrificially. Many Ethiopians have low-paying jobs. However, they are faithful in tithing and giving to church."[86] Concerning the desire to share their faith, almost all Ethiopian evangelical churches in the US organize evangelism outreach campaigns once a month. One of the participants stated, "It is good that American churches have the passion for reaching out to other nations. However, they must not forget that their Jerusalem requires missions today,

---

81. Survey participant 26, November 18, 2020.
82. Zoom Interview, second generation participant 1, December 8, 2020.
83. Zoom Interview, first generation participant 2, December 12, 2020.
84. Zoom Interview, first generation participant 4, December 15, 2020.
85. Zoom Interview, first generation participant 1, December 7, 2020.
86. Zoom Interview, first generation participant 5, December 20, 2020.

and Ethiopian Christians in America can help in reaching out to their people here."

Simplicity is another strength of Ethiopian diaspora churches in the US Simplicity is welcoming people to ministry based on their call, not expertise. It is good to have evaluation methods when recruiting people for ministry, but these requirements should not be hurdles to those who have a genuine calling. One of the online survey participants noted, "American churches and mission organizations tend to focus on status, expertise, and professionalism for ministry. However, Ethiopian churches do not worry much about those things. They are only looking for people who are willing and have the sense of calling."

Here, it fits to share the story of this researcher's friend. After many years of service among Ethiopian diaspora churches, he wanted to engage in a cross-cultural ministry with a US Baptist church. He joined them as a church planter. At that time, he was the only non-Western participant on his team, and the way they do church was entirely different from his experience. He was a highly respected person within his community, but the least accepted in the church planting team. Moreover, the lengthy paperwork and assessment process was odd to him. Consequently, he did not succeed as a church planter among Americans and he had to return to his Ethiopian community in the US to find his spot. He eventually moved back to Ethiopia.

Another area that needs simplicity is the expensive way of doing church and missions work. One of the interview participants from the second generation stated:

> One of the things I have learned from Ethiopian diaspora churches in America is that I do not need much to fulfill the mission. I know how to trim down, do without a lot and be fine with that. American churches can take their lesson from Ethiopian diaspora churches how much it can be done without and still accomplish missions.[87]

Family model versus business model is another area that needs to be simplified. A second-generation interview participant pointed out:

---

87. Zoom Interview, second generation participant 3, December 11, 2020.

> How churches operate here in America feels more like a business. I have been around pastors who have mega-churches. Even deciding where to establish their church and vision is controlled by money. On the other hand, Ethiopian churches are more like family. As a new church planter, the business model bothers me a lot, and I am constantly asking myself how we can be excellent without losing the sense of family.[88]

The cultural resourcefulness is another strength of Ethiopian diaspora churches in the US One of the participants said, "The fact that we have already 'crossed' culture (not only border) to come here allows us to share the gospel from a different perspective." Another participant added, "Today, Ethiopian diaspora are dispersed all over the world, which enables their children to grow up in these cultures and communicate the gospel with the hosting community in their language" An interview participant also stated:

> As a second-generation, I struggled growing up in this culture because I had to speak and act in a certain way to be accepted by Americans. However, my Ethiopian side gave me the ability to understand someone else and appreciate the story's power. Everybody is on a different journey, and everybody has a culture to celebrate. My way is not the way, but it is a way. This is freeing, unlike the American culture that dictates how to do church or community in a certain way.[89]

Another second-generation interview participant noted:

> As second-generation Ethiopians, we see a push back about Christianity in America. This push back is fueled by racial issues like associating Christianity with a white religion. However, growing up in the Ethiopian context gives us another story to defend this push back. We can tell how Ethiopia is one of the oldest countries that practice Christianity.[90]

---

88. Zoom Interview, second generation participant 1, December 8, 2020.
89. Zoom Interview, second generation participant 2, December 11, 2020.
90. Zoom Interview, second generation participant 3, December 11, 2020.

Another strength of Ethiopian diaspora churches concerning culture is that they can help US mainstream churches reach out to the United States' current diverse context through cultural collaboration. One participant shared his experience.

> American mainstream churches are mostly homogeneous. When they consider Ethiopians or other African migrants, perhaps they tend to perceive them as charity cases that need financial help, and they may not see them as equal brothers and sisters. Diaspora churches like ours can help American churches to reshape their views of migrants. In our city, we have a large population of the Somali community. There are different ministries that white people run to reach out to the Somalis. They do tutor to gain a relationship with them. One time, they invited me to a Somali woman's home to do English tutoring, and they were surprised at how open and very welcoming the Somali woman was towards me versus how long it took them even to have a normal relationship with her. I have met many white people who have the burden for the Somali community, even those who moved all the way to Somalia to open schools and do missions. I always appreciate their passion, but I think they would be more effective if they collaborated with us because we are the direct neighbors where we have proximity by look and culture. Therefore, equipping the direct Christian neighbors and collaborating with them in missions would significantly benefit American churches.[91]

In this case, one can note that the cultural flavors in each generation are beneficial tools to communicate the gospel effectively with Americans and beyond. Also, US mainstream churches can benefit from the cultural richness of the diaspora communities through partnerships in missions.

Weakness of Ethiopian Diaspora Churches in Missions

According to participants' responses, staying in a comfort zone is one of the weaknesses of Ethiopian diaspora churches in the US One participant said,

---

91. Zoom Interview, second generation participant 2, December 11, 2020.

"We are exclusive to our own culture and avoid going out of our comfort zone. This approach leads us to focus more on survival mentality than taking the initiative to reach out to other communities."[92] Another participant added, "Staying in our comfort zone is restricting our children and us. We are not taking steps to learn English or raise our children in a way that they can effectively reach out to communities beyond our own."[93] Still another participant noted, "We are self-centered and survival focused. It is not common to do missions outside of our community; we need to wake up to utilize our potential and opportunities."[94] Another participant also said, "Ethiopian Christians have the passion for sharing their faith, but they are timid because of lack of experience. They are very closed off from other communities, and as a result, there is fear of the unknown and lack of confidence to go beyond our own culture."[95]

Another weakness of Ethiopian diaspora churches is restricting missions to occasional evangelism outreach. A participant indicated:

> There is a lack of awareness among Ethiopian diaspora churches that missions is more than street preaching and passing out gospel tracts. Ethiopian churches in America need to establish methods on how to reach out to non-Ethiopian communities and platforms like planting English-speaking churches to disciple new converts.[96]

It is good that Ethiopian diaspora churches have the zeal to proclaim the gospel. However, in this chapter, participants also reflected that missions demands crossing cultures and living among the community God has called us to serve. On the contrary, evangelism outreach practices among Ethiopian diaspora churches in the US look more like one-time encounters with people, and there may not be another opportunity to meet those people again.

Based on participants' responses, lack of vision and mission planning is another weakness of Ethiopian diaspora churches. One of the participants stated, "There is poor leadership and resource allocation in our church regarding

---

92. Zoom Interview, independent ministry participant 1, December 10, 2020.
93. Zoom Interview, first generation participant 4, December 15, 2020.
94. Zoom Interview, first generation participant 2, December 12, 2020.
95. Zoom Interview, first generation participant 5, December 20, 2020.
96. Zoom Interview, 1.5 generation participant 1, December 16, 2020.

missions. There is a lack of emphasis in equipping members for cross-cultural missions work and developing strategies to reach out to the city."[97]

Church splitting is another weakness that affects the missions work of Ethiopian diaspora churches in the US. Participants pointed out, "One of the biggest problems among first-generation leaders is that they get divided for every little reason. This creates a huge burden on the second and 1.5 generations, as it makes the rebuilding process so difficult."[98] An interview participant from the second generation said:

> One of the sad things is that we had church splits several times in the church I grew up. Even the churches that departed from us split themselves. I do not think that the first-generation understand how that affects the second-generation. It is okay for most Ethiopian church pastors as long as they have 25–50 members. However, the ones who are affected the most is the second generation. Church division is like divorce. When parents get divorced, they defend themselves and blame the other person for their differences. However, the ones who suffer the most are their children, who are torn between these two families. Our church was the only church with youth ministry, and youth from other churches joined us to benefit from the ministry. However, because of the church split, other churches were unwilling to send their youth to our church. They would always promise them that they would have youth ministry and hire a youth pastor for them. However, none of these came to reality because of a lack of financial resources and the inability to find the ministry's right person. Therefore, church division is so detrimental because it makes us focus on internal matters and miss the whole objective of engaging in the mission of God.[99]

In addition to negatively impacting the second and 1.5 generations, church splitting makes Ethiopian diaspora churches more inwardly focused than outward facing for missions. One participant stated, "Church conflict is one

---

97. Survey participant 34, November 22, 2020.
98. Survey participant 37, November 21, 2020.
99. Zoom Interview, second generation participant 2, December 11, 2020.

of the weaknesses of Ethiopian diaspora churches. Church politics consumes all the energy of these churches. Consequently, the leaders are striving for survival, and they are not missional in their vision."[100]

Based on the survey results above, one can conclude that church division affects Ethiopian churches' strength in unity. Division brings church politics to the forefront, which casts a shadow on spiritual growth, and creates many small churches that lack the necessary resources to disciple their children and focus on missions here and beyond.

Challenges of Ethiopian Diaspora Churches in the US

This section presented research findings on the challenges of the first- and second-generation church congregations in missions.

Challenges of the First-Generation Churches in Missions

Based on survey results, the two main challenges of Ethiopian diaspora churches in missions are the language barrier and the lack of a missional mindset. Thirty-two participants indicated that the language barrier is the most challenging factor in the missions work of Ethiopian diaspora churches. Meanwhile, almost the same number of participants showed that lack of a missional mindset is one of the most challenging missions. A fair number of participants (sixteen) indicated that lack of theological training and experience are also barriers to missions in Ethiopian diaspora churches.

The language barrier is a common challenge of every missionary who crosses cultures for the sake of the gospel; therefore, Ethiopian diaspora churches cannot use the language barrier as an excuse for their weak engagement in missions. As indicated in the survey results, what is mainly lacking is a missional heart and training in missions. American and European missionaries come to Ethiopia as missionaries, not because they know Amharic or any other ethnic language in Ethiopia, but because they have the necessary training and the heart for missions. Hence, lack of a missional mindset and lack of training, which takes intentionality, are the main factors that contribute to the poor engagement of Ethiopian diaspora churches in missions. One of the interview participants expounded on these factors,

---

100. Zoom Interview, second generation participant 1, December 8, 2020.

> The misconception that missions are a White man's burden is one of the challenges contributing to the lack of missional mindset among Ethiopian diaspora churches in America. We have given the missions work to Christians in the West, and we thought that our responsibility is only for our own community. When Ethiopians think of missions or missionaries, it is almost synonymous with the White people's responsibility. This thought may not be visible openly, but it is there subconsciously, and we need to change this mindset first.[101]

When explaining the consequences of this misconception, one participant said, "Ethiopian diaspora churches do not see America as their mission field. Their focus is still on reaching out to their Ethiopian fellow migrants in the USA."[102] Another participant added, "We need to revisit the way we run our church. We have so many diverse skills that can help us reach out to all kinds of people in the USA. However, we are not maximizing this opportunity yet."[103]

According to survey results, this misconception that says, "missions is a Western duty, not ours," affects how Ethiopian diaspora churches reach out to even their own children in the diaspora. Ethiopian diaspora churches tend to focus on the work back in their home country rather than crossing cultural barriers to reaching out to their children in the US. One of the second-generation interview participants noted:

> Missions is right here in our church. Our children are not disciplined properly. We need to make sure why they are even coming to the church. Is it because their parents are bringing them to the church? If so, perhaps they are waiting until they finish high school to make their own decisions whether to stay in the church or leave. We should research all these over again. It is the churches' responsibility to build the transition from their children and youth ministry to adult's church service; otherwise, no wonder that they will withdraw from the church when they finish high school. The mission field is not out there, but it is

---

101. Zoom Interview, independent ministry participant 2, December 10, 2020.
102. Zoom Interview, independent ministry participant 1, December 10, 2020.
103. Zoom Interview, independent ministry participant 2, December 10, 2020.

right there in our backyard. To use our church as an example, the first and 1.5 generations still have a lot of "babies," they are still building their families. There are close to 350 children in the children ministry, and there are close to 150 youth in the youth ministry.[104]

The misconception about missions as Westerners' responsibility also leads the Ethiopian diaspora churches to lack intentionality in missions. An interview participant noted, "It is the children and youth ministry that suffers the most because of lack of intentionality and the poor resource allocation in the Ethiopian diaspora churches. It is the last priority to invest in the second-generation ministry after the church distributes the budget on everything."[105] Another participant also said:

We lack intentionality in training church members for missions work. We do not have the department, the budget, or the planning for missions. I understand that some churches are working for their survival, but other churches have the finance and other resources and yet are not utilizing it for missions purpose.[106]

First generation immigrants have the language and cultural barriers, but even if they cross these barriers, they often lack confidence as they have a fear of the unfamiliar, and a sense of inadequacy. When discussing the minority syndrome, one participant pointed out:

Ethiopian evangelical believers were the minority in Ethiopia for a long time, negatively impacting their missional mindset. Ethiopian church pastors are focused on protecting numbers in their comfort zone where they never want to be missional. The dichotomy approach sees the church as a safe hiding place from the dangerous world out there. This approach contributes to the lack of a missional mindset. Currently, evangelicalism is rapidly growing in Ethiopia, and we need the shift from hiding as a minority to going out for missions globally. If Ethiopian diaspora churches want to be effective in missions here in America, they

---

104. Zoom Interview, second generation participant 1, December 8, 2020.
105. Zoom Interview, second generation participant 2, December 11, 2020.
106. Zoom Interview, first generation participant 3, December 17, 2020.

should overcome their minority syndrome and the fear of being swallowed by the majority culture in America.[107]

Following visits to many Ethiopian children and youth ministries across the US, one of the participants has observed that their teaching is highly affected by a minority syndrome. The participant stated:

> The church and parents are worried about protecting their children from some issues in the majority secular context of America including atheism, sexual immorality and improper use of social media. There is a huge difference between the effort they make to protect their children from these issues and their effort to teach them the gospel. In other words, their effort is more focused on reactive and defensive approaches, which has gone further than the zeal for the gospel, and Christ is the foundation of these children. This approach is dangerous because it is a fear-based false shield that alienates our children from the majority culture with a lack of compassion, and it leads our children to a misconception that Christianity is all about morality. However, what these children need the most is the gospel and Christ being the foundation of their lives.[108]

Based on the above survey results, one can assert that the language barrier is a common problem when people want to serve beyond their community. However, it is much more difficult if a person also lacks a missional mindset and lacks training. Ethiopian diaspora churches in the US face all three of these challenges, which hinders their missions endeavor to reach out to non-Ethiopian communities in the US, and their efforts to reach out to their own children who were born and raised in the US

Challenges of the Second-Generation Churches in Missions

Survey results indicated that lack of discipleship, lack of ethnic diversity, and lack of stability are the main challenges of the second-generation Ethiopian churches in the US.

---

107. Zoom Interview, independent ministry participant 1, December 10, 2020.
108. Zoom Interview, 1.5 generation participant 2, December 16, 2020.

Concerning lack of discipleship, participants emphasized that church and family roles should not be mixed up in the process of discipling the second generation. One of the second-generation pastors noted, "During the time I was responsible for children and youth ministry, parents expected me to do everything that falls under parental responsibility including tutoring them and even going to school to follow up with their situation at school."[109] Another participant said, "As a youth pastor, everything was dropped on me. Particularly, during church services or occasional spiritual conferences, parents enjoy their experience with God in the main sanctuary while I had to watch the kids, teach them and make sure they do not destroy anything in the church facility."[110] The participant added,

> I was fortunate because my Dad is very intentional in making sure that I am learning something at church. He always asked me to share what I have learned at church on our way back home. If I did not give him an adequate answer, he would go straight to my Sunday school teachers and challenge them about the matter. However, it is unfortunate that most parents do not have that practice. When I look back, I appreciate my Dad's contribution to who I am today.[111]

Most participants indicated that parents need to take the primary role of discipling their children, and the church should supplement that effort. Many members of second-generation churches have had poor discipleship. Consequently, second-generation pastors have members with low spiritual maturity. One of the second-generation pastors said:

> The children and youth ministry at Ethiopian churches does not focus on discipleship, and that is detrimental for our second-generation church. Parents told them to read their Bible and pray, but most were not taught how to do that. Therefore, as a second-generation church, we are putting much effort into teaching our members what they should have know earlier in time, how to pray, and study their Bible. If we had that

---

109. Zoom Interview, second generation participant 3, December 11, 2020.
110. Zoom Interview, second generation participant 2, December 11, 2020.
111. Ibid.

foundation built, it would have been easy to use the second-generation for missions in more effective ways. However, we are still talking about the challenge of maturing our congregation right from the basics.[112]

Another participant added:

Parents in the Ethiopian diaspora churches have the issue of priority. They do not want their children to be Christians but good Ethiopian students. This difference makes the discipleship process very challenging. Most parents complain when their children are not good at school or get ear piercings or tattoos. These concerns are more cultural than they are gospel-driven.[113]

Regarding lack of ethnic diversity, the second-generation pastors indicated that over 95 percent of their congregation consists of Ethiopian descendants. This implies that the second generation is following the pattern of the first generation, as it mainly, if not exclusively, serves its own community. One factor contributing to the lack of ethnic diversity is the isolationist approach that comes down from their parents. One participant pointed out,

Our parents' isolationist lifestyle affected us to the extent that we feel like we were kept in a box. We did not see our parents engage in social matters with Americans. We did not even see them talking to their American neighbors. Therefore, we did not have a head start we needed, and we were not ready for the real world.[114]

Another factor contributing to the lack of diversity among the second-generation church is the name "Ethiopia" attached to the churches. When people from other ethnic backgrounds see the name, they do not feel they belong to the church. An interview participant said:

Usually, second-generation churches have a different name that fits their English-speaking context than the first-generation churches. However, since most of the English-speaking young

---

112. Zoom Interview, second generation participant 1, December 8, 2020.
113. Ibid.
114. Zoom Interview, second generation participant 3, December 11, 2020.

adult ministries are within the same building and location as Ethiopian churches, it is challenging to invite other ethnic communities to our English-speaking congregation; otherwise, they have to be able to ignore that this is an Ethiopian church. The Ethiopian church where we grew up allowed us to continue our ministry in their building and remain to be our own independent church. However, we decided to have a different facility at one of the American interdenominational churches because it is better for us and other communities who want to join us.[115]

Moreover, second-generation churches are dealing with a lack of stability because their demographics predominantly consist of the young adult age groups. One of the second-generation pastors stated,

The advantage with higher age demography is that it would help have more financial resources and members stability. One of the challenges we have as a second-generation church is that many people are still in their transitionary life because most our members are predominantly young adults who are running to make their lives. Most of them are not homeowners. Either they are still living with their parents or renting apartments. We do not know when they will leave for a job or other opportunities, or they may leave the city simply because they do not like the state or the weather. In short, we do not have long-term stability in terms of who will be here in the next five years; it is really up in the air. Nevertheless, if these people have a family with children, they could consider being more stable in the city as they want to raise their children in the same community.[116]

Based on the above survey results, the blurring of church and family responsibilities in discipling the second generation has created a second-generation church with low spiritual maturity and poses a significant challenge for the second-generation pastors' ministries. Other challenges facing missions in the second-generation churches include lack of diversity due to

---

115. Zoom Interview, second generation participant 2, December 11, 2020.
116. Zoom Interview, second generation participant 3, December 11, 2020.

the influence of their parents' isolationist approach, and lack of stability due to the young adult demographics of their members.

Chapter Summary

This chapter discussed research findings on the definition, practices, strengths, weaknesses, and challenges of Ethiopian diaspora churches in missions. This researcher assessed participants' responses on factors that have shaped their definition of missions. These factors include biblical views of missions, missionary sending and receiving countries, and missionaries' activities in the recipient countries. This researcher discovered that these factors shaped the participants' definition of missions. Interview participants have a broader historical and Biblical understanding of missions than online survey participants. Participants' definition of missions reflected that missions is partnering with God in his mission, missions involves both gospel proclamation and humanitarian work, going to all nations, and disciple-making.

Based on these definitions, it is encouraging that most participants view missions as God's calling to all believers and that most of them are focused on disciple-making to join God on his mission. However, participants' responses indicated that Ethiopian Christians in the US need to revise their views on the connection between gospel proclamation and humanitarian work. They also need to shift from organizing occasional evangelism campaigns, to engaging in missions work by going to nations beyond their own and living among them to share the gospel.

Regarding missions practices among Ethiopian diaspora churches, this researcher explored the mobilization and recruitment, organizational structure, and transnationalism. Regarding mobilization, Ethiopian diaspora churches in the US desire to be involved in missions work, yet they lack training and practical actions. The monetary allocation to missions is still minimal. In terms of organizational structure, Ethiopian churches have no intentional programs designed to mobilize their members for missions. For instance, there is no missions department run by a full-time staff, and they mostly organize occasional evangelism outreach campaigns using volunteers. When it comes to transnationalism or a cross-cultural ministry or missions-sending experience, this researcher discovered that the primary focus of Ethiopian churches in the US is their own community. In other words, their missions endeavors focus inward because they emphasize reaching out to Ethiopians here in the US or back in their home country. Cross-cultural ministry, such as establishing church services for English-speaking communities and building partnerships with US churches, is also weak.

This study showed that community, spiritual fervency, simplicity, and cultural resourcefulness are some of the strengths of Ethiopian diaspora churches in the US On the contrary, staying in their comfort zone, restricting missions to occasional evangelism outreach campaigns, lack of vision and planning, and church splitting are some of the weaknesses of Ethiopian diaspora churches in the US This researcher discovered that language barrier, lack of a missional mindset, and lack of training are the three significant challenges of first-generation churches. Meanwhile, participants also reported that lack of discipleship, lack of ethnic diversity, and lack of stability are the main challenges of second-generation Ethiopian churches in the US.

CHAPTER 6

Conclusion and Recommendations

Conclusion

The purpose of this research was to establish an understanding of missions from the Ethiopian diaspora churches in the US by analyzing their history, intergenerational dynamics, definitions, and practices of missions, including their mobilization, recruitment, missions to future generations, and transnationalism. This study further develops comprehensive mission strategies to effectively mobilize Ethiopian diaspora churches for global missions.

Chapter one established the introduction, including the need for this study. The need for scholarly research on the missional character of Ethiopian diaspora churches in the US is three-fold. First, very little scholarly research has been done thus far on missions in Ethiopian diaspora churches. Second, missions to the diaspora receives much emphasis in many diaspora missiology works with less focus given to missions by the diaspora. Third, there is lack of a comprehensive study into Ethiopian diaspora churches' intergenerational context and its impact on missions.

Chapter two provides the history of Ethiopian evangelical diaspora churches in the US Many Ethiopian evangelical churches were planted in the US during the second wave of Ethiopian migration to the US between 1974–1991. The churches' primary purpose during this period was to provide spiritual and community services through home fellowships and spiritual conferences. The church members were predominantly single male refugees with a survival mentality. This mindset impaired their missions endeavor, including reaching out to communities beyond their own, preparing platforms for their children (the second generation), and partnering with US mainstream churches. Ethiopian evangelical churches grew exponentially during the third wave, between 1991 and the present day. During this period, they experienced much growth while contending with the second-generation crisis, a leadership crisis, and widespread church splitting.

Chapter three developed an understanding of the intergenerational dynamics of Ethiopian evangelical churches in the US The chapter contains three sections. The first section focuses on defining, describing, and offering Biblical examples of the first, second, and 1.5 generation migrants. The second section highlights the nature, process, and challenges of the cultural adjustments among the three generations. These issues were explained using the different sociological acculturation models, including separation, integration, assimilation, and marginalization. The third section of this chapter deals explicitly with the intergenerational dynamics within Ethiopian evangelical churches in the US This researcher argued that integration is the healthiest model for migrants to follow, as it fosters migrants' growth in bi-cultural and bi-lingual competencies.

Chapters four and five presented research findings. This study encompasses participants between the ages of twenty-one and seventy. Most participants' motivation to join ministry is to fill the needed gaps in the church, and it is not necessarily missional. On average, the Amharic-speaking congregations have between 300–350 members and the English-speaking congregations have between 50–150. Migration, not missions, is the primary source of the membership increase. The Amharic-speaking ministry is designed solely to meet the needs of its own community. Most English-speaking congregations also look like children, youth, and college ministries, made up of predominantly Ethiopian descendants.

Ethiopian diaspora churches have a good number of members. However, their establishment, ministry approach, and growth are not missional as they are exclusively focused on reaching out to their own community. The language barrier is not the primary barrier to interaction across generational lines. Instead, focusing exclusively on one's own generation while neglecting the others is responsible for the generational gaps. The feeling of not being understood by their parents is the major challenge of the second generation. The first and 1.5 generations focus on tackling economic challenges in the diaspora, while the second generations face more social, mental, and spiritual challenges.

Regarding church practices, most second generation immigrants leave their parents' ethnic church when they finish high school, and they either join US mainstream churches or stop going to church altogether. Others may consider going to churches planted by second-generation pastors if there is one in their area. Most participants agreed that the first, second, and 1.5 generations need to participate in church together to narrow the generational gap and foster effective missions. Also, most participants support the "two church service" approach – one in English and the other in Amharic. However, participants were unsure if doing church together would be practical, and if each generation would be open to the "two church service" model. Despite these uncertainties, most participants still suggested that the first generation is responsible for providing English-speaking church services in addition to their already established Amharic services.

Regarding the definition of missions, factors such as a biblical view of missions, missionary-sending and receiving countries, and missionaries' activities in the recipient countries have shaped the participants' definitions of missions. Interview participants reflected a broader historical, global, and Biblical understanding of missions than online survey participants. Participants' definitions of missions reflected the following areas: (1) missions mean to partner with God in his mission, (2) missions involves both gospel proclamation and humanitarian work, (3) missions involves going to all nations or going beyond one's own community, and (4) missions involves disciple-making.

When it comes to mission practices, most Ethiopian diaspora churches tend to have members, particularly among the young adults, who desire to be involved in missions work. However, their participation is often hampered by: (1) lack of mobilization—including failure to provide the necessary training—and lack of financial resources (2) poor organizational structure with only occasional evangelism outreach campaigns run by volunteers.

Transnationalism, or a cross-cultural ministry or missions-sending experience, revealed that the missional framework of Ethiopian diaspora churches is inwardly focused and is limited to addressing the needs of Ethiopians in the US or back in their home country. Cross-cultural ministry, such as establishing church services for English-speaking communities and building partnerships with US churches, is also weak.

This study showed that community, spiritual fervency, simplicity, and cultural resourcefulness are some of the strengths of Ethiopian diaspora churches in missions. Conversely, staying in a "comfort zone," restricting missions to occasional evangelism outreach campaigns, lack of vision and planning, and church splitting are some of the weaknesses of Ethiopian diaspora churches in the US This study also found that language barrier, lack of a missional mindset, and lack of training are the three significant challenges of first-generation churches. Meanwhile, lack of discipleship, lack of ethnic diversity, and lack of stability are the main challenges of second-generation congregations.

Recommendations

This section presents strategic recommendations offered by participants and the present researcher himself. At the end of the questionnaire, participants were asked to give their further thoughts regarding this study, and most of them reflected their hopes that this study would help them increase their engagement in missions as diaspora. One of the participants stated, "This is an eye-opening study that will challenge our church to go out of its comfort zone and do mission as a church in the diaspora."[1] Another participant said, "I believe this study will provide insights on how to handle the intergenerational situation in the Ethiopian diaspora churches in America."[2] Another participant added:

> This research will help many Ethiopian churches to revise their ministry in the diaspora. We do not have a reference for the history of these three generations as they are just appearing now. Such that, knowing and understanding this will benefit all generations and save many families' lives.[3]

This researcher draws recommendations from the study's findings to meet participants' expectations and fill the gap in the study of diaspora missiology. Moreover, the recommendations are meant to encourage and motivate Ethiopian diaspora churches to engage in missions by intentionally utilizing

---

1. Survey participant 36, November 21, 2020.
2. Survey participant 20, November 17, 2020.
3. Survey participant 27, November 18, 2020.

their intergenerational dynamics. In other words, this researcher hopes that the recommendations will help to develop comprehensive mission strategies that can bring the first, second, and 1.5 generations together for effective missions. The recommendations are presented as follows.

Continue Spiritual Fervency and Community Life

Addressing the spiritual and community needs of Ethiopians in the US was the initial purpose of the Ethiopian churches at their establishment. These elements continue to be the strengths of Ethiopian diaspora churches in the US In other words, members of Ethiopian diaspora churches, including the first, second, and 1.5 generations, show a relatively higher commitment to their faith in their prayer, teaching of the scripture, and evangelism outreach practices than the local US churches. Also, they all value community over the individualistic lifestyle common in the US Even the second generation admires the communal cultural heritage from their parents. The way they grieve together, their freedom in asking for help, and how they celebrate different events together are some of the ways that they take the opportunity to share the gospel in their community. This researcher recommends that Ethiopian diaspora churches continue this spiritual fervency and live out their faith as a community.

Grow From Inward to Outward Focus

Survey results indicated that the first, second, and 1.5 generation congregations are not missional at their core. In other words, Ethiopian diaspora churches in the US are primarily self-focused in their ministry approach, and the emphasis given to reaching out to communities beyond their own is minimal. The first and 1.5 generation ministries are exclusively designed to serve Ethiopians. Even though there is minimal diversity among the second-generation churches, they are still predominantly Ethiopian descendants. Moreover, survey results indicated that most Ethiopian diaspora churches in the US have missions initiatives in their home country while none have the practice of sending missionaries globally, beyond Ethiopia. This indicates that Ethiopian diaspora churches are inwardly focused because they solely reach out to their community. Engaging with their own community is a default for many people, and that tendency is not necessarily wrong. However, Ethiopian diaspora churches need to grow outwardly for the gospel's sake. The gospel requires us to go beyond our community. For instance, Matthew 28:16–20 tells us that the Great Commission requires believers to go to all nations.

Similarly, Acts 1:8 shows that believers are called to be witnesses of the gospel in Jerusalem, all Judea and Samaria, and to the ends of the earth. Going beyond one's own community for the gospel's sake takes a missional mindset and intentionality. To grow from the inward (self-focused) ministry approach to the outward (beyond one's own community) missional approach, this researcher recommends that Ethiopian diaspora churches carefully consider the following points.

Cultivate a Missional Mindset

This researcher recommends Ethiopian diaspora churches examine the lack of a missional mindset among their members and their churches. Many of them believe that language and lack of finances are the two significant factors contributing to the lack of a missional mindset. While the language barrier is indeed a challenge for anyone wishing to serve cross-culturally, it is actually the lack of a missional mindset that makes cross-cultural ministry more difficult. US missionaries keep going to Ethiopia not because they know the Ethiopian languages but because they have a missional mindset. The missional mindset enables us to overcome the language barrier to reach out to communities beyond our own. Ethiopian diaspora churches in the US need to cultivate a missional mindset among their members instead of using the language barrier as an excuse for their poor engagement in missions. Learning the language (in this case English) is very important as it helps to communicate the gospel with English speaking communities in the US. However, knowing the language is not central to cultivating a missional mindset. For instance, the second generation speak English so well, but this doesn't guarantee that they will get involved in missions just because they know the language. They need a missional mindset. One of the second-generation pastors noted:

> The second-generation is imbedded in the majority culture but being embedded in the missional mindset is the issue of discipleship. In other words, the second generations are suited in the community so well, but they may not take Christianity as

Conclusion and Recommendations

their primary identity, and therefore that is where discipleship is needed.[4]

Regarding finances, it is true that the church needs financial support for ministry, but missions is not necessarily dependent on finances. Ethiopian diaspora churches need to understand that money is not a determining factor for missions. It is not our bank accounts that transform people's lives, but the gospel. We are called and empowered by God to preach the gospel (Acts 1:8; 1 Cor 1:18; 4:19–20; 1Thes 1:5). We do not do missions because we have the finances, but because we have the heart for nations. One participant noted, "We are self-focused, and we will never finish the work among our community. We should consider living for someone else beyond our own community and grow outward. Missions is not about having the financial capacity, but it is more about having the missional heart."[5]

Understanding missions as expensive is a traditional approach that implies missions from the West (the haves) to the rest (the have-nots). This study's online survey participants reflected such a mindset in their definition of missions. They see missions as a Westerners' burden because they have the "resources." They view Africa as the only missionary recipient while none view the West as a missionary recipient. In this case, they are missing the missional aspect of their movement to the US because they do not perceive the US as a mission field.

On the other hand, their focus is on their country of origin, and Africa in general, because they perceive that missions work is needed only in Africa. These participants represent the wider Ethiopian diaspora church communities in the US Therefore, Ethiopian diaspora churches need to change their mindset that missions is associated with having or not having resources and maximize the missional aspect of their movement as African missionaries to the US Consideration is next given to ways in which churches can gain a missional mindset.

Work on Awareness Creation and Training

Awareness creation and training on missions is crucial to help Ethiopian Christians increase their engagement in missions. Survey results indicated

---

4. Zoom Interview, second generation participant 1, December 8, 2020.
5. Zoom Interview, independent ministry participant 1, December 10, 2020.

that most participants believe that they are missionaries in the US, but they do not know what it means or how to engage in missions practically. Awareness creation and training on missions are needed among Ethiopian diaspora churches in the US for three reasons.

First, missions initiatives among Ethiopian diaspora churches in the US are weak or absent at the individual, family, and church levels. One participant stated:

> I feel like missions is missing in most of us today (first or second-generation). Life has become more of an individual survival to make it to heaven and not be a missionary. The spiritual battles and the compromises we make in our spiritual life is affecting our missionary life, which is the actual life of a Christian.[6]

Another participant said, "There are many young people in the Ethiopian diaspora churches who have the sense of calling for ministry, yet they are restricting their calling only to their community while they have the potential to reach out to non-Ethiopian communities."[7]

Participants indicated that the first generation lacks a missional mindset at a family level when raising their children in the US A participant pointed out, "For most first-generation, sending their children to medical or engineering school is everything, but to send them to a Bible school or preparing them for missions in line with any other passion they may have is the last thing they want."[8] This shows that the first generation does not prioritize their faith but the American dream. Another participant added, "The first-generation need the awareness about the importance of missions. They need to work on changing their mindset towards reaching out to their children who are living in-between two cultures."[9]

At a church level, a participant noted, "Missions has not been given enough emphasis among Ethiopian churches, be it here in the diaspora or back in our home country. We are very self-focused, while missions is more

---

6. Zoom Interview, first generation participant 1, December 7, 2020.
7. Zoom Interview, 1.5 generation participant 1, December 16, 2020.
8. Zoom Interview, first generation participant 4, December 15, 2020.
9. Zoom Interview, first generation participant 2, December 12, 2020.

Conclusion and Recommendations 185

outward-focused. We need to refocus because missions is not about us; it is about others."[10]

The second reason awareness creation and training on missions is needed among Ethiopian diaspora churches is that the context where they are living is different from their country of origin. Participants stated, "Providing training and awareness on missions is important because we are living in a different context. This is America; we are not in Ethiopia. We cannot change the gospel, but how can we be relevant to this context without losing our cultural flavor?"[11]

Third, inter-generational dynamics require a collaborative front for missions. One participant noted:

> Missions is like a glue that connects the different generations in our church and helps us to work together for a common purpose. Therefore, our preaching, teaching, and ministry activities should be focused on missions because I believe that when people learn about missions, they want to work together regardless of their age or the generational dividing lines.[12]

Survey results indicated that interview participants have a broader mission perspective than the online survey participants. Interview participants include those who have independent ministries, second-generation church planters, and some first and 1.5 generations who are believed to be influential among the Ethiopian church communities in the US This group of people have a deeper understanding of the global, historical, and Biblical missions. Ethiopian diaspora churches can use these groups to train and mobilize their members for global missions. The church can also consider providing training for trainers on some missions courses such as the Kairos course, Perspectives on the World Christian Movement, and the Bridges course.

Assess the Irony of Growing in Number

Both survey results and the history of Ethiopian diaspora churches discussed in chapter two agree that the church has been growing numerically since

---

10. Zoom Interview, first generation participant 4, December 15, 2020.
11. Zoom Interview, independent ministry participant 2, December 10, 2020.
12. Zoom Interview, first generation participant 3, December 17, 2020.

its establishment in the 1980s. However, the growth was not on account of missions. Instead, it was due to the migration of Ethiopian Christians from Ethiopia or different cities within the US Ethiopians are still coming to the US, and currently, they comprise the second-largest number of African immigrants in the US It is good that Ethiopians are enjoying their large community in the US However, the influx of Ethiopians to the US may not continue in such a manner.

For instance, the Diversity Visa Lottery Program is one of the primary means of many Ethiopians' migration to the US Currently, migration means are declining due to migration quota and policy changes in the US If this trend continues, it may impact the Ethiopian diaspora churches in the US as the primary source of church growth. This impact may not be seen soon because they currently have many young adults in their churches. However, if the decline continues, it may cause the Ethiopian diaspora churches to lose their impact as the second-largest African population in the US and eventually die out in the long run. Therefore, this researcher recommends that Ethiopian diaspora churches consider reaching out to the second generation and other communities beyond their own for a better future.

Evaluate the Move to Buy Church Buildings

Most Ethiopian diaspora churches in the US are on the move to buy their church buildings, or they already have them. It is not wrong to own a church building. However, Ethiopian diaspora churches need to examine this movement from the standpoint of missions for two reasons.

First, ownership of church buildings could foster their isolationist approach. This study revealed that the tendency of the first generation is to preserve their culture in the diaspora. Building compounds or camps in the countries they went to was one of the weaknesses of the Western missionaries that led to them isolating themselves from the community they serve. Similarly, buying a facility can led to the alienation of Ethiopian diaspora churches from US mainstream churches and encourages them to have their own island in the diaspora. When people see the name "Ethiopian Evangelical Church" on their buildings, they automatically know that they do not belong there because the name itself implies that it is a church for Ethiopians. That is one of the reasons why the second generation does not want to stay at their parent's ethnic churches. The second generation usually prefers to move to a different location and have a different name for their church that fits their English-speaking context. Pathway, Perazim, Avenue, and Overflow City Church are examples of churches planted by second-generation Ethiopian Americans. One of the interview participants from the second generation pointed out, "When we planted our church, the first-generation was willing to give us a space in their building, but we did not want to accept the offer. Instead, we moved to an interdenominational American mainstream church where there is no mental barrier for other ethnic communities to come join us."[13] One can see how Ethiopian diaspora churches could become disconnected from their children and the local US churches.

This researcher recommends that Ethiopian diaspora churches take the following practical actions. First, Ethiopian diaspora churches can consider inviting US churches to use their facilities and partner with them in a meaningful way beyond sharing their space. Second, Ethiopian churches can also consider changing their church names so that other ethnic groups who want to join them feel they belong in their churches. Third, allow the second generation to take over the church building, do their church service as the primary service in that building, and give them the freedom to name that church in a way that is welcoming to the diverse community around them. This recommendation does not imply dissolving the first-generation congregation. The first-generation church service can continue, but not as the leading service in that building. It would take humility for the first generation to work under the second generation.

Fourth, the movement to buy church buildings could redirect their funds to building rather than missions. In this case, the Ethiopian diaspora churches' fundraising, and fund management efforts would be diverted to buying and maintaining the building. One of the participants noted, "Ethiopian diaspora churches are good at fundraising for building, but they lack motivation when it comes to raising funds for missions."[14] Instead of raising funds for building, Ethiopian diaspora churches need to consider raising funds for missions. To those churches that have not bought their church buildings yet, this researcher recommends that they consider redirecting building funds toward a missions fund instead.

---

13. Zoom Interview, second generation participant 2, December 11, 2020.
14. Zoom Interview, 1.5 generation participant 1, December 16, 2020.

Consider Integration Model

Every generation has its own way of dealing with the process of adjusting to life in the diaspora. The first generation is more focused on cultural preservation as they apply a separation model that leads to minimizing or avoiding the hosting culture. The second generation mostly follows the assimilation model to fit into the hosting culture while detaching themselves from their parents' culture. Most of the 1.5 generation resemble the pattern of the first generation because they feel that they are not Americanized enough.

Unlike the separation and assimilation cultural adjustment models, the integration model enhances bicultural and bilingual competencies, creating an openness to home and host cultures. This researcher recommends the first, second, and 1.5 generations consider an integration cultural adjustment model for two reasons. First, the integration model helps the diaspora community to increase their cultural competency for the missions of God, as it fosters openness to embracing other cultures. Second, the integration model helps narrow the generational gap among the diaspora communities and effectively engage in missions together.

This study revealed that the second-generation ministry has been receiving the least priority among Ethiopian diaspora churches in the US This researcher recommends that the first and 1.5 generations reach out to the second generation for two reasons. First, the second generation is the future of the church. Participants stated, "Missions is about looking for the future and passing down the gospel to the next generation. Ethiopian diaspora churches in America need to focus on the future generation. They need to choose their children above their language and culture."[15]

Second, from the missions point of view (Acts 1:8), the second generation is their new Jerusalem in the diaspora. Reaching out to their Jerusalem (the second generation) leads to reaching out to their uttermost part of the earth (Americans). In other words, the second-generation is well versed in the hosting culture, and therefore, Ethiopian diaspora churches can have effective missions in the hosting culture through discipling the second generation.

---

15. Zoom Interview, 1.5 generation participant 1, December 16, 2020.

Grow from Evangelism Campaigns to Missions

Remarkably, almost all Ethiopian diaspora churches in the US organize evangelism outreach campaigns at least once a month. However, they need to go beyond the evangelism campaign program because it cannot replace missions. Missions require the commitment to going, crossing cultures, and living among those we desire to serve. "Going" refers to deciding to leave one's own community. "Crossing culture" includes the willingness to learn their language and culture so we can communicate the gospel on their terms. The "living" refers to identifying ourselves with those we want to evangelize. It also indicates the time and process that missions tend to take.

On the contrary, the evangelism campaign does not require all these elements because it is done only once in a while. The infrequent nature of these evangelism campaigns means that particpants encounter people they may never talk to again, and the need to study language and culture is not as necessary. Missions were not the motivation for most Ethiopian Christians to come to the US Migration (search for a better life) brought them to the US This researcher encourages and challenges Ethiopian diaspora Christians in the US to see the missional aspect of their movement beyond evangelism campaigns. Ethiopian diaspora Christians can be missional in the US in two ways: first, by intentionally developing relationships and friendships with non-Ethiopians; and second, by intentionally sending believers from the first, second, and 1.5 generations as missionaries among Americans. These missionaries will carry their evangelism zeal with them and leave their comfort zone for the sake of the gospel. They live among Americans and other migrant communities in their cities and church plants.

Work on Unity

Church division is one of the main challenges among Ethiopian diaspora churches in the US Personal ego and lack of platform for those who want to engage in ministry are the significant causes of church division. One of the participants said that the first-generation pastors have a "club mentality" where they form their own unions at the city and national levels. Ethiopian Churches' Fellowship in North America, Leaders Accountability Team, and Ethiopian Pastors Congress are some of these clubs at a national level. The second generation and the missions work are two areas that suffer the most due to church division. This researcher recommends that a more missional and unifying institution be established to focus on mobilizing Ethiopian diaspora churches for missions. In line with this point, a participant remarked, "I wish there could be a central place or board that can organize the youth and young adults with the first-generation so that all of them can collaborate in the work of God together."[16] Moreover, this researcher would encourage and challenge the second and 1.5 generations to do a better job keeping their unity in their city and across the states at the national level.

Consider Family Approach

Ethiopian diaspora church leaders, the hosting communities and parents need to consider the family dynamics of the diaspora to better serve them. The first-generation Ethiopian diaspora leaders are not serving the whole family. For instance, the first-generation pastor caters his ministry exclusively to parents while neglecting the second generation. The responsibility of pastoring the second generation is given to volunteers who may or may not have a ministry calling. This creates a gap between parents and children in their discipleship process. One of the participants noted, "The gap between the second-generation and their parents is not only cultural but also spiritual. Parents are struggling to pass their faith down to their children."[17] This researcher recommends that Ethiopian church pastors consider discipling the whole family, because that is what it takes to be a pastor in the diaspora. The church can facilitate platforms to bring parents and children together for open discussion. A participant stated, "It is essential to know each other well beyond worship and prayer. The church can create stable parent-children conversation platforms such that they can have open and honest talks to express what each of them are experiencing."[18] Here, the 1.5 generation can play an instrumental role in bridging the gap between the first and second generation by taking the initiative to facilitate such workshops, forums, and conferences in the church.

The hosting communities also have a similar problem, in that they do not perceive migrants as a family. When they want to help, they either focus on the first or the second generation individually. For instance, they have strategies

---

16. Zoom Interview, first generation participant 5, December 20, 2020.
17. Zoom Interview, second generation participant 1, December 8, 2020.
18. Zoom Interview, 1.5 generation participant 2, December 16, 2020.

like English as a Second Language (ESL) and citizenship classes to reach out to the first generation, which does not work for the second generation as they already know the language and they are US citizens by birth. Supporting the first generation in those areas is right. However, to reach out to the migrants more effectively, this researcher recommends that the hosting communities develop strategies that work for the whole family. For instance, being hospitable for the whole family could be one strategy. Here, family to family connection is very important. For example, instead of going as an individual to help with ESL or citizenship classes, hosting communities could consider sending whole families as missionaries to the migrant family next door.

Migrant parents also struggle to manage their family dynamics. This researcher identifies four problems and their recommendations regarding the issue of how parents need to address their whole family.

Lack of time is one of the problems. Parents do not carve out time to sit down with their children. They are busy working 16 hours a day to provide for their family and achieve the American dream. This researcher recommends the following two points for parents to consider. First, parents would be wise to live a simple life so as to make time for their children. Second, parents need to know that earning a living for the family is not enough. They also need to win their children's souls. This goes beyond providing food on the table, and includes addressing the spiritual, emotional, social, and mental aspects of their children in the diaspora.

Lack of commitment and knowledge of carrying out parental responsibility is another problem. One of the challenges of the children and youth ministry leaders is that they are required to do everything that falls under parental responsibilities. One of the participants stated, "Narrowing the gap between the first and second-generation should start at home, not at church. If parents are not in the lives of their children at home, how can they do church and missions together?"[19] This researcher recommends that parents take the primary responsibility of discipling their children. This includes tutoring, discipling, doing devotional time for prayer and Bible reading, and following up on what their children are learning at church. One participant said, "I believe parents should be part of children's ministries and know what their children

---

19. Zoom Interview, second generation participant 3, December 11, 2020.

are learning."[20] Another participant suggested, "Parents and children can study together about one nation every week. Where is the country located? What is lifelike in that country? What is the gospel coverage look like? And they can pray for that nation. By doing so they can cultivate a missional mindset as a family."[21] In this respect, the church's responsibility is to play a supplementary role, such as supporting parents with training and other necessary resources to help them effectively raise their children in the diaspora.

Lack of communication is another problem for families in the diaspora. One participant said, "Most parents do not know their children and vice versa." Another participant added, "I doubt whether parents know the passion and interest of their children. Parents need to ask how their children are doing and encourage them to share if they struggle with anything. Then, they need to listen to their children without judging them."[22]

Parents need to take additional steps to learn their children's world. One participant pointed out, "The cultural change is required to come from the first-generation, not from the second-generation, because it is the parents' cultures and worldviews that are different from the American context. For instance, as parents, we cannot impose a shame and honor culture on our children who were born and raised in America."[23] Learning their children's context involves learning language, how to talk about issues that concern their children in this different cultural context, and how to use technology.

Misplaced authority is another problem regarding the issue of family. Children are well assimilated within the US culture, which may lead them to see their parents as traditional or uneducated because they do not speak English or speak English with a heavy accent. Moreover, parents may not be able to understand the US context fully. Consequently, children may avoid their parents and seek guidance from their peers. Replacing authority figures may lead parents to become more authoritarian, which could cause conflict between them and the second generation. This researcher recommends that both children and parents consider humility. Children may feel prideful about how much they know that their parents do not. Children need to

---

20. Zoom Interview, second generation participant 2, December 11, 2020.
21. Zoom Interview, independent ministry participant 1, December 10, 2020.
22. Zoom Interview, second generation participant 3, December 11, 2020.
23. Zoom Interview, first generation participant 2, December 12, 2020.

humble themselves and change their view toward their parents. Parents are not illiterate just because they do not speak English well. On the other hand, proving their authority is the parents' point of pride. They need to humble themselves to accept a reverse mentorship. Since children have a better grasp of the hosting language and culture, parents need to acknowledge this and learn from their children.

Partner with Local US Churches and Mission Organizations

The partnership between Ethiopian diaspora churches and local US mainstream churches as one body of Christ is crucial for effective missions in the US and beyond. US mainstream churches need to see migrants as mission fields and mission forces. This researcher recommends that US churches consider the following practical actions.

First, local US churches need to revise their outreach strategy to migrants. Classes such as English as a Second Language (ESL), citizenship training, and cooking could be relevant for new arrivals who have not built their community in the diaspora or are not connected with their communities yet. However, once immigrants and refugees are connected with their own communities, they may not be interested in having further relationships with the local people. Immigrants may choose to separate themselves from the hosting community to conserve their culture. Therefore, local US churches and mission organizations must realize that not all migrants are new and needy. They need to consider studying the settlement patterns of immigrants to revise their ministry strategy accordingly.

Second, local US churches need to consider utilizing the unique opportunity to reach the second generation. Reaching out to the growing number of second generation migrants in the US is a tremendous opportunity for several reasons. First, it is comparatively strategic for future missions than reaching out to the first generation. It is true that first generation immigrants or young adult international students have a better attachment with their home country and reaching out to them may lead to taking the gospel back to their country of origin. However, reaching out to the second generation creates even more opportunities for the global missions endeavor. Their upbringing in their parents' and hosting cultures, and the fact that they are friends with people of many different ethnic backgrounds gives them a global citizen identity, making them a perfect fit for global missions in our globalized world. Second, it is easier to evangelize the second generation because they do not have a language barrier like the first generation. Third, the second generation is more open to accepting new things, including the gospel, than the first generation. Fourth, compared to the first generation, reaching out to the second generation may lead to national transformation because their upward mobility in the socioeconomic and political status in the hosting nation enables them to impact the hosting nation and beyond.

Again, local US mainstream churches and missions organizations need to consider revising their mission strategies to reach the second generation. For instance, mission strategies like ESL and citizenship classes do not help reach the second-generation migrants. The second generation does not need to take ESL because they already know English. Similarly, they do not need citizenship classes because they are already citizens by birth. Therefore, local US churches and missions organizations need to realize the intergenerational dynamics of the diaspora communities and cater a relevant ministry to each generation accordingly.

Third, local US churches and missions organizations need to revise the traditional missions approach that limits itself to overseas missions. US mainstream churches need to realize that God has brought the mission fields to their doorstep. Due to migration, the uttermost end of the earth is their Jerusalem. While still doing the overseas missions, US mainstream churches and mission agencies need to refocus on reaching out to nations coming to their doorstep.

Regarding migrants as a missions force, US mainstream churches and missions agencies must maximize the opportunity to partner with believing diaspora communities in missions. This researcher recommends the following two ways by which US mainstream churches and mission organizations can engage in the mission of God together with diaspora churches.

First, equip and mobilize the next generation for missions. Due to the increasing presence of migrants, the ethnic demography in the US is changing faster than ever before. The first generation typically did not grow up in a multi-ethnic community. However, it is now normal for the next generation to grow up in today's diverse community. This researcher recommends that the US mainstream churches and missions organizations grow in their diversity so that their children can have a platform that resembles their context. For instance, US missions organizations can consider recruiting and sending missionaries from the 1.5 and second generation believing Ethiopians, along with US missionaries.

US mainstream churches can consider a partnership with Ethiopian diaspora churches to help equip the second generation. Due to language and culture barriers, discipling the second generation in the US is challenging for the first generation. In line with this point, participants said, "Would it be a bad idea to bring outside help (from people who are not Ethiopian) until leaders from the 1.5 and second-generation are established? Would this still fall under the victim or receiving mentality?"[24] The answer to this question is "no." US mainstream churches can partner with Ethiopian diaspora churches to fill this gap by sending missionaries to help the Ethiopian churches in their children and youth ministries.

US mainstream churches and missions organizations can also consider partnering with Ethiopian diaspora churches in helping the second-generation young adults find a church platform to grow them spiritually. This study indicates that many second-generation Ethiopians leave their parents' ethnic church once they finish high school because of a lack of platform. These people join US mainstream churches or churches planted by their second-generation peers if there is one in their city. In this case, this researcher recommends that US churches consider helping the second-generation church planters establish their churches. This researcher also recommends that US churches welcome the second-generation Ethiopians who want to join them. US churches need to be ready to embrace the second generation's unique stories and encourage them to engage in the church ministry.

Second, US churches need to learn to be on the receiving end of missions initiatives. Missionaries are needed to help revitalize churches in the US today. Ethiopian diaspora churches can send missionaries to help in this area. For instance, the researcher himself is engaged in revitalizing one of the US mainstream churches in his city.

Another area that US Christians can benefit from Ethiopian diaspora Christians is cultural intelligence. There is a cultural and story proximity among most migrants. Therefore, US Christians can increase their cultural intelligence by learning and engaging in missions with diaspora communities.

---

24. Survey participant 20, November 17, 2020.

For instance, US missionaries can collaborate with Ethiopian diaspora Christians in the US to reach out to the Somali people in their city.

US mainstream churches and missions organizations can also benefit from the leadership of believing migrants in the US The findings of this study reveal that most Ethiopian diaspora churches are part of US church denominations. The partnership between the Dallas Baptist Convention and Ethiopian Evangelical Baptist Church Dallas is an excellent example of a healthy partnership that engages diaspora churches at a leadership level.

Evaluate Church Structure

The findings of this study indicated that Ethiopian diaspora churches need to consider revising their church structure for two reasons. First, they are self-focused. There is lack of a missional mindset among Ethiopian diaspora churches because their ministry is designed to serve their community solely, and they are not reaching out to communities beyond their own. Second, they do not have a platform that brings the first, second, and 1.5 generations together for missions. The current structure does not help to address the intergenerational dynamics of the church. Much emphasis is given to the first generation, while the second generation is left to volunteers. Most of the 1.5 generation follows the pattern of the first generation, while a few are volunteering in the second-generation ministry. Now the question is: what kind of church structure can bring the first, second, and 1.5 generations together for effective discipleship and missions? This researcher presents the following five kinds of church models with their strengths and weaknesses. This researcher put forth recommendations based on how these models help Ethiopian diaspora churches to be more missional.

Church Model 1: Joint Service Occasionally

Most participants suggested this model as a working church model to bring the first, second, and 1.5 generations together. The strength of this model is that it is simple to implement. Participants suggested that it would be good if their churches had such a joint service once a month. Most Ethiopian diaspora churches in the US already have such a service, mainly during the holidays. However, the weakness of this model is threefold. First, it does not help to open up to other ethnic communities to join them regularly. Second, this model is like parents saying to their children to come home once in a while. Therefore, the result of this model is that the second generation does not feel they belong in their parents' church. Third, churches cannot prepare the second generation for missions using such occasional services. This researcher does not recommend this model because it does not help the Ethiopian diaspora churches to have effective intergenerational discipleship and be more missional in reaching out to communities beyond their own.

Church Model 2: Joint Sunday Service

This model suggests that the Ethiopian churches have two church services, one in Amharic and another in English. This model aims to bring parents and children together in the English service, and in the following service, parents would have their service in their heart language. To effectively manage the English-speaking church, the first-generation pastors can collaborate with the second and 1.5 generation leaders who have the linguistic and cultural skills. Putting the two generations together is not easy, but a participant noted that humility is one element that can help narrow down the generational gap:

> It starts with what might sound simple enough but lacks consistency between these generations, which is humility and building trust. There needs to be a sincere desire to get down to each group level and connect with them. Sometimes this means not even doing anything but simply being present at different gatherings which can show support and be so encouraging to that group.[25]

The strength of this model is twofold. First, it allows the first generation to disciple their children early on. One of the participants pointed out:

> Regarding establishing the English-speaking church for English speaking members, whatever plan is put in place should not be for the college-age now, rather this is something that would be foundational for years to come where students who are in middle school and high school would see that the church is a viable option for them even as they go to college.[26]

---

25. Zoom Interview, second generation participant 2, December 11, 2020.
26. Zoom Interview, first generation participant 3, December 17, 2020.

The second strength of this model is that it helps the Ethiopian diaspora churches to become more missional by opening their doors to non-Ethiopians to join them in the English-speaking church service.

The weakness or challenges of this model is that there may be a lack of willingness from the first generation to have church service in English together with their children and vice versa. The other weakness is that it could be challenging for their congregation to diversify due to the dominance of the Ethiopian culture. The name "Ethiopian Evangelical Church" itself implies that it is just for Ethiopians, and other ethnic communities may not feel they belong.

This researcher recommends this model to the Ethiopian diaspora churches with predominantly younger children below college level. New church planters from the 1.5 generation can also consider this model from the start.

Church Model 3: Plant an English-Speaking Church Led by the 1.5 or Second Generation

So far, according to our research, second-generation pastors have planted only four English-speaking churches across the United States. This indicates that most Ethiopian churches are still stuck in the children and youth ministries. The first generation desires to see the growth of the English-speaking ministry in their city. However, they still do not know how they can come alongside to support the initiative of the second and 1.5 generation church planters. A participant stated:

> There is a desire now more than I have seen before from the first-generation to see the second-generation church grow. The second-generation church is viewed less as "babysitting" and more as a ministry. They differ in their knowledge and approach to helping the second-generation grow. They want to help, but they are not sure how.[27]

Due to not receiving the necessary support from the first generation, there is frustration among the second and 1.5 generation church planters. When one of the participants reflected on his frustration, he said, "I hope and pray that the current Ethiopian leaders resign with honor and give their platform to the second and 1.5 generation leaders that God calls, are ready for

---

27. Zoom Interview, second generation participant 1, December 8, 2020.

leadership and are more well versed about the issues of the day than them." When another participant from the first generation confessed on behalf of his generation, he said:

> We bring Christian values and plant churches in America with high commitment. However, we have not stayed relevant to the time and context of America for the effective continuity of our churches. We have not prepared successors who stay current with the social dynamics and can navigate through new strategies. Many young adults are willing to lead the church, but we do not know how to let our position go and pass it over to them. We lack vision, and therefore we grip on our position so we will not lose our identity, significance, and financial security. I feel sorry for the second and 1.5 generations because they are not given a chance, and it is so frustrating that they are losing their golden age where they can actively engage in ministry.
>
> Here is my advice for the second and 1.5 generation young adults. They need to make the commitment we had when we first planted our churches in America. There was not much support back then, but we were resilient. In the same way, they may not get support from the first-generation, but they need to have a high commitment to plant churches so that many unchurched second generations would get a platform to grow in their spiritual lives. They need to recognize that this is their season. They should not wait for the church (the first-generation). The church would not support because it is not their concern or vision.[28]

The strength of this model is that it can be very missional in terms of engaging non-Ethiopian communities and growing toward a multi-ethnic church. However, the weakness of this model has to do with the age demography. Most church members in this model would be young adults, and therefore they need to work to grow intergenerationally. Otherwise, their ministry tends to reflect a youth ministry that would not welcome those who are a bit older than them. Such people are looking for a place to settle with their families. By contrast, most young adults are single and less financially

---

28. Zoom Interview, first generation participant 4, December 15, 2020.

stable. Consequently, they may move to a different location to follow jobs, education, or marriage opportunities.

This researcher recommends that the 1.5 and second-generation leaders utilize this model and plant more churches across the US to rescue unchurched second generations and reach out to the diverse community in their cities.

Church Model 4: Join US Mainstream Churches

Some parents move from Ethiopian diaspora churches to US mainstream churches so that their children will benefit from the English service. In this case, these parents are there because of their children, not because they have the missional mindset. Since their motivation is not missional, these parents may not engage with the US church they join. However, this model is different from the approach taken by these parents, and is more missional at its core. This model refers to one or more families' decision to join US mainstream churches as missionaries. These families can also be missionaries sent by their Ethiopian diaspora churches. The bottom line here is that they are not there just to be numbers. They are there to contribute to leadership or any other ministry capacities.

This model also refers to the decision of an Ethiopian diaspora church to merge with a US mainstream church to engage in missions together. In this case, the Ethiopian congregation would engage in the US church service with the second generation, and at a different day or time, they may have their service in their heart language. Both the US and Ethiopian churches would have a mutual obligation to support the English and the Amharic service in order to be missional to each other's community. In this case, Ethiopian diaspora churches need to educate US mainstream churches about their intergenerational context, including a partnership to reach out to the second generation.

The strength of this model is that it helps Ethiopian diaspora churches to recognize the missional aspect of their migration to the US They intentionally join US mainstream churches as a family or church to engage in missions with them. However, the weakness of this model is that Ethiopian diaspora believers could be dominated by the US church they join. This could lead to an unhealthy partnership where the two churches are not on equal standing. The other weakness of this model is that Ethiopian diaspora believers could face challenges if they feel that US churches are not welcoming them and embracing their stories in their churches.

This researcher highly recommends this model to all Ethiopian diaspora churches in the US because it helps all the generations (first, second, and 1.5) to live out their missional call in impacting each other's lives across the generational lines and reaching out to communities beyond their own. The summary of suggested church models is depicted in the table on the next two pages.

Further Recommendations

This researcher makes the following recommendations for future studies to expand the research in missions from the Ethiopian diaspora churches.

First, this researcher recommends a mixed-methods study be done with Ethiopian diaspora churches around the world. One of the limiting factors of this study was that it is focused only on Ethiopian diaspora communities in the US, but there are Ethiopian diaspora churches in the Middle East, Europe, Canada, South Africa, and Australia as well. Consequently, this research gave a limited perspective on missions from Ethiopian diaspora churches. This researcher recommends that a similar kind of study be done in three or more Ethiopian diaspora churches from three or more nations outside the US Engaging further study in such a manner helps develop a broader perspective on the impact of missions from the Ethiopian diaspora churches globally.

Second, this researcher recommends a comparative study be done to gain a broader understanding of missions from the diaspora churches. Diaspora communities, such as South Koreans, Hispanics, and the Chinese, lived in the United States long before Ethiopians arrived. This researcher recommends a further study to compare the missions practices among churches from these diaspora communities and Ethiopian diaspora churches in the US Such further study helps Ethiopian diaspora churches learn from other diaspora churches in the US.

Finally, this researcher recommends that a further study be done to research how US mainstream churches and missions organizations engage in missions work with diaspora churches such as Ethiopian diaspora churches in the US A researcher could interview US mainstream church pastors, their members, and leaders of missions organizations to better understand the challenges and opportunities of engaging in missions with the diaspora believers next door.

Church Model 1 Joint service occasionally	Church Model 2 Joint Sunday service
Strengths It is simple to implement.	**Strengths** - It helps the Ethiopian diaspora churches to become more missional by opening their doors to non-Ethiopians. - It allows the first generation to disciple their children from an early age.
Weakness / Challenges - It is not open for other ethnic communities to join the church. - The second generation still does not feel they belong in their parents' church. - It does not help to prepare the second generation for missions.	**Weakness / Challenges** - Lack of willingness from the first generation to have church service in English together with their children and vice-versa. - The dominance of the Ethiopian culture may impact their growth in ethnic diversity.
Remarks Not recommended because it does not help with the intergenerational discipleship process, and it is not missional in reaching out to non-Ethiopians.	**Remarks** Recommended for: - Ethiopian diaspora churches that have younger children below college level. - New church planters from the 1.5 generation can also consider this model at the start.

Final Words

To effectively engage in the work of the Great Commission (Matt. 28:16–20), Ethiopian diaspora churches in the US need to see the missional dimension of their migration and be intentional in mobilizing their unique intergenerational context for missions. This researcher has developed comprehensive missions strategies to help the first, second, and 1.5 generations be more effective in missions together. These strategies were developed around elements such as spiritual fervency and community life, inward versus outward missions approach, partnering with local US churches and missions organizations, prioritizing family discipleship, and evaluating church structures.

It is the author's hope that Ethiopian diaspora churches would respond to the call of the sovereign God who led them with their families to a different

Church Model 3 Plant English-speaking church led by the 1.5 or second generation	Church Model 4 Join US mainstream churches
Strengths - It is very missional in engaging non-Ethiopians and growing toward a multi-ethnic church. - It provides a platform for the unchurched second generation.	**Strengths** - Ethiopian diaspora churches intentionally live out their missional call as a family and church.
Weakness / Challenges - They may not get support from the first generation. - Young members that make the church look like a youth ministry. - Single members who could move any time.	**Weakness / Challenges** - Difficulty understanding English for parents' generation. - They may be dominated by the US church they join. - US churches may not be ready to embrace Ethiopian diaspora churches
Remarks - Highly recommended for 1.5 and second-generation leaders. - It helps to rescue unchurched second generations and reach out to the diverse community in the cities.	**Remarks** -Highly recommended for all Ethiopian diaspora churches in US - It helps the first, second, and 1.5 generations to live out their missional call as a family and church.

nation to fulfill his mission. The global church cannot afford to leave out diaspora churches in missions at this critical time where people are on the move more than ever. With this work, the author cries out to the Lord who himself said, ". . . The harvest is plentiful, but the workers are few. Ask the Lord of the harvest, to send out workers into his harvest field" (Matt. 9:37–38).

Appendix 1

Online Survey for Church Ministers and Members

By continuing with this survey, you indicate your willingness to participate in this study, which is designed to assess missions from Ethiopian diaspora churches in the US: an intergenerational perspective. The entire survey should take only 25–30 minutes, but you are free to stop at any time. Your response will be anonymous. Your specific work and location will not be mentioned in the study. Thank you for your participation!

Part 1. Demography

1. What is your age?
   - ☐ 21–31
   - ☐ 31–40
   - ☐ 41–50
   - ☐ 51–60
   - ☐ 61–70

2. Gender?
   - ☐ Male
   - ☐ Female

3. What is your ministry in the church? (If you do not have any ministry, you can just say member. If you have an independent ministry, please write independent ministry.

4. Your ministry in the church is
   - ☐ Full time
   - ☐ Voluntary
   - ☐ Other

5. What motivated you to join this ministry initially?
   - ☐ Desire to help full the needed gap in the church
   - ☐ My own personal life experience
   - ☐ I was looking for a job
   - ☐ Ministry calling
   - ☐ Other

Part 2. Church Feature

6. When was the Amharic speaking church/congregation established/planted? (Example 3 years ago)

7. Based on your observation, how many members does the Amharic congregation have? (Example 50–100)

8. Based on your observation, what is the average attendance of the Amharic congregation during Sunday service? (Example 50–100)

9. Is your church growing since its establishment? If yes, please explain what makes the church grow. If no, please explain why your church is not growing.

10. How do you describe the Amharic speaking congregation? Please check all that apply.
    - ☐ It is designed just for the Amharic speaking group.
    - ☐ It is designed in a way that parents can worship together with their children.
    - ☐ It is designed in a way that other ethnic groups (non-Ethiopian) can worship with them
    - ☐ Other

11. If the second generation in your church have established an English-speaking church, when was that congregation planted? (Example 1–3 years ago or you can say - there is no church established by the second generation)

12. How many members does the English-speaking second-generation church have? (Example 50–100)

13. What is the average Sunday service attendance at the English-speaking second-generation church? (Example 50–100)

14. Choose the top three that describe the characteristics of the ministry provided to the English-speaking second generation in your church?
    - ☐ It is more like a children ministry
    - ☐ It is more like a youth ministry
    - ☐ It is more like a college ministry
    - ☐ It is more like Sunday school
    - ☐ It is a church that predominantly consists of Ethiopian descendant second generation.
    - ☐ It is an independent church established by the second generation and it has a diverse age and ethnic group.
    - ☐ Other

15. If you have a young adult ministry for Amharic-speaking 1.5 generation, please describe the nature of their ministry. Please check all that apply.
    - ☐ It is designed just for the Amharic speaking young adult group
    - ☐ It is designed in a way that English-speaking second generation can worship with them
    - ☐ Its service is similar to the Sunday service except it is run by the young adults
    - ☐ Other

Part 3. Definition and Practices

16. In your opinion, what nations are well known in sending missionaries globally? (If you want to respond to this question orally, you can just write your phone number)

17. Where are they mostly sending their missionaries? (If you want to respond to this question orally, you can just write your phone number)

18. What are some of the activities they do in the countries they go to? Please share 2 or 3 activities. (If you want to respond to this question orally, you can just write your phone number)

19. Based on your answers in questions 14–16, how do you define missions? (If you want to respond to this question orally, you can just write your phone number)

20. What is your personal definition of missions? (If you want to respond to this question orally, you can just write your phone number)

21. Based on your definition of missions, who could be a missionary? (If you want to respond to this question orally, you can just write your phone number)

22. Based on your answers in questions 18 and 19, what are the main activities that missions need to include? (If you want to respond to this question orally, you can just write your phone number)

23. Do you see yourself as a missionary in the US?
    - ☐ Yes
    - ☐ No

24. If you say "YES" to question 23, what are some of the activities you do as a missionary in the US? If you say "NO" why?

25. List Bible verses that have shaped your views and practices in missions?

26. From the 66 books in the Bible, which ones have shaped your views and practices in missions?

27. Do you have educational background in theology and missions?
    - ☐ Yes
    - ☐ No

28. What are the top two cultural challenges that your church is facing in reaching out to non-Ethiopians in the US?
    - ☐ Language barrier
    - ☐ Survival mentality (Our church is under the tension between conserving and risking the Ethiopian culture)
    - ☐ Lack of a missional mindset (Lack of willingness to go beyond the Ethiopian community)
    - ☐ Lack of theological training and experience on how to address the secular cultural context of the US
    - ☐ We have no cultural problems
    - ☐ Other

29. What are the top two things your church is doing to effectively function in the US context?
    - ☐ Help our church members to settle in the US
    - ☐ Our church has an English service that is welcoming to the non-Ethiopian communities
    - ☐ We offer trainings on cross-cultural ministry to reach out to non-Ethiopian communities
    - ☐ We have partnership with US churches or mission organizations
    - ☐ Other

30. How is your church partnering with US churches/mission organizations? Please check all that apply.
    - ☐ We are renting or sharing space at a US church building
    - ☐ We are supporting US missionaries financially
    - ☐ We are part of a US church denomination for administration support and resource sharing
    - ☐ We have one or more missionaries that we sent through US mission organization
    - ☐ We have no partnership with US churches or mission organizations
    - ☐ Other

31. What resources are available in your church for missions? Please check all that apply.
    - ☐ Financial resource (We always have a budget for missions)
    - ☐ Training (We have training materials and trainers on missions)
    - ☐ Human resource (We have members who have passion/zeal for missions)
    - ☐ Experience (We have members who have experience in the work of missions)
    - ☐ Other

32. How much of your churches' finance presently goes to mission work?

33. What does your church organizational structure look like in relation to missions? Please check all that apply.
    - ☐ We have a missions department with a full-time worker
    - ☐ We have occasional outreach programs in our city
    - ☐ We have short term missions program in different countries
    - ☐ We have a long-term missions program in different countries
    - ☐ Other

34. Does your church send missionaries globally (in countries other than Ethiopia)?
    - ☐ Yes
    - ☐ No

35. If you say "YES" to the above question, please describe to which countries your church has sent missionaries and the activities you do in those countries.

36. Does your church have missions work in Ethiopia?
    - ☐ Yes
    - ☐ No

37. If you say "YES" to the above question, please describe what your church is doing in Ethiopia. (If you want to respond to this question orally, you can just write your phone number)

38. Who mostly goes on these mission trips? Please check all that apply.
    - ☐ Our pastor (Our pastor travels to different places where our church has missions work)
    - ☐ Church members who take individual initiative to go for missions
    - ☐ Members of young adult ministry
    - ☐ The second-generation youth ministry
    - ☐ Members of the English-speaking second generation
    - ☐ Other

39. How do you mobilize believers in your church for missions? Please check all that apply.
    - ☐ We have mission-focused trainings
    - ☐ We support our members who have personal initiative for missions
    - ☐ Most sermons in our Sunday services are mission-focused
    - ☐ Other

40. In the city where your church is located, your church is more focused on: (Please check all that apply).
    - ☐ Sharing the gospel with Ethiopians
    - ☐ Sharing the gospel with non-Ethiopian communities
    - ☐ Other

41. Your church is not established in Ethiopia. It is planted in the US. Share three suggestions that can help your church be more effective in the US context. (If you want to respond to this question orally, you can just write your phone number)

42. What are some of the strengths of Ethiopian diaspora churches in the US that can help them to effectively do missions? (If you want to respond to this question orally, you can just write your phone number)

43. What are some of the weaknesses of Ethiopian diaspora churches in the US regarding missions? (If you want to respond this question orally, you can just write your phone number)

Part 4. Intergenerational Aspect

44. How open are the second generation (children who were born and raised in the US) to learn their parents' context?
    - ☐ Second generation are open to learn their parents' language
    - ☐ Second generation are open to go back to Ethiopia to learn the culture and contribute transnationally
    - ☐ Second generation are open to join their parents in the Amharic service
    - ☐ Second generation are willing to take over and continue their parents' ethnic church in the future
    - ☐ Second generation are not open for any of the above options
    - ☐ Other

45. How open are the first generation (older generation or parents of second generation) to learn the context of their children?
    - ☐ First generation are open to learn English
    - ☐ First generation are willing to open an English-speaking church and have English-speaking service together with their children
    - ☐ First generation are open to learning the US culture to better understand their children's worldview
    - ☐ First generation are not open to any of the above options
    - ☐ Other

46. How open are 1.5 generation (young adults who came to the US at a young age) to play their bridging role between the first and second generation?
    - ☐ 1.5 generation are encouraging and challenging the first generation to engage in the English service with their children
    - ☐ 1.5 generation are more open to engage in the first-generation Amharic service and they do not have much connection with the second generation
    - ☐ 1.5 generation are not playing their bridging role properly because they are mostly busy achieving their personal economic and professional dreams.
    - ☐ 1.5 generation are more open to engage in the second-generation English service and they do not have much connection with the first generation.
    - ☐ Other

47. Most second-generation English-speaking young adults are interested in learning Amharic so that they can continue the Amharic service
    - ☐ Agree
    - ☐ Disagree

48. Most second-generation English-speaking young adults leave their parents' ethnic church when they finish high school.
    - ☐ Agree
    - ☐ Disagree

49. If you agree with the above statement, what are the reasons for their departure from their parents' church?
    - ☐ There is no platform that can fit them (the Sunday school they had until high school is more for children and adults church service is for Amharic speaking congregation)
    - ☐ There was already a gap from the very beginning because of the church structure that divides between parents and children (parents go to the main sanctuary while children go to their Sunday school rooms.)
    - ☐ Other

50. From the following options select only the top three areas where the second-generation could end up after high school?
    - ☐ They join our college ministry
    - ☐ They go to US churches
    - ☐ They join churches planted by Ethiopian second generation themselves
    - ☐ They join their parents' ethnic church
    - ☐ Join another Ethiopian church in another city (If they went for college)
    - ☐ They stop going to church all together
    - ☐ Other

51. From the following options select only the top two challenges that the second generation is facing in their relationship with the first generation in the church.
    - ☐ Second generation are not well understood by the first generation
    - ☐ Second generation are not given enough financial resources and space compared to the first generation
    - ☐ Second generation have not had the chance to do church together with the first generation and therefore there is a disconnect in sharing spiritual experiences between each other.
    - ☐ Second generation are always considered as youth
    - ☐ Other

52. From the following options select only the top two challenges that the first generation (parents generation) is facing in their relationship with the second generation?
    - ☐ First generation does not communicate well with the second generation because of language barrier
    - ☐ First generation do not get a chance to do church with the second generation and that creates a huge disconnect in sharing spiritual experiences between each other.
    - ☐ First generation is focused only on the Amharic ministry because they do not know how to do ministry with their children (second generation) in the US context.
    - ☐ Second generation are not willing to listen to the first generation
    - ☐ Other

53. In the process of adjusting to the US culture what are the top two challenges of the second generation?
    - ☐ Mental health (depression, trauma, and suicidal thoughts)
    - ☐ Addiction and substance abuse
    - ☐ Social prejudice (discrimination because of skin color or accent)
    - ☐ Economic opportunity (lack of access to decent jobs)
    - ☐ Spiritual (Ungodliness, secularism, and atheist lifestyle)
    - ☐ Other

Online Survey for Church Ministers and Members 215

54. In the process of adjusting to the US culture what are the top two challenges of the 1.5 generation?
    - ☐ Mental health (depression, trauma, and suicidal thoughts)
    - ☐ Addiction and substance abuse
    - ☐ Social prejudice (discrimination because of skin color or accent)
    - ☐ Economic opportunity (lack of access to decent jobs)
    - ☐ Spiritual (Ungodliness, secularism, and atheist lifestyle)
    - ☐ Other

55. The first generation (parents) need to have a missional mindset that crosses the cultural barrier between them and their children (second generation), so that they can reach out to their children more effectively.
    - ☐ Agree
    - ☐ Disagree
    - ☐ Other

56. Parents (the first generation) and children (the second generation) need to do English church together to effectively engage in missions together.
    - ☐ I agree with this statement, but our church does not have this structure
    - ☐ I disagree with this statement because it is impossible to do church together
    - ☐ Other

57. Our church would be willing to have two services, one in English where parents can worship together with their children and one in Amharic for the first generation to worship in their heart language.
    - ☐ I agree with this statement and our church is doing that
    - ☐ I agree with this statement, but our church does not have this structure
    - ☐ I agree with this statement, but our church does not have enough space to do that
    - ☐ I disagree with this statement because we already have two services both in Amharic.
    - ☐ I disagree with this statement because our pastor does not have the capacity to do that
    - ☐ Other

58. The first generation need to take responsibility for opening an English service to worship with their children.
    - ☐ I agree with this statement because it is the responsibility of the first generation to disciple their children in the US context.
    - ☐ I agree with this statement but most first generation (parents) would not be willing to worship with their children in English
    - ☐ I agree with this statement but most second generation (children) would not be willing to worship with their parents in English
    - ☐ I disagree with this statement because it is the responsibility of the second generation to open an English service as they know the language better.
    - ☐ I disagree with this statement because our children can learn Amharic and join us in the Amharic service
    - ☐ I disagree with this statement because this will never happen
    - ☐ Other

59. Please give a strategic recommendation. What other options do you suggest that can help your church to narrow the generational gap among the first, second and 1.5 generations and bring the desired unity to do church service and missions together? (If you want to respond to this question orally, you can just write your phone number).

60. What potential do you see in each generation (first, second, and 1.5 generation) that can be utilized for missions? (If you want to respond to this question orally, you can just write your phone number).

61. Please share any other thoughts that may add value to this study. (If you want to respond to this question orally, you can just write your phone number).

62. Can I call you if I have any question on your responses? If yes, please write your number.

Appendix 2

Interview Questionnaire for Independent Ministry Leaders

By continuing with this survey, you indicate your willingness to participate in this study, which is designed to assess missions from Ethiopian diaspora churches in the US: an intergenerational perspective. The entire interview will take 1 hour and 15 minutes, but you are free to stop at any time. Your response will be anonymous. Your specific work and location will not be mentioned in the study. Thank you for your participation!

Part 1. Definition and Practices of Missions

1. In your opinion, what nations are well known in sending missionaries globally?
2. Where do they mostly send their missionaries?
3. What are some of the activities they do in the countries they go to?
4. Based on your answers in questions 1–3, how do you describe missions (What are the main elements that a Christian mission needs to include?)
5. As a believer in diaspora, what are some of the missions activities you do in the US?

6. What is your personal definition of missions?

7. Based on your definition of missions, who could be a missionary?

8. List Bible verses that have shaped your views and practices in missions?

9. From the 66 books in the Bible, which ones have shaped your views and practices in missions?

10. What are some of the cultural challenges that diaspora Ethiopian Christians in the US face in reaching out to non-Ethiopians in the US?

11. What are some of the strengths of diaspora Ethiopian Christians in the US that indicate their potential for missions?

12. What are some of the weaknesses of diaspora Ethiopian Christians in the US regarding missions?

Part 2. Intergenerational Aspect

The Ethiopian diaspora church have the first generation (older generation), 1.5 generation (young adults who came to the US at a young age), and second generation (those who were born and raised in the US).

13. Challenges -What are some of the challenges regarding mobilizing the different generations for missions?

14. Opportunities - What potential do you see in the first, second 1.5 generations that can be utilized for missions?

15. Give a strategic recommendation on how diaspora Ethiopian Christians in the US can narrow the generational gap among the first, second and 1.5 generations and be effective in missions together?

16. What can the US mainstream churches learn from Ethiopian diaspora churches in missions?

Please share any other thoughts that may add value to this study

Appendix 3

Interview Questionnaire for Second Generation Church Planters

By continuing with this survey, you indicate your willingness to participate in this study, which is designed to assess missions from Ethiopian diaspora churches in the US: an intergenerational perspective. The entire interview will take 1 hour and 15 minutes, but you are free to stop at any time. Your response will be anonymous. Your specific work and location will not be mentioned in the study. Thank you for your participation!

Part 1. Definition and Practices of Missions

1. In your opinion, what nations are well known in sending missionaries globally?
2. Where do they mostly send their missionaries?
3. What are some of the activities they do in the countries they go to?
4. Based on your answers in questions 1–3, how do you describe missions?
5. What is your personal definition of missions?
6. Based on your definition of missions, who could be a missionary?
7. What are the main elements that a Christian mission needs to include?

8. List Bible verses that have shaped your views and practices in missions?

9. From the 66 books in the Bible, which ones have shaped your views and practices in missions?

Part 2. Intergenerational Aspect

The Ethiopian diaspora church have the first generation (older generation), 1.5 generation (young adults who came to the US at a young age), and second generation (those who were born and raised in the US).

10. Describe the demography, size, and structure of your church.

11. How is mission practiced in your church? What do you do locally in the place where you are established and globally outside the US?

12. What has the second-generation congregation learned from the first-generation congregation in the work of missions?

13. What makes the second generation uniquely positioned for missions?

14. What are some of the challenges that the second-generation church face in the work of missions?

15. Give strategic recommendation how diaspora Ethiopian Christians in the US can narrow the generational gap among the first, second and 1.5 generations and be effective in missions together?

16. What can the US mainstream churches learn from Ethiopian diaspora churches in missions?

17. Please share any other thoughts that may add value to this study.

Bibliography

Books

Adeney, Miriam. "Latino Diaspora Ministries in the USA." In *Scattered and Gathered: A Global Compendium of Diaspora Missiology*, edited by Sadiri Joy Tira and Tetsunao Yamamori, 423–429. Oxford: Regnum Books International, 2016.

Alemu, Zeleke. ሕይወቴ እና ጽንጠቆስጠጤአዊ እንቅስቃሴ አጀማመር በኢትዮጵያ. Gaithersburg: Signature Book Printing, 2009.

Alba, Richard, and Victor Nee. *Remaking the American Mainstream: Assimilation and Contemporary Immigration.* Cambridge: Harvard University Press, 2003.

Bonk, Jonathan. *Missions and Money: Affluence as a Western Missionary Problem.* Maryknoll: Orbis, 1991.

Creswell, John W. *Qualitative Inquiry and Research Design: Choosing Among Five Approaches.* 3rd ed. Los Angeles: SAGE Publications, 2012.

Elliston, Edgar J. *Introduction to Missiological Research Design.* Pasadena: William Carey Library, 2011.

Hanciles, Jehu J. *Beyond Christendom: Globalization, African Migration, and the Transformation of the West.* New York: Orbis Books, 2008.

Korcho, Mehari. "The Case for Missions in Ethiopian Diaspora Churches of America." In *Churches on Mission: God's Grace Abounding to the Nations*, edited by Geoffrey Hartt, Christopher Little, and John Wang. Pasadena: William Carey Library, 2017.

Kwiyani, Harvey. *Our Children Need Roots and Wings: Equipping and Empowering Young Diaspora Africans for Life and Mission.* CreateSpace Independent Publishing Platform, 2018.

Larkin, William J. Jr., and Joel F. Williams. *Mission in the New Testament: An Evangelical Approach.* Maryknoll: Orbis Books, 1998.

Looney, Jared. *Crossroads of the Nations: Diaspora, Globalization, and Evangelism.* Portland: Urban Loft Publishers, 2015.

Metaferia, Getachew, and Shifferaw Maigenet. *The Ethiopian 2nd Revolution of 1974 and the Exodus of Ethiopian's Trained Human Resources.* Lewiston: The Edwin Mellen Press, 1992.

Neill, Stephen. *Creative Tension.* London: Edinburgh House Press, 1959.

Skinner, Robert P. *Abyssinia of Today: An Account of the First Mission Sent by the American Government to the Court of King of Kings, 1903–1904.* Whitefish: Kessinger Publishing, 2010.

Solomon, Getahun A. *The History of Ethiopian Immigrants and Refugees in America 1900–2000: Patterns of Migration, Survival and Adjustment.* New York: LFB Scholarly Publishing, 2007.

Tennent, Timothy. *Invitation to World Missions: A Trinitarian Missiology for the Twenty-first Century.* Grand Rapids: Kregel, 2010.

Tira, Sadiri Joy, and Tetsunao Yamamori. *Scattered and Gathered: A Global Compendium of Diaspora Missiology.* Oxford: Regnum Books International, 2016.

Tesema, Tesfai. *Hope for the Second Generation: How Children of Immigrants Can Rekindle Christianity in the West.* N.p: Tenth Power Publishing, 2022.

Udall, Jessica. "The Ethiopian Diaspora: Ethiopian Immigrants as Cross-cultural Missionaries; Activating the Diaspora for Great Commission Impact." In *Diaspora Missiology: Reflections on Reaching the Scattered Peoples of the World,* edited by Michael Pocock and Enoch Wan. Pasadena: William Carey Library, 2015.

Wan, Enoch. *Diaspora Missiology: Theory, Methodology, and Practice,* 2nd ed. Portland: Institute of Diaspora Studies, 2014.

Wu, Jeanne. *Mission Through Diaspora: The Case of the Chinese Church in the USA.* Carlisle: Langham Academic, 2016.

Journal Articles

Garcia, Maria "Cross-Cultural Identity of Second-Generation Immigrant Youth." *Saint Louis University* (2019): 1–9.

Habecker, Shelly. "Becoming African Americans: African Immigrant Youth in the United States and Hybrid Assimilation." *Africology: The Journal of Pan African Studies* 10, no. 1 (2017): 55–75.

Mevludin Hasanovic, Dina Smigalovic, and Magbula Fazlovic "Migration and Acculturation: What We Can Expect in The Future." *Psychiatria Danubina* 32, no. 3 (2020): 386–395.

Jenkins, Philip. "From Lagos to All Nations." *The Christian Century.* (2018): 44–45.

John, Stanley. "Are Migrant Churches Missional? A Case for Expanding Our Geography of Missions." *International Bulletin of Mission Research* 41, no. 1 (2017): 8–17.

Kim, Rebecca Y. "Second Generation South Korean American Evangelicals: Ethnic, Multiethnic, or White Campus Ministries?" *Sociology of Religion* 65, no. 1 (2004): 19–34.

Krabill, Matthew and Allison Norton. "New Wine in Old Wineskins: A Critical Appraisal of Diaspora Missiology." *Missiology* 43, no. 4 (2015): 442–455.

Asamoah-Gyadu, Kwabena J. "Migration, Diaspora Mission, and Religious Others in World Christianity: An African Perspective." *International Bulletin of Missionary Research* 39, no. 4 (2015): 189–192.

Kwiyani, Harvey. "Rethinking Mission in Europe: An African Contribution." *Vista Research Based Information on Mission in Europe* 34 (2019): 10–12.

Lee, K. Samuel. "Navigating Between Cultures: A New Paradigm for South Korean American Cultural Identification," *Pastoral Psychology* 54, no. 4 (2006): 289–311.

Salerno, Stacy, John Taylor, and Quentin K. Kilpatrick. "Immigrant Generation, Stress Exposure, and Substance Abuse Among a South Florida Sample of Hispanic Young Adult." *SAGE Journals*, no. 5 (2019):1–10.

Sam, David and John Berry. "Acculturation: When Individuals and Groups of Different Cultural Backgrounds Meet." *SAGE Journals* 5, no.4 (2010): 472–481.

Tesema, Tesfai. "Ethiopian Immigrant Children: What Church Fits Them?" *Lutheran Mission Matters* 56, no. 1 (2020): 114–121.

Wan, Enoch and Sadiri J. Tira. "Diaspora Missiology and Missions in the Context of the Twenty-First Century." *Torch Trinity Journal* 13, no. 1 (2010): 45–56.

Xie, Yu and Emily Greenman. "Segmented Assimilation Theory: A Reformulation and Empirical Test" *University of Michigan* (2005): 1–56.

Online Sources

Global Atlanta Snapshots. "A Look at Ethnic Communities in the Atlanta Region." Accessed October 17, 2020. http://documents.atlantaregional.com/gawsnapshots/ethiopian.pdf

Brown, Susan K., and Frank Bean. "Assimilation Models, Old and New: Explaining a Long-Term Process." *Migration Information Source*, October 1, 2006. Accessed March 20, 2021. https://www.migrationpolicy.org/article/assimilation-models-old-and-new-explaining-long-term-process

Bays, Daniel H. "The Foreign Missionary Movement in the 19th and Early 20th Centuries." National Humanities Center. Accessed January 22, 2022. http://nationalhumanitiescenter.org/tserve/nineteen/nkeyinfo/fmmovement.htm.

Britannica. "Ethiopia-Ethnic Groups and Language."Accessed October 15, 2020. https://www.britannica.com/place/Ethiopia/Ethnic-groups-and-languages

Camp, Ken. "Kelile Nominee for BGCT Second Vice President." *Baptist Standard*. July 2020. Accessed October 20, 2020 https://www.baptiststandard.com/news/texas/kelile-nominee-for-bgct-second-vice-president/

Christianity Today. "Hudson Taylor: Faith Missionary to China." Accessed on January 22, 2022. https://www.christianitytoday.com/history/people/missionaries/hudson-taylor.html

The Ethiopian Diaspora in the United States. Migration Policy Institute (MPI), (2014).

Ethio-Visit. "Ethiopia Basic Facts." Accessed October 15, 2020. https://www.ethiovisit.com/ethiopia-basic-facts/64/

Jeffrey, James. "How did US and Ethiopia Become so Close?" *BBC News*. April 8, 2019. Accessed October 19, 2020. https://www.bbc.com/news/world-us-canada-47203691

Jordan, Sarah-Claire. "Top Four Languages of Ethiopia." *Alpha Omega Translations*. September 2015. Accessed October 27, 2020. https://alphaomegatranslations.com/foreign-language/top-4-languages-of-ethiopia/

Gutierrez, Manuel J. "Missions from a Personal Latin American Perspective." https://missionexus.org/missions-from-a-personal-latin-american-perspective/.

Kobel, Paul S. "Ethiopian Americans." *Countries and Their Cultures*. Accessed October 17, 2020. https://www.everyculture.com/multi/Du-Ha/Ethiopian-Americans.html

Limon, Elvia. "Ethiopian Evangelical Baptist Church Gets New Texas Site." *The Dallas Morning News*. June 8, 2020. Accessed October 20, 2020 https://www.news-journal.com/features/religion/ethiopian-evangelical-baptist-church-gets-new-texas-site/article_1e806b9e-69c2-11e8-945c-878ef1147c82.html

The International Organization for Migration. *Mapping of Ethiopian Diasporas Residing in the United States of America*. Accessed October 17, 2020. https://ethiopia.iom.int/sites/default/files/document/Final%20Mapping%20of%20Ethiopian.pdf

Boundless Immigration. "The Diversity Visa Lottery Explained: Find out About Timeline, Cost, and How to Apply for the Green Card Lottery." Accessed October 20, 2020. https://www.boundless.com/immigration-resources/diversity-visa-lottery/

Center for Immigration Studies. "The Legacy of the 1965 Immigration Act." September 1, 1995. Accessed March 21, 2021 https://cis.org/Report/Legacy-1965-Immigration-Act

Weissbourd, Richard, Milena Batanova, Virgina Lovison, and Eric Torres. "Loneliness in America: How the Pandemic Has Deepened an Epidemic of Loneliness and What We Can Do About It." *Making Caring Common*.

February 2021. Accessed January 25, 2022 https://mcc.gse.harvard.edu/reports/loneliness-in-america

The UN Refugee Agency. "What Is a Refugee?" Accessed October 17, 2020. https://www.unhcr.org/what-is-a-refugee.html

UNICEF Data. "Children Migration." April 2021. Accessed September 12, 2021. https://data.unicef.org/topic/child-migration-and-displacement/migration/

Papers and Presentations

Little, Christopher. "Biblical Theology of Missions." Class Notes for BIB/ICS 6030. Lecture presented at Columbia International University. 2016

Theses and Dissertation

Halche, Yared. "A Socio-Cultural Analysis of Leadership Approaches in Ethiopian Immigrant Churches in the United States: Leadership Styles and Implications for Missions." PhD diss., Concordia Theological Seminary, 2008. ProQuest Dissertations & Theses Global.

Kim, Sinyil. "South Korean Immigrants and Their Mission: Exploring the Missional Identity of South Korean Immigrant Churches in North America." PhD diss., Asbury Theological Seminary, 2008. ProQuest Dissertations & Theses Global.

Mussa, Mohammed. "Sociocultural Problems Experienced by Ethiopian Immigrants in the United States and Communication of the Gospel." PhD diss., Fuller Theological Seminary, 2005. ProQuest Dissertations & Theses Global.

Nwoji, Stanley. "The Missional Status of African Christians in Diaspora: A case of the African Christian Fellowship and African-led Churches in the United States of America." PhD diss., Asbury Theological Seminary, 2009. ProQuest Dissertations & Theses Global.

Nyanni, Caleb. "The Spirits and Transition: The Second Generation and the Church of Pentecost -UK." PhD Diss., The University of Birmingham, 2018. ProQuest Dissertations & Theses Global.

Tesema, Tesfai. "Global Nomads: Identity and Assimilation of 1.5 and Second-Generation Ethiopian Christians in the United States." PhD diss., Concordia Theological Seminary, 2009. ProQuest Dissertations & Theses Global.

Langham Literature, with its publishing work, is a ministry of Langham Partnership.

Langham Partnership is a global fellowship working in pursuit of the vision God entrusted to its founder John Stott –

> *to facilitate the growth of the church in maturity and Christ-likeness through raising the standards of biblical preaching and teaching.*

Our vision is to see churches in the Majority World equipped for mission and growing to maturity in Christ through the ministry of pastors and leaders who believe, teach and live by the word of God.

Our mission is to strengthen the ministry of the word of God through:
- nurturing national movements for biblical preaching
- fostering the creation and distribution of evangelical literature
- enhancing evangelical theological education

especially in countries where churches are under-resourced.

Our ministry

Langham Preaching partners with national leaders to nurture indigenous biblical preaching movements for pastors and lay preachers all around the world. With the support of a team of trainers from many countries, a multi-level programme of seminars provides practical training, and is followed by a programme for training local facilitators. Local preachers' groups and national and regional networks ensure continuity and ongoing development, seeking to build vigorous movements committed to Bible exposition.

Langham Literature provides Majority World preachers, scholars and seminary libraries with evangelical books and electronic resources through publishing and distribution, grants and discounts. The programme also fosters the creation of indigenous evangelical books in many languages, through writer's grants, strengthening local evangelical publishing houses, and investment in major regional literature projects, such as one volume Bible commentaries like the Africa Bible Commentary and the South Asia Bible Commentary.

Langham Scholars provides financial support for evangelical doctoral students from the Majority World so that, when they return home, they may train pastors and other Christian leaders with sound, biblical and theological teaching. This programme equips those who equip others. Langham Scholars also works in partnership with Majority World seminaries in strengthening evangelical theological education. A growing number of Langham Scholars study in high quality doctoral programmes in the Majority World itself. As well as teaching the next generation of pastors, graduated Langham Scholars exercise significant influence through their writing and leadership.

To learn more about Langham Partnership and the work we do visit langham.org

www.ingramcontent.com/pod-product-compliance
Lightning Source LLC
Chambersburg PA
CBHW051540230426
43669CB00015B/2669